Accelerating International Growth

Executive Development from IMD

Marchand, D.A.	Competing with Information – A Manager's Guide to Creating Business Value with Information Content ISBN 0-471-89969-0
Strebel, P.	Focused Energy – Mastering Bottom-Up Organization ISBN 0-471-89971-2
Rosenzweig, P., Gilbert, X., Malnight, T. and Pucik, V.	Accelerating International Growth ISBN 0-471-49659-6

Accelerating International Growth

Philip Rosenzweig
Xavier Gilbert
Thomas Malnight
Vladimir Pucik

JOHN WILEY & SONS, LTD
Chichester • New York • Weinheim • Brisbane • Singapore • Toronto

Copyright © 2001 by John Wiley & Sons, Ltd, The Atrium, Southern Gate,
Chichester, West Sussex PO19 8SQ, England
Telephone (+44) 1243 779777

Email (for orders and customer service enquiries): cs-books@wiley.co.uk
Visit our Home Page www.wileyeurope.com or www.wiley.com

Reprinted December 2005

Other Wiley Editorial Offices

John Wiley & Sons Inc., 111 River Street, Hoboken, NJ 07030, USA

Jossey-Bass, 989 Market Street, San Francisco, CA 94103-1741, USA

Wiley-VCH Verlag GmbH, Boschstr. 12, D-69469 Weinheim, Germany

John Wiley & Sons Australia Ltd, 33 Park Road, Milton, Queensland 4064, Australia

John Wiley & Sons (Asia) Pte Ltd, 2 Clementi Loop #02-01, Jin Xing Distripark,
Singapore 129809

John Wiley & Sons (Canada) Ltd, 22 Worcester Road, Etobicoke, Ontario M9W 1L1

Wiley also publishes its books in a variety of electronic formats. Some content that
appears in print may not be available in electronic books.

British Library Cataloguing in Publication Data

A catalogue record for this book is available from the British Library

ISBN-10: 0-471-49659-6 (hbk)   ISBN-13: 978-0-471-49659-5 (hbk)

Typeset in 10/12pt Garamond by Best-set Typesetter Ltd., Hong Kong
Printed and bound by CPI Antony Rowe, Eastbourne
This book is printed on acid-free paper responsibly manufactured from sustainable forestry, in which at
least two trees are planted for each one used for paper production.

Contents

Part Five Adapting the Global Organization

Part Six Putting it Together

Foreword

I believe that Nokia provides a good example of what this book is all about: how a medium-sized company can quickly become a leading global firm by thinking globally right from the start.

In 1992, Nokia could be characterized as a regional, diversified corporate with the majority of its sales coming from northern Europe. Our portfolio included a broad variety of businesses such as cables, cable machinery, televisions, aluminium and tyres, in addition to telecommunication businesses. Our financial results were not at the level we wanted. We also witnessed the early globalization of our markets.

At that point in time we decided – with the leadership of Jorma Ollila – to take a much more focused approach and concentrate our efforts on globalizing a few of our businesses. We redefined our strategic intent to guide our decision making. The key elements of the new intent were: focused, telecom-oriented, global and high added-value.

At the time of this decision, the new focus areas – telecommunications systems and mobile phones – constituted only 28% of the Nokia Group's sales. The rest we decided to divest. With the combined sales of the two remaining business groups at only about £0.7 billion in 1991, we were a small player in the telecommunications industry.

Most industry experts did not bet on our success. However, the industry was facing two simultaneous shifts, both proving more significant than most people could foresee. These were the digitalization of mobile communications and the deregulation of the telecommunications operator industry. These shifts began to drive the growth and globalization of the mobile communications industry – and Nokia.

In addition to renewing our strategic intent, we also defined core Nokia values in order to grow a uniform culture within the company. The values were defined based on our existing strengths and what we expected would be important in the future. We realized that the fit between these two was extremely good, culminating in four values: customer satisfaction, achievement, respect for the individual and continuous learning.

We then started to communicate these values and to integrate them in our processes. In many countries – especially those with an authoritarian local culture – it required a major effort to firmly embed the values in our operations there. However, it has certainly been worthwhile. Nokia's globally consistent value base has enabled fast global learning. It has functioned as the glue bringing everything together into one whole.

The third decision was to aim for a global presence as fast as possible. The attitude was to be global "right from the start".

We realized we were presented with a huge opportunity: unlike our competitors, we were free of the burden of heavy multidomestic assets. We began to establish R&D centres close to leading telecommunications clusters and universities, and to build factories in major markets. We made sure that we were developing an interrelated, synergistic network with the capability to add value as a combination of both a global and local presence.

In 1997, about 85% of our sales derived from our global communications business. Up to that time, the two core businesses had operated relatively independently of each other. The reason for that was a decision to focus our attention on ensuring that we utilize all growth opportunities to the fullest within both businesses. Following this, it was time to enter a new phase: to create much more uniform business support processes for the whole of Nokia. This was necessary in order to attain the flexibility needed for fast renewal.

In 2000, our sales were £30.4 billion. The average annual growth of our communications business from 1992 to 2000 was about 50%. Our biggest market was the US, followed by China, the UK, Germany and Italy. Due to the global scope of our business, our domestic sales constituted less than 2% of the total. Although that is not much in relative terms, our market position in Finland is very strong. This is fundamentally important, because Finland continues to be one of the world's leading markets in the evolution and utilization of mobile communication devices and services.

I think Nokia is a good example of a medium-sized regional company that was able to become a global industry leader in a short period of time. In other words, it can be done.

Matti Alahuhta
President of Nokia Mobile Phones

Preface

This book is designed to help you – the practising manager – navigate your company's international growth.

It's no secret that international growth is one of the most important challenges facing companies today. Companies of all sizes and in almost all industries know that building a strong international position isn't an option – it's a necessity. The reasons for growing internationally vary, but include a need to reach new customers, or to drive down costs, or to gain access to leading expertise. But whatever the reasons, the result is the same – a need to expand around the world. And the more quickly, the better.

Yet international growth remains complex. The difficulties are enormous. Many companies grow swiftly and smoothly at home, only to stumble – or worse – when they move abroad.

Our objective with this book is to make the journey a bit easier, its obstacles more predictable, its success more certain. My colleagues and I have written a book that's practical, relevant, up to date and full of examples. Each chapter is short, with an overview and a summary, and with key learning points. Our aim is to improve practice, not to advance the limits of theory.

What's different about this book

In the last decade, dozens of books have appeared exhorting managers to "go global". This one is different in a few important respects.

First, we understand *international growth as a process*, not a single step. We think of growth as a series of steps that raise different challenges and pose different obstacles along the way. Successful growth depends on exactly this approach – patience, adaptability, marshalling resources toward one objective and then the next.

Second, we identify and explain *five capabilities needed for successful growth*. Some books remain at the level of strategy but never broach issues of organization or staffing; others examine alliances but never touch on learning. We've tried to cover the range of interrelated capabilities needed for successful growth: global strategic thinking, managing international partnerships, rapid staffing, global learning and organizational adaptation. We provide a complete and a systematic look at what it takes to succeed at rapid international growth.

Third, we pay special attention to *mid-sized and small firms*. One of the most striking features of international growth today is the high participation of small companies – yet so far little has been written for them. Over the last several years, we've worked closely with hundreds of companies, large and small, on the topics of strategy and international growth. We've been struck by the reaction of many managers when reading about the likes of ABB, Shell and other large multinationals. "*If only,*" they exclaim. "*If only* we had their resources. *If only* we had their depth of managerial talent. Their deep pockets. Their supplier network." In fact, many companies face the need for rapid international growth but lack the resources. They also lack the safety net – the steady profits from established markets that can offset failure in a new market, or the lengthy record of success that makes investors patient. While the need for international growth is high, the means to achieve it are scarce. Hence our interest in this book in the particular challenges of mid-sized and small companies.

About the authors

This book is a collaboration among four colleagues at IMD, based in Lausanne, Switzerland. In addition to our experience at IMD, we've served on the faculties of leading business schools including Harvard, Wharton, Michigan and Cornell. Each of us has worked closely with hundreds of managers in dozens of firms over the past years. We bring expertise in a variety of fields – strategy, organization design, human resources – as well as in industries including pharmaceuticals, telecommunications, building materials, aluminum, hotels and lodging, and many more.

Just as important, we've collaborated over the past five years; we've taught a programme for executives called *Accelerating International Growth*. Many of the ideas in this book have been developed for that course, then tested in discussions and classroom debates with scores of managers. The models, examples and concepts we present here have benefited many companies, and we trust they'll be of high value to you.

Acknowledgements

My colleagues and I have received the help of many people during the preparation of this book. Our publisher at Wiley, Claire Plimmer, has been a source of support and encouragement from the time the project was conceived up until its final completion. We're grateful for her steadfast support. Our editor and collaborator, Laura Mazur, immersed herself in the intricacies of international growth for several months. She has helped organize, focus, clarify and edit the entire manuscript, as well as stimulate us to keep the momentum. Laura's contribution has been central to this project, and we've been fortunate to have her as a colleague.

Finally, our home institution, IMD, has provided us with the most important of all resources – a stimulating environment rich in contact with practising managers. Our programme, *Accelerating International Growth*, has given us a lens through which to organize our thinking, as well as a forum to work with managers concerned with exactly this issue. The many other programmes we teach provide valuable complementary experiences and make clear, as we state in the following pages, that international growth is everyone's business.

Philip Rosenzweig
Lausanne, Switzerland

1

Overview: International Growth is Everybody's Business

In the modern global economy, companies of all sizes and in most industries have to think about how to grow internationally and, even more critically, how to accelerate the process. In industry after industry companies of all sizes are expanding internationally. In this chapter, **Philip Rosenzweig** looks at the reasons why, and outlines the five capabilities necessary for rapid international growth.

Overview

International growth is no longer limited to large companies – today, companies of all sizes and in almost all industries are expanding abroad. Reasons for the surge in international growth include greater opportunities for expansion – thanks to changes in public policy, growing economic convergence around the world, and improved means of managing internationally – as well as growing competitive imperatives. For many companies, international growth is no longer an option, it's a necessity.

Yet today, successful international growth demands a new set of capabilities. Companies must learn to do five things well: they must think strategically on a global basis; manage partnerships effectively, including both alliances and acquisitions; staff effectively through expatriation and localization; manage the learning process on a global basis; and adapt the organization structure as its needs shift. These five capabilities are addressed in detail over the subsequent chapters.

What is successful international growth?

Who comes to mind when you think of successful international growth?

You might think of global giants like Unilever and Nestlé, Sony and Philips, General Motors and Toyota. These companies have dominated their industries for decades – in no small part because they were successful in managing international expansion. Each was among the most influential multinationals in the 1970s, remained strong through the 1980s and 1990s, and each one still ranks among the leading companies today.

In the last decade, these older multinationals have been joined by a new generation of companies, many in high-tech industries. Consider these examples:

- Cisco Systems, the world leader in networking hardware and software for the internet, was focused on its home market – the United States – from its founding in 1984 until the early 1990s, then turned its attention toward international growth. After a breathtaking series of acquisitions and new entries in Europe, Asia, and elsewhere, Cisco now operates in more than 75 countries and employs more than 30000 people worldwide.
- Nokia Oy was a stodgy diversified Finnish manufacturing company until it dedicated itself to wireless telephony equipment in the early 1990s. Now it's the world's leader in mobile phone handsets, with sales of 128.4 million handsets in 2000, for a 32% share of the global market. Nokia employs 60000 people in 50 countries, with R&D conducted in 15 countries around the world.
- Vodafone has grown from its founding in 1985 to become a giant in wireless telecommunications. From its base in the United Kingdom, Vodafone expanded into countries as far removed as Australia, South Africa, and the US, in addition to more than 20 countries in Europe. In the last two years,

Vodafone pulled off two of the most ambitious international acquisitions ever – AirTouch in the US and Mannesmann in Germany – to consolidate its position as the world's leading wireless telecommunications operator.

Not just large companies

Rapid international growth isn't just limited to large companies. The internet has dramatically lowered barriers to international growth, making it possible – and sometimes even essential – for companies to reach customers in many countries in just a few years. In fact, many internet-based companies are rewriting the rules of global expansion, moving rapidly to build worldwide positions. After setting up a website in 1996, E*Trade has offered on-line stock trading services to investors in more than 20 countries. Its core strategy is to leverage a strong US base to reach new markets. "The fastest growing markets will be outside the US," according to E*Trade's chief executive, Christos Cotsakos. "The US [provides] the basic infrastructure in technology that we can leverage." Other financial service companies are rushing to keep up with E*Trade. Blake Darcy, chief executive of DLJDirect, another brokerage firm, argues that a domestic position – even in a large market like the US – isn't sufficient: "Our vision of the company is really to be a global financial services firm." A few years ago, global ambitions for a small company would have been preposterous – today they're essential.

Not just high tech

No one is surprised to read about rapidly growing high-technology companies. But what's surprising is that in many traditional industries, companies are setting their sights on international growth. Take a look at some very low-tech industries like tea and cigars. You might think there is nothing much happening there. But in both instances, companies are pushing abroad.

For example, the world's leading brand of tea is Lipton, sold in hundreds of countries, and owned by global giant Unilever. It enjoys a strong brand name, deep financial resources and extensive distribution channels. How can a local brand of tea compete with Lipton? Tata Tea, based in India, decided it needed a global position and its own strong brand name. The result? Tata bought Tetley Tea, one of Britain's leading independent brands. The managing director of Tata Tea explained: "The reason we are interested in Tetley is very simple. If we want to remain in the tea business, we have to compete with Unilever" (Guha, 1999). Now, with its own well-known brand and larger revenues, Tata Tea can compete with Lipton from a stronger position.

Cigar producers have traditionally been local or at best regional, selling worldwide through exports, but never building a global position for the manufacture and sales of cigars. Spain's Tabacalera Cigars International, had a different idea. Antonio Vasquez, managing director, observed: "There are European companies which are European players, and US companies that are US players. But there is no company that has had a big platform in both markets" (White, 1997). Spotting an opportunity to develop a global position, Tabacalera acquired distribution channels and manufacturing in the US, and factories in Honduras and Nicaragua, and now has 11% of the world market. With activities on both sides of the Atlantic, greater scale in production, and a global network for distribution, Tabacalera has rewritten the rules of competition in the cigar industry.

The legal profession has been local almost by definition – until recently. As more and more companies have expanded abroad, they've required legal support on a global basis, prompting law firms to set up offices around the world. In one example, Clifford Chance, a prominent UK law firm, merged with Rogers & Wells, a New York-based firm, and then with Puender, Volhard, Weber, & Axster, a large German firm. Today the combined company has 30 offices around the world with 2700 lawyers, and is able to provide superior coverage and service to its corporate clients, who are themselves global firms.

So, in industry after industry, companies are expanding internationally. A few decades ago, the list of global companies was dominated by heavy industries like petroleum, automobiles and chemicals. Today the list of global companies includes everything from retailing to insurance, from software to food. Companies of all kinds, and of all sizes, find they need to expand abroad in order to remain competitive. One CEO put it this way: *"Either you grow abroad or you shrink. There's no middle ground."*

Fifteen years that changed the world

The explosion of international growth is seen in the rise of foreign direct investment, or investments abroad that involve managerial control of a production or service enterprise.

Foreign direct investment, or FDI, totalled about $60 billion in new investment in 1985, which was already a large increase from 1970, but nothing like what we've seen in subsequent years. In the years following 1985 FDI rose sharply, reaching $240 billion by 1990. After a brief slowdown in the early 1990s, due to the Gulf War and recessions in some leading countries, the pace picked up again, reaching $350 billion in 1995. Just when we imagined the numbers couldn't get much bigger, they took another leap. Thanks to massive cross-border mergers and acquisitions, including British Petroleum's takeover of Amoco and Daimler Benz's purchase of Chrysler, FDI in 1998 topped $800 billion. The pattern is illustrated in Figure 1.1.

Of course, a few large companies contribute disproportionately to these sums, but the real story is the sheer number of companies growing internationally (Table 1.1). In 1990, there were 37 000 companies classified as "multinational", meaning they owned and operated activities in more than one country. They managed 170 000 affiliates abroad, an average of 4.6 per company. By 1998, there were 63 000 multinationals, an increase of 70%, with 690 000 foreign affiliates, up more than 300%. The average multinational in 1998 had more than 10 affiliates around the world – more than twice the number from the start of the decade (United Nations, 2000).

The composition of investment has shifted, too. Companies investing abroad are increasingly diverse in geographic region, size and industry (United Nations, 2000).

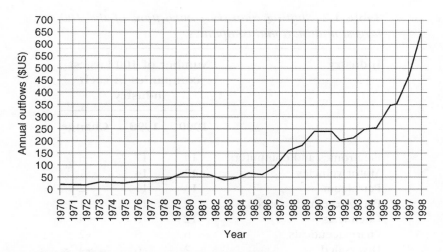

Figure 1.1: *Foreign direct investment, 1970–1998*
Reproduced by permission of United Nations Publications from *World Investment Report 2000.*

Table 1.1: *The growth of multinational companies*

	1990	1998	
Multinational companies	37 000	63 000	+70%
Foreign affiliates	170 000	690 000	+300%
Average affiliates per company	4.6	10.9	

Reproduced by permission of United Nations Publications from *World Investment Report 2000.*

A decade ago, more than 80% of FDI took place among the major industrialized regions of Europe, North America and Japan. Today, FDI increasingly includes the emerging markets of Asia, Latin America, and central and eastern Europe, not only as recipients of investment, but as the home of companies that are expanding abroad. Companies like Mexico's Cemex and South Africa's SAB are among the new breed of multinationals from emerging markets.

The size of companies undertaking FDI has also changed. Until recently, companies expanded abroad when they had exhausted their domestic market. They tended to be large and mature. And they had to be large, with deep pockets, to afford the considerable costs of international expansion. No longer. Companies, much earlier in their lives, and much smaller in revenues and assets, are identifying and pursuing international opportunities.

The change in industry composition of the largest companies is seen in Table 1.2. Through the 1980s, FDI was dominated by major industries including automobiles,

Table 1.2: *Shifting industry composition of the 100 largest multinational companies*

Industry	Number of 100 largest companies in each industry		
	1990	1998	Change
Electronics and computers	14	17	+3
Motor vehicles	13	14	+1
Petroleum	13	11	−2
Food/beverage/tobacco	9	10	+1
Chemicals	12	8	−4
Pharmaceuticals	6	8	+2
Diversified	2	6	+4
Telecommunications	2	6	+4
Trading	7	4	−3
Retailing	0	3	+3
Utilities	0	3	+3
Metals	6	2	−4
Media	2	2	+0
Construction	4	1	−3
Machinery/engineering	3	0	−3
Other	7	5	−2
Totals	100	100	

Reproduced by permission of United Nations Publications from *World Investment Report 2000*, p. 78.

chemicals, electronics and petroleum. By 1990, the largest 100 multinational companies consisted of 14 each in electronics and computers, 13 each in motor vehicles and petroleum, and 12 in chemicals. By 1998, electronics, motor vehicles, and petroleum remained at the top of the list, but elsewhere there were significant shifts. Several companies in chemicals, metals and construction were replaced by large multinationals in newly global industries of retailing, utilities and telecommunications.

Who are these new multinational firms? In telecommunications, Telefónica SA (Spain), Nortel Networks (Canada) and SBC Communications (USA) are soon to be joined by Vodafone (UK); in retailing, Wal-Mart (US), Carrefour (France) and Royal Ahold (Netherlands); and in utilities, deregulation coupled with privatization has led to the international expansion of Texas Utilities Company (USA), RWE Group (Germany) and Southern Company (USA).

Explaining the surge in FDI

What's behind this enormous growth in foreign expansion? Two words: *opportunity* and *imperative*. Companies have greater opportunity than ever before to expand internationally. But as more and more companies grasp the opportunity, other companies feel that it is imperative to do likewise. Pressure from both competitors and customers often demands international growth (Figure 1.2).

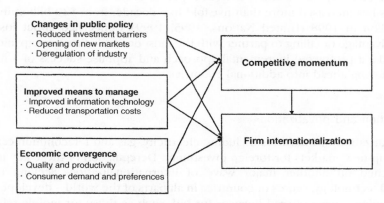

Figure 1.2: *Forces for international growth*

Greater opportunities for international growth arise from three main factors:

* *changes in public policy*, including reduced barriers to investment, the opening of new markets and privatization in key industries;
* *growing economic convergence* among markets, which allows companies to find customers and producers in many more countries than just a few years ago;
* *improved means of managing internationally*, thanks to revolutions in information technology and transportation.

Changes in public policy

Lower investment barriers

Growth in foreign investment has been greatly helped by the liberalization of investment laws. During the 1990s, more than 1000 laws were changed governing foreign investment, 94% of which created a more favourable climate. Governments have eased laws restricting investment, often allowing foreign firms to take majority ownership of local affiliates rather than rely on minority joint ventures. Many countries that were once ambivalent – or even hostile – toward inward investment now place a premium on attracting foreign investment to stimulate their economies and create jobs.

Newly opened markets

Geographic patterns of foreign investment have been transformed over the last decade. Following the fall of communism, western companies have invested heavily in central and eastern Europe. Investment also surged in South Africa, where apartheid was discarded after decades. South-east Asia, India and other regions have begun to receive inward investment and also to invest abroad to a greater extent than before. To capitalize on these opportunities, many western companies, large and small, have entered many new markets in a short period of time. Investment to developing countries has increased more than five-fold in a decade, from $29 billion in 1989 to $166 billion in 1998 (United Nations, 1995, 1999). Concerned about losing first-mover advantage or failing to partner with the most desirable firms, companies can no longer take a protracted incremental approach and appraise success of a first entry before moving ahead into additional countries.

Deregulation and privatization

The privatization of industries including electricity, gas and telecommunications has opened up new markets for foreign investment. Deregulation of these key industries has touched off another major wave of internationalization. Seeking the most advanced technology, scores of countries in all parts of the world – developed as well as developing – have offered licences for bid, such as those for mobile telephones. Given the finite number of licences in each market, firms must tender when these licences are offered or run the risk of being shut out by competitors. A careful process of sequential entry is not possible; compressed or accelerated entry is necessary. Deregulation allows firms in these industries to shift from a multidomestic strategy to a more global business structure, creating global product offerings for business clients while retaining the local requirements for individual customers.

Economic convergence

Growing convergence among economies has been a powerful force for international growth, both on the production side and the demand side.

Quality and productivity

A few decades ago, world-class manufacturing was restricted to industrialized countries, while less developed countries often handled labour-intensive production of relatively simple products. Today, high-technology products are manufactured in Mexico, China, Malaysia, and other countries once mainly attractive for low wages. Intel microprocessors, one of the most sophisticated products in the world with their extreme precision and extraordinary sensitivity to contamination, are now produced in wafer fabrication shops on four continents. Even products usually associated with low sophistication and low wages, such as toys, are now made in Asia with sophisticated moulds engineered in local factories.

Consumer demand and preferences

Whereas many products retain important local adaptations – notably in food, fashion, construction and a variety of other industries – other products cater to an increasingly standardized set of tastes. Until recently, examples like Coca-Cola and McDonald's were among the few "global brands". Now they have been joined by many others, ranging from software (Microsoft) to clothing (Benetton) and more. Anglo-Dutch giant Unilever's recent shedding of hundreds of brands, followed by its 2000 acquisition of Bestfoods to gain its global brands, is testimony to this trend toward convergence in consumer demand.

Improved means to manage

Improvements in technology have meant that companies can identify opportunities for growth and manage global activities in a way unimaginable a few years ago.

Improvements in information technology

A sweeping change affecting internationalization is the revolution in information technology. The current obsession with the internet and mobile telephony is only the latest step. Previously, the emergence of global IT architectures, with common operating environments, has transformed the ability to coordinate global activities. Information technology allows firms to connect any location around the world, allowing them to manage globally integrated activities in a way unimaginable just a few years ago, with instantaneous information sharing on operating activities and knowledge sharing among employees.

Improvements in transportation

Transportation costs and shipment times have dropped dramatically over the past decades, increasing the economic benefits of producing goods far from the markets where they are sold. Container shipments have increased scale efficiencies and driven down prices. Over the past 20 years, unit-transport costs on the key Asia–US route have fallen by one-third, or about two-thirds in inflation-adjusted terms, bringing shipping costs to only 1% of the total merchandise cost (Taggart, 1999). While 95% of world cargo volume still moves by ship, air freight companies such as DHL and Federal Express provide air express services to speed time-sensitive shipments. In addition, logistics information systems have been developed to communicate shipment status information real-time over the internet to improve shipment efficiency, reduce the time to clear customs and reduce paperwork costs.

Improved communication and transportation mean that companies can spread their activities around the world, performing each step in the most advantageous location. Companies can perform data entry in India, locate call centres in Ireland and the Philippines, and set up manufacturing in Mexico, Indonesia, Vietnam, China or any of a dozen other countries.

Taken together, these trends have combined to transform the nature of production around the world. The United Nations stated it clearly: "Liberalization and new technologies increasingly allow [companies] to locate their production and other functions wherever it is most efficient and strategically appropriate for them" (United Nations, 2000).

Competitive momentum

As some companies expand abroad, others feel that it is imperative to follow suit. For some, it's a matter of *pull* – that is, important customers expand abroad and ask for local support. Suppliers of everything from components to packaging, and from professional services to package deliveries, are asked to provide local inputs. For example, Mercedes-Benz's plant in Vance, Alabama, cost $3 billion and created about 600 jobs. But to support the plant, Mercedes asked key suppliers to locate nearby, bringing nine additional companies and more than 1200 jobs.

Many companies are pulled abroad thanks to what one manager calls the "slip-stream". In some ways, entering a new market in order to serve an existing customer is attractive. One of the most difficult uncertainties of foreign expansion – *"Will I find local customers?"* – is removed. But being pulled abroad means that you don't pick the timing. You go abroad when a customer asks you, not when you're ready.

Other companies aren't pulled abroad by customers. They're pushed by competitors. As major rivals take positions abroad, others feel compelled to follow. Allowing a rival to set up in a new market unchallenged, and seize first-mover advantage to build market share, establish a brand, lock up distribution and attract the best local talent, is worrisome indeed. As we saw earlier, Unilever's Lipton brand pushed Tata Tea to acquire Tetley. Heineken's expansion to Vietnam accelerated the entries of Carlsberg and San Miguel. As retailers like Carrefour expand abroad, others like Royal Ahold and Wal-Mart build their positions; and as Wal-Mart expands rapidly, Carrefour joins with Promodes.

The new rules of international growth

More and more companies expand abroad, but many find themselves unprepared for the challenges they face. It's not just a matter of different circumstances abroad – differences in currency, culture, language and so on. Companies expanding abroad today do so under a different set of circumstances. *In recent years, the capabilities needed for successful growth have changed.*

The way it was

Many of the best-known global companies built their positions over several decades. Many were already large companies with a strong position in their home markets. In fact, a dominant home-market position sometimes meant the companies had exhausted prospects for continuing rapid domestic growth.

For decades, successful internationalization involved a number of common features. Companies entered new markets in a careful, sequential process, usually moving from closer and more similar markets, to ones that were further away and increasingly different. American firms often ventured first to Canada and other English-speaking countries; British firms expanded to their colonies and former colonies; European firms to their neighbours and colonies. International expansion was a logical, measured process, with success in one market established before additional resources were committed in the next one (Table 1.3).

Table 1.3: *Changing imperatives for internationalizing firms*

	Conventional view	Current view
Firm size	Large with abundant financial resources	Firms of varied size, resources
Markets for entry	Radiating from home	Opportunistic, global search
Timing	Measured, incremental	Pressure for rapid entry
Mode of growth	Primarily greenfield	Alliances and acquisitions
Mode of entry	Export to direct investment	Versatility among modes
Subsidiary role	Stand-alone business	Complex integration
Staffing	Main emphasis on expatriates	Greater emphasis on localization
Use of resources	Sequential	Simultaneous

Growth was often pursued organically, and many firms relied on a single mode of entry, often moving from exports to finally greenfield expansion. Foreign subsidiaries often duplicated the home-country business model.

Foreign subsidiaries were also staffed with expatriates, who could transfer expertise and hire local employees to handle most activities. Given the measured and incremental nature of internationalization, expatriates could be deployed successively. A team of expatriates might start one country subsidiary and move on to another when the first country was operating successfully. Successful companies made sequential investments to gain experience, build on internally controlled financial and human resources, and limit the total risk exposure at any one time.

Many companies developed in this manner, including some of today's best known and respected multinationals such as Heineken, Colgate-Palmolive, Hewlett Packard and Sony. Given the era when they expanded abroad, and the relatively low competitive pressures they faced, their approach was entirely appropriate.

CASE STUDY: STEADY INTERNATIONAL GROWTH AT HEINEKEN

Heineken, the world's leading global beer, operates today in more than one hundred countries worldwide. Its global position was built over more than a century. First it expanded from its Dutch home market into neighboring countries, then into Dutch colonies in Asia, next into Africa and North America. By now, it owns and manages under license breweries all over the world.

Heineken expanded in a slow, incremental process. In most new markets, Heineken first imported its beer, introducing its brand and establishing an image of high quality. If successful, Heineken would then license a brewer to produce locally, building its volume in that market and overseeing the brewing process to ensure high quality, while reducing the costs of transportation. If that worked, Heineken would often take a limited ownership position, buying a share of the local brewer or entering into a joint venture to build a greenfield brewery. If limited ownership was successful, Heineken would often increase its ownership stake, eventually taking full ownership in the local brewer. While Heineken sometimes deviated from this sequence, taking advantage of opportunities as they arose, for the most part it retained a disciplined and incremental approach to international expansion.

Adapted from Jacobs and Maas (1992).

CASE STUDY: COLGATE-PALMOLIVE, HEWLETT PACKARD AND SONY: EXAMPLES OF CONVENTIONAL INTERNATIONAL GROWTH

Colgate-Palmolive, the US-based consumer products company, initially expanded abroad in the early decades of the 20th century, first to Canada and Mexico, then to English-speaking countries including Great Britain and Australia, and only later to industrialized European countries. In each country, its local subsidiary performed a full range of activities except basic research – procurement, manufacturing and marketing. To staff these newly formed subsidiaries, Colgate-Palmolive dispatched expatriates who hired local employees. Consistent with conventional views, the process was incremental, unfolding over decades and at a measured rate.

Hewlett Packard, the US-based electronics and computer firm, also internationalized in a measured, incremental manner. Founded in 1939, HP set up its first manufacturing plant in Germany in the 1950s, then France in the 1960s and Singapore in the 1970s. It relied on greenfield entries – with the exception of Japan, where regulations forbade majority ownership and HP established a joint venture with Yokogawa Electrical Works.

Sony, the Japanese electronics company, relied entirely on exports through the 1960s. In 1972, it set up a television assembly plant near San Diego, US. Two years later, it stepped up its US investments with new business lines in magnetic tape and audio equipment. Over the next years, Sony expanded into the UK, setting up a television plant in 1975, and then established magnetic tape and audio equipment manufacturing in Europe. Again, the approach to international expansion was measured and incremental.

International growth: the new realities

For companies expanding internationally today, the approaches of Heineken, Colgate-Palmolive, Hewlett Packard and Sony seem leisurely – and even quaint. More importantly, it would be dangerous for many companies today to adopt such a slow approach. Most don't have the luxury of a slow, incremental approach. Successful growth today calls for a new set of capabilities.

Rather than choose adjacent markets, companies can search broadly to identify the best opportunities anywhere, both for markets and for costs. And rather than relying on themselves, they can look to partnerships. In terms of entry mode, reliance on organic growth is no longer possible. Rather, joining with existing firms, whether through joint ventures, non-equity alliances or even acquisitions, is critical for success. Firms must be able to enter unfamiliar markets with limited people and capital resources before a competitor closes a market opportunity. While an acquisition or joint venture is often more difficult to implement than a greenfield investment, it may be the only way to establish a strategic position, gain access to key knowledge, or secure an installed base. The best firms today do not rely on a single entry mode, but are adept at greenfield entry, alliances and acquisitions.

Rather than a reliance on expatriates, today's successful companies find it necessary to look more to local managers. Companies that are rapidly expanding abroad typically don't have enough experienced people within the organization, so they hire from outside, using some combination of a local workforce, expatriates or external supply networks. This is especially true when the companies are young, growing rapidly at home, and constrained in terms of management talent. Global success is a matter of human capital: building a first-class workforce and leveraging its expertise on a global basis. Robert Corti, chief financial officer at Avon, the cosmetics giant, explained his company's outstanding record: "Avon can draw on its human capital to solve crises and seek opportunities half a world away. And it can do it fast" (Leander and Thurston, 1998).

Some firms face all of these together. The new shape of international growth is expressed by Didier Benchimol, CEO of an internet firm, iMediation:

The old, restricted view that you can start in your domestic market and then progressively expand, taking countries one by one, is completely obsolete. . . . (We) launched the company simultaneously in Germany, the UK, France and the US. There's a new wave of managers and leaders who can quickly build up a company and take that company global. They start up in many countries at once, so that after 12 months the company has a balanced business in Europe, the US and Asia.

For many companies, it's not quite this extreme, but it's getting there. Incremental, sequential expansion is replaced by rapid, compressed growth. And this in turn calls for a new set of capabilities.

CASE STUDY: FAILING AT INTERNATIONAL GROWTH: THE CAUTIONARY TALE OF LINCOLN ELECTRIC

Can a company attempt to grow internationally too quickly? Of course!

Lincoln Electric has been a leader in the US arc welding equipment industry. In the early 1990s, faced with slowing growth in its domestic market, coupled with foreign competitors entering the US, Lincoln Electric set its sights on international growth. Over the next three years it expanded aggressively, spending $325 million on new plants in Japan, Venezuela and Brazil, and acquiring eight plants in Germany, Norway, Great Britain, the Netherlands, Spain and Mexico. The result was disaster: unprecedented losses in Europe that threatened the survival of the company.

What went wrong? Just about everything. Lincoln Electric's most fundamental failure was one of strategy. There was little clarity of motivations for growth, a lack of vision regarding competitive success and how international growth would contribute to it, and almost no careful preparation of foreign markets.

A second failure had to do with staffing. The company had no executives with international experience – in fact, some key managers didn't even own a passport. Unable to staff its new affiliates with capable expatriates, it relied on newly-hired local citizens who had little understanding of Lincoln Electric's unique management approach. Reckless growth outstripped the company's management resources.

A third failure was in knowledge management. Lincoln Electric had no way to transfer its technical and managerial expertise to its new affiliates, and it created no processes to share expertise among them. Furthermore, the pace of growth was so rapid that there was no time to digest the lessons from initial entries before embarking on subsequent ones. There was no explicit recognition that successful international growth depends on leveraging knowledge.

Lincoln Electric's fourth and final failure was one of organization. Rather than set up a new division that would provide resources and managerial oversight to its growing European activities, Lincoln Electric had all new subsidiaries to report directly to the CEO – ostensibly to give them prominence, but a bad decision as it overloaded the CEO while providing inadequate dedicated managerial support.

By 1992, three years into its foreign adventure, Lincoln Electric had piled up staggering losses – so great they jeopardized the company's survival. Over the next years, Lincoln Electric did an about-face, rationalizing some foreign subsidiaries and eventually closing or selling others. It also learned that, contrary to its earlier assumptions, the German market could accept imports from the US. The upshot of this painful tale stresses the need for preparation, for anticipating human, knowledge and organizational needs, and to manage the process of growth carefully. And finally, speed doesn't guarantee success – for the unprepared company, speed can compound problems.

Five capabilities for rapid international growth

Many companies are struggling with international growth. They understand the need, and they're persuaded of the importance, but they find successful international growth to be elusive. The reason is clear: they're facing today's challenges with yesterday's capabilities. Other companies are succeeding at rapid international growth. They include prominent companies in high-tech industries like Cisco, Nokia and Vodafone; but also many smaller companies in a wide variety of industries. What do these companies have in common? First, they've set aside the lessons of the previous generation. They're not tied to incremental, sequential growth.

Today, successful rapid international growth calls for five capabilities:

- *a strategic capability*, involving an ability to think strategically on a global basis, and scan the globe for opportunities;
- *a partnership capability*, involving the effective management of alliances and acquisitions;
- *a staffing capability*, involving the rapid staffing through expatriation and localization;
- *a learning capability*, involving both the creation of new knowledge and the ability to transfer it effectively through processes;
- *an organizational capability*, involving the continual adaptation of organization design to meet shifting needs.

These capabilities form the structure of this book, as follows:

Part One: Developing Strategic Capability

We start at the broadest level, with a consideration of firm strategy and the motivations for international growth. Successful international growth calls, first of all, for a change of mindset. It means thinking about strategy in a new way. The best companies don't think one country at a time – they grasp the entire globe at once. They don't replicate their business model in each country, but look for the best way to spread their business system across the world. They're guided by one broad question: *how can I best reconfigure my business system on a global basis?* To do this, they need to understand their industry, their firm and markets. In Chapter 2, *Grasping the Globe*, Philip Rosenzweig shows how companies can identify ways to take advantage of global opportunities at each step of the value chain. In some instances, they may undertake global sourcing of inputs, and in others they may rely on trade, but for more and more companies, the answer is to undertake foreign direct investment, meaning the ownership and management of activities abroad. In Chapter 3, *Crafting an International Growth Strategy*, he describes the implementation of a global strategy in terms of marshalling scarce resources in a sequential fashion. He addresses two critical dimensions of growth – what countries to enter, and what products to introduce – and provides practical guidelines for both.

Part Two: Managing Global Partnerships

Rapid international growth calls for partnerships, whether alliances or acquisitions. Many of today's leading multinationals expanded abroad mainly by setting up green-field operations. Today, that approach is often too slow. Alliances – non-equity alliances as well as joint ventures – and acquisitions are vital to building a global position rapidly. In Chapter 4, *Competing through Alliances and Joint Ventures*, Vladimir Pucik sets forth the range of issues and challenges companies face when it comes to dealing with alliances, which are increasingly being used to speed up the process of international growth. An alliance isn't a one-off deal, but a complex process that needs to be managed carefully. Nor are alliances static – they evolve over time. Successful alliances are based on effective relationship building among partners. They call for skilful negotiation and preparation; communication, trust building and dispute resolution; staffing and resource sharing during the alliance's formative stages; and the ability to secure resources in the later stage. In Chapter 5, *Mergers and Acquisitions*, he examines the relentless pace of mergers and acquisitions in the global marketplace, and shows how critical it is to ask fundamental questions about both the strategy behind the merger and how it will be implemented. There is little doubt that these deals, particularly those that work across borders, are increasingly complex and difficult to get right, particularly since mergers and acquisitions are far more than an exercise in financial transfer of accounts and much more about the softer, less tangible aspects of management.

Part Three: Staffing the Global Company

The scarcest resources for companies expanding internationally are often human resources. A strong global position demands an excellent local staff. Attracting and retaining outstanding talent are hard enough for a domestic company, and the challenges multiply when expanding abroad. The best companies have built two capabilities – expatriation and localization. In Chapter 6, *Managing Expatriation*, Vladimir Pucik examines keys to successful expatriation management. He describes the expatriate cycle – selection, preparation, support and repatriation – and offers particular insights on the challenges facing mid-sized firms. In Chapter 7, *Developing Local Talent*, Philip Rosenzweig addresses the recruitment and development of local managers. He argues that successful international growth requires companies to bring local citizens into responsible positions, making full use of their talent and also reducing the need for expatriates.

Part Four: Fostering Global Learning

Rapid international growth is closely linked to managing knowledge. In Chapter 8, *The Global Learning Imperative*, Xavier Gilbert asserts that to succeed at international growth, companies can no longer just focus on replicating their proven strategies, processes and approaches. Copying, even if done smartly, is bound to be inadequate. The emphasis increasingly has to be on effective and rapid learning. In Chapter 9, *Deploying the Domestic Business Model Internationally: The Inside-Out Approach*, he stresses the need for companies which are expanding abroad by using their domestic model to look more fundamentally at the expected competitive advantages they hope to gain and to be open to new knowledge that will help accelerate their internationalization process. A business model taken internationally is a learning agenda to be shared by all. Finally, in Chapter 10, *Stretching the Business Model Globally: The Outside-In Approach and the Learning Intent*, he looks at how companies can move beyond the learning from local adaptation to use the learning as a basis for the future business model they want to deploy globally.

Part Five: Adapting the Global Organization

As companies expand abroad, their organizations have to adapt. The wrong structure is like a strait-jacket – it inhibits growth. In Chapter 11, *Changing Perspectives on Global Strategy and Organization*, Thomas Malnight looks at how organizational designs are adapting to cope with the global environment. In Chapter 12, *Managing Subsidiary Evolution*, he discusses how national affiliates are evolving to play both a local and global role.

Part Six: Putting it Together

Although we present strategic, partnership, staffing, learning and organizational capabilities one at a time, successful companies don't address them in sequence, one at a time, but balance them simultaneously. In our concluding chapter, *Accelerating International Growth – And Succeeding*, Philip Rosenzweig takes an integrative approach and considers all five capabilities together.

SUMMARY

Companies of all sizes and in almost all industries are expanding abroad – to capture new opportunities and to keep up with competitive pressures. Foreign direct investment has exploded since 1986, and the number of multinational firms continues to rise.

Yet successful international growth remains difficult – in part because the capabilities that once ensured success are no longer enough. Successful growth today calls for a new set of capabilities, ranging from a global approach to strategy formulation, to effective management of partnerships, to rapid staffing, worldwide learning and organizational adaptation. Failure at international growth can often be explained as the failure to develop one or more of these capabilities.

LEARNING POINTS

- Companies of all kinds – young and old, high tech and traditional – are expanding abroad.
- Foreign direct investment has soared, both from greenfield investment and from acquisitions.
- The growth in foreign direct investment reflects both greater opportunities, but also the heightened imperatives facing companies.
- To expand abroad rapidly, companies have to develop a new set of capabilities: developing strategic capability, managing global partnerships, staffing the global company, fostering global learning and adapting the global organization.

References

Guha, K. (1999) Tata Tea seeks Strength through Western Infusion, *Financial Times*, 27 July 1999.

Hastings, D.F. (1999) Lincoln Electric's Harsh Lessons from International Expansion, *Harvard Business Review*, May–June 1999.

Jacobs, M.G.P.A. and Maas, N.H.G. (1992) *Heineken History*, Amsterdam.

Leander, T. and Thurston, C. (1998) Companies with Global Muscle, *Global Finance*, **12**(10), 24–27.

Taggart, S. (1999). The 20-ton Packet, *Wired*, October, 246–255.

United Nations (1995) *World Investment Report 1995*, UNCTAD.

United Nations (1999) *World Investment Report 1999*, UNCTAD.

United Nations (2000) *World Investment Report 2000*, UNCTAD, p. xv, and p. 18.

White, D. (1997) Smoke Signals, *Financial Times*, 13–14 September 1997, p. 7.

Part One
Developing Strategic Capability

CHAPTER 2

Grasping the Globe

Companies used to have the luxury of expanding
internationally on a country-by-country basis. Now they
have to think about their expansion strategies in a holistic
way, identifying global opportunities on a global basis.
Philip Rosenzweig explains how different industries have
addressed international growth, and looks at the
motivations for foreign direct investment.

Overview

In Chapter 1, we focused on the most important development in international growth: foreign direct investment (FDI). We'll spend most of this book on foreign direct investment, defined as owning and operating productive activities outside the home country – but for now, let's put FDI in its proper context.

Foreign direct investment isn't the only way to grow internationally. Some companies fail because they jump right to FDI, setting up manufacturing around the world, when they'd be better off relying on exports. Undertaking international growth should be based on a careful analysis of how companies compete, and how they achieve and maintain a competitive advantage. What's the key? It's a capability we call *grasping the globe*. Rather than thinking about one country at a time, it means taking a holistic approach and identifying opportunities on a global basis.

Understanding the value chain

The place to begin is the *value chain*, which identifies the steps that contribute to customer value. A typical value chain for a manufacturing industry is shown in Figure 2.1. The first step is research and product development, the creation of a product for customers. Next is procurement of inputs and manufacturing. Logistics bring the product to customers, encompassing sales and customer support. Supporting these steps are key functions: finance, legal, marketing, information technology and human resources. In service industries, a different sequence of events contributes to customer value, but for the sake of simplicity, we'll use the standard manufacturing value chain.

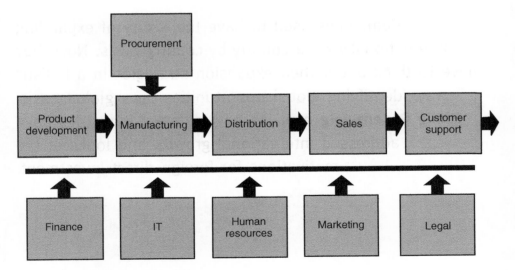

Figure 2.1: *The value chain*

The value chain does more than just list steps. It lets us isolate the costs at each step, so we have a clear picture of how improvements at each step contribute to improved performance. We can also use the value chain to ask customers where they perceive most value. Companies are often surprised to find that the steps customers perceive as most valuable may not be those that involve the most addition of costs. The value chain also lets us see where our assets are used, and can shed light on steps that are relatively asset intensive, especially relative to the value they contribute. Finally, by performing a similar analysis of competitors – at least to the extent that information exists to allow such an analysis – we can compare ourselves systematically, in terms of costs, assets, perceived value and so forth.

A number of actions flow out of value-chain analysis. Most fundamental is to ask which of the many steps should be performed in-house, and which should be left to others. For example, a step that offers little perceived added value to customers but ties up substantial assets is obviously a good candidate for outsourcing. Many decisions to work with contractors or original equipment manufacturers (OEMs) stem from such an analysis. At one extreme, a company can be completely vertically integrated, performing everything from product development to manufacturing to logistics to sales. At the other extreme, a company may focus on just a few key activities, and look to other companies to perform other activities. In recent years, the disaggregation of activities has become more and more widespread, with companies focusing on a select few activities, and looking to others for a range of activities including logistics, information technology and manufacturing. Nike, world leader in athletic shoes, focuses on just those activities where it contributes superior value – product design and marketing – while outsourcing the others.

From competitive analysis to global strategy

Now let's introduce the geographic dimension. At each step of the value chain, a company can examine how worldwide opportunities may contribute to improved performance, whether by lowering costs, finding higher productivity or reaching new markets. The hallmark of a global strategy is precisely this analysis: thinking about global opportunities at each stage of the value chain.

WHAT'S A *GLOBAL STRATEGY*?

A company pursues a global strategy if it identifies and takes advantage of opportunities on a worldwide basis. The result may be importing components from around the world, or reaching markets through export, or FDI. It's not the form that is important, but the process of identifying opportunities on a global scale and responding accordingly.

The phrase "global strategy" is sometimes used by other managers and researchers to indicate the location of activities or the consistency of management. Let's look at both:

• *Global location of activities. A company is sometimes said to have a global strategy if its revenues, assets and employees are spread across the world. The broader a company's distribution of revenues, assets and employees, the more it's global. This definition is reflected in the United Nations Conference on Trade and Development's (UNCTAD) index of transnationality. We believe that measuring the global distribution of activities is useful, but it's one result of a global strategy, not the strategy itself. Some companies, like Dubai Aluminium, clearly have a global strategic vision, but don't find any advantage in foreign investment.*

• *Global consistency of management. Others use the term global strategy to denote a single, consistent approach to key decisions worldwide. They use the term global in contrast to local – if a company adapts products, marketing or human resource policies to each local environment, it is said to have a local strategy; if it handles these and other elements in a consistent way worldwide, it's said to pursue a global strategy. Again, it's often very important to understand the pressures for global consistency versus those for local adaptation, but they refer to an approach to management – which we believe is different from a company's strategy.*

In our view, as long as a company examines each stage of the value chain and asks how and where it can make full use of global opportunities, then its strategy – its position relative to competitors, and how it seeks to achieve high performance – is global.

Professor Howard Perlmutter of the Wharton School has described the evolution of global management as following three stages (Perlmutter, 1969). First is *ethnocentric* management, where the home country is the point of reference. Decisions about investments, management policies and more, are all made with a home country focus. Next, as companies evolve internationally, and compete in additional markets, they may adopt a *polycentric* approach, thinking of themselves as competing in several regions, and needing to respond and adapt to each one.

Finally, the most advanced stage, which Perlmutter noted very few companies had yet reached, is *geocentric*, which denotes an integrated and comprehensive approach to global operations. The hallmark of a geocentric approach was to ask *"Where in the world?"* – that is, where in the world shall we procure our inputs, shall we find customers, shall we raise capital, shall we locate manufacturing, shall we conduct product development and so forth. Such an approach teases out the many stages of the value chain and asks, separately for each, how the company can best take advantage of global opportunities. *Geocentric*, in Perlmutter's terminology, is what we mean by a global strategy.

Examining each step of the value chain

Opportunities to improve performance may differ at each step of the value chain, as follows.

Where should we conduct research and develop products?

Is R&D best performed at a single location worldwide or distributed in multiple locations? Is it best performed in our home country, or close to customers, or in countries that boast specific skills? Eli Lilly, the giant US-based pharmaceuticals company, has performed 80% of its R&D at its Indianapolis home. In late 2000, it announced it would step up R&D abroad in order to gain access to scientists and technologies around the world. Dr August Watanabe, vice president for research and development, named the UK, Spain, Germany and Belgium as likely sites, explaining: "There are certain countries in Europe that have a history of being strong in drug discovery, such as the UK" (Michaels, 2000). Likewise, automobile companies have set up design centres in California, software companies have programming centres in India, and speciality chemical firms conduct research in Germany. In each case, their overall competitive position benefits from leading expertise around the world.

Where shall we procure inputs?

Should it rely on local sources, perhaps advisable when inputs are widely available, and when any benefits of coordinated procurement are offset by transportation costs? Or are there ways to improve significantly costs, quality and delivery time by scanning the world for suppliers and new inputs? Companies have long scanned the world for key inputs – commodities grown or mined in particular parts of the world, or electronic components from Taiwan or Japan. Today, with the expansion of e-commerce – and *e-procurement* – the opportunities to rationalize purchasing on a company-wide basis and search for the best opportunities anywhere in the world are becoming a reality.

Where shall we manufacture?

Do economies of scale force companies toward one or a few very large plants, resulting in low per-unit costs? Or do transportation costs outweigh scale economies, and push companies to set up multiple plants, each close to final customers? Sometimes the answer is a mixture, with components manufactured in a few central plants, then shipped to local factories for final assembly. In many instances, companies benefit by performing activities in countries with favourable factor costs, such as labour-intensive manufacturing or service activities in countries where wages are low. Any of these options might make sense, depending on variables including scale economies in plant production; which sometimes dictate central production; transportation costs, which if high relative to the value of the product might force multiple local plants; and relative labour costs and productivity.

Where shall we find customers?

Many multinational companies expanded incrementally from their home market, first looking to new customers in adjacent markets, or in countries with a similar culture or language, and over time expanding further afield. Today, information technology allows companies to identify and tap customers in distant lands with ease. One small company in the United States designed software systems for hospital bedside monitoring units. They identified their market as any hospital in the world where English was spoken, where a specific kind of bedside monitoring unit was in use, and where the health-care reimbursement system would allow such a purchase. The company's first sale was in New Jersey; its second sale was in Singapore.

Where shall we perform customer support?

Some forms of support require activities next to the customer, but remote support – call centres and contact centres – can be located almost anywhere. Today, thanks to a combination of language and communication skills, wage rates and their position in key time zones, countries like Ireland and the Philippines are home to outstanding call centres.

How shall we market our products?

How shall we handle branding, product positioning, advertising, promotions and other aspects of marketing? Are there benefits to global coordination, in terms of cost efficiencies, ability to provide standardized products to globally mobile customers, and the like? Or do the needs of customers push us toward a local or regional approach?

Where shall we raise capital?

Are we best raising capital in our home market, or can we tap superior sources of capital in foreign markets? In recent years, numerous European and Japanese companies have listed shares in New York. Several large South African companies, including South African Breweries, Old Mutual, Billiton and Dimension Data, have listed on the London exchange to take advantage of the lower cost of capital, as well as to avoid some exchange controls in the home market. They remain committed to their home country but in this one step of the value chain they are searching globally for the best source of funds (Skapinker, 2000).

Where shall we recruit our employees?

Are we best recruiting in our home country, or are there advantages to attracting talent on a global basis, either for specific technical skills, or more broadly for young professionals? Where we hire isn't necessarily where we perform our activities. For example, until the late 1990s, Microsoft located all of its software development on a single large campus in Redmond, Washington, US. The idea was to locate software developers so they could easily work together and interact closely. However, although it performed all its software development at one site in the United States, its software developers included a wide variety of nationalities and backgrounds.

CASE STUDY: SEQUENCE OF ANALYSIS

Is there a sequence in which a company should examine its value chain for global opportunities? We've followed the conventional sequence, but R&D isn't always the place

to start. Shall we start with customers, identify where in the world to sell our goods
and services, and then work backwards to manufacturing and sourcing?

In fact, there's no single right answer. The process of evaluating one's value chain,
and understanding opportunities for improvement by seizing worldwide benefits, is a
holistic process.

As a general rule, however, begin at the stage that represents a distinctive compe-
tency, or what sets you apart from competitors and where, at the end of the day, your
core resides. Often that will be a distinctive product or technology, a unique service
offering or a value proposition that is hard for customers to imitate. For many com-
panies this leads to distinctive brands, superior service delivery, outstanding manu-
facturing, a unique technology, or perhaps the ability to learn and innovate faster than
the competition. These are the places to begin. From there, identify the secondary steps,
sometimes manufacturing, which leads to procurement, and finally to support activi-
ties. Not surprisingly, many of these lend themselves to outsourcing.

Comparing industries: a few examples

Value-chain analysis highlights the similarities and differences among industries in
global opportunities. In some industries, there are benefits to a global strategy at
almost all steps of the value chain, resulting in a strong need for a global position. In
other industries, a global strategy is rewarded in some steps but not others. And in
still other industries, the benefits of a global strategy are few and far between, which
means that those companies find little or no advantage to a global approach, and that
local companies are at no real disadvantage against large global firms.

Automobiles

The automobile industry benefits from a global position at all stages. In fact, it's
hard to imagine a successful automobile company today without a global position. Huge development costs demand global scale. Trends are best analysed and
captured in parts of the world like southern California, where several Japanese
companies now locate design centres. Procuring inputs on a global basis produces
substantially lower costs. In manufacturing, automobile plants offer such high-
scale economies that the minimum efficient scale of production typically surpasses
the size of all but the largest national markets. In other words, there are virtually no
national markets, aside from the United States, large enough to warrant a dedicated
automobile plant.

The result, for many leading automakers, is a value chain spread across the globe.
Take the example of a car produced by one of the large US automakers. Design takes
place in Germany, worth about 7.5% of the car's value. Components and advanced
technology come from Japan, basic assembly takes place in Korea, and minor parts
come from Taiwan and Singapore. Advertising and marketing services are based in the
United Kingdom, and data processing is handled in Ireland and Barbados. Altogether,

nine countries are involved in some aspect of production, marketing and selling. Only 37% of the production value of this "American" car is generated in the United States (David, 1997).

Household appliances

Household appliances – so-called *white goods*, including refrigerators, washing machines, ovens, and the like – reward a global strategy at some steps of the value chain but not others. Upstream, in components, there are enormous economies of scale awaiting a global player. Yet final products must be adapted to the tastes and traditions of local markets. Final products are heavy, bulky and expensive to ship compared to the price of the good. Customers are mainly local citizens, reducing the benefits for global brands.

The result: there are important benefits to global coordination in procurement and component manufacturing, and a country-by-country or regional approach to product design, final assembly and marketing. Electrolux, the Swedish appliance company, recognized the benefits awaiting an appliance company that pursued a global strategy. It rewrote the rules of the game by expanding, often through acquisition of small appliance makers throughout Europe, and consolidating them to achieve scale economies. It transformed what had been a multidomestic business and has given it a competitive edge as it coordinated its activities on a global basis. And, in its wake, other companies, notably Whirlpool, found that to survive they needed a global approach, as well.

Beer

Beer has historically been a local industry, with many local and national brands competing. Research and development tends to be fairly small as a share of total cost, product quality is stable, and inputs are abundant and inexpensive. Economies of scale in brewing aren't great relative to the final price, the product is expensive to ship, and freshness is important. Finally, most customers buy in small quantities. For all these reasons, a global strategy hasn't bestowed important competitive advantages.

Yet in recent years, some brewers have found ways to derive benefits from an international position. Heineken built and leveraged a global brand, and also benefited from sharing expertise around the world. And as Heineken forged a global brand, others, did too, including Belgium's Interbrew – which recently purchased Labatt in Canada, Dos Equis in Mexico and Rolling Rock of the United States, among other brands – and South African Breweries – which added Pilsner Urquell of the Czech Republic to its long list of brands (Thornhill, 2000). Today the beer industry includes a number of global giants, deriving the benefits of global branding and economies of scale and scope, competing side-by-side with many small local brewers. Unlike, say, automobiles and pharmaceuticals, where R&D costs and plant scale make it impossible for small players to survive, the beer industry bestows benefits to global companies while still allowing small firms to be competitive in local markets.

Roofing tiles

Many European homes and buildings have roofs with clay or concrete tiles, which are rather different from the shingles on most American homes. The European roofing tile industry includes dozens of national and regional companies. Roofing tiles are fairly simple products and, although some advanced material science is involved, the industry isn't R&D intensive. Inputs of mainly clay and concrete can be found almost anywhere. There's little benefit to procuring them on a global basis, since they're inexpensive to buy but expensive to ship. Manufacturing doesn't lend itself to major economies of scale. In fact, the high cost of transportation for tiles means that the economic radius is about 100 km – any per-unit benefits in production costs are wiped out by higher transportation costs. As a result, production is scattered among many small plants, each close to its final customers. Customers tend to be local: not only final users who reside in the building, but architects and contractors who design and build. There may be some benefit to a well-known brand name as a symbol of quality and durability, but there are essentially no multinational customers or global accounts.

What are the benefits to international growth for a roofing tile company? Local companies compete quite well in this industry, but multinationals like Lafarge can take advantage of their size and scale in a few ways. They can pursue research into materials science in a way that small local firms cannot; they can share process expertise among plants; and they can attract and retain outstanding people by offering greater career opportunities. Even if the physical product doesn't move among countries, either in raw materials or finished tiles, there are benefits to a global strategy, mainly from coordination among activities.

Fresh food

At first glance one might be tempted to say fresh foods offer little advantage of a global position. High risk of perishability, relatively low-scale economies, high transportation costs compared to value – these and other factors make fresh food a local industry. Your neighbourhood bakers don't need to serve global clients, nor can they benefit from mixing dough in a low-wage country, baking it in a low-energy-cost country, and shipping it to a third country. The same holds for fresh milk – there's little to be gained from global growth. But now consider fresh fruits and vegetables. Winter in the northern hemisphere is summer in the southern hemisphere; and some fruits grow in the tropics but not in temperate climates. Many fruits and vegetables command a sufficient price, and have long enough shelf life, to warrant international shipping. Hence the very important market in the northern hemisphere for produce from Chile, fruits from New Zealand and from Israel, and more. Even in fresh fruit, until recently an improbable example of a global industry, we see benefits present for companies that can expand their value chain across the globe.

This quick survey of a handful of very different industries makes two points. First, industries vary widely in the rewards or requirements of a global strategy. In automobiles, competition *requires* companies to grasp global opportunities at almost every stage of the value chain – economies of scale, of transportation, design costs and competitive pressures make it imperative. For industries like household appliances, it's necessary to capture global opportunities at some stages – upstream, in that case – but a global strategy contributes less downstream, in manufacturing and marketing. And in some other industries, like beer or roofing tiles, there are *rewards* to a global strategy, but it is hardly a requirement. Second, we find that most industries offer benefits to companies that understand their value chains and can pursue global opportunities. Even with roofing tiles and fresh food, where benefits may be small, they are appreciable. This might not be at all stages of the value chain, of course, but there will be sufficient advantages in specific stages to bestow important advantages.

Basic options: trade and foreign investment

A company pursues a global strategy if it examines each step of the value chain, determines which it should perform and which are best left to others, and takes full advantage of global opportunities to optimize its activities. The result of strategic analysis can lead to sourcing intangible assets like knowledge and technical expertise, or recruiting employees from abroad. It may lead to sourcing inputs from abroad, including raw materials, components and other inputs, which is scored as imports, and sending products for sale abroad, which is scored as exports. Or it may lead to FDI.

The test is whether a company makes the right choice at each step. Some companies pursue a global strategy by relying on imports of raw materials and components, and exports for sales of finished products, but perform all key activities in their home country. Dubai Aluminium, known as Dubal, is a world-class producer of foundry, billet and high-purity aluminum based in the United Arab Emirates. By any definition, Dubal pursues a global strategy, and ranks among the leading companies in its industry worldwide. Yet as described in the case study Dubal has concentrated its production in Dubai, where it runs the largest single site smelter in the western world. It pursues a global strategy without any FDI.

Yet for many companies – and an increasing number, as we saw in Chapter 1 – a global strategy calls for more than worldwide sourcing, and for more than exports to markets around the globe. It calls for performing some key activities abroad, or FDI.

CASE STUDY: DUBAI ALUMINIUM, GLOBAL STRATEGY WITHOUT FOREIGN INVESTMENT

Dubai Aluminium, known as Dubal, is one of the leading producers of aluminium in the world. Located in Dubai, in the United Arab Emirates (UAE), on the shores of the Persian Gulf, Dubal has a production capacity of 600 000 tons per year, and produces some of the best foundry, billet and high-purity aluminium in the world.

Dubal has constantly asked "Where in the world?" Ninety-five per cent of its customers are located outside of the UAE, mostly in Asia but also in Europe and North

America. Its sourcing of inputs, including bauxite, comes from traditional supplying countries like Australia and Jamaica. Its source of talent includes not just citizens of the Emirates, but Europeans and North Americans. In all these ways, Dubai actively scans the world for ways to improve.

Yet for production, it is located entirely in Dubai. Why? World-class aluminium production requires access to four things: proximity to shipping, for inbound and outbound logistics; abundant water for cooling in the smelting process; abundant energy; and a large-scale smelter to achieve economies of scale. Dubai is a superb location for production on all counts. The result: Dubai pursues a global strategy, yet optimizes its activities by locating one enormous smelter in Dubai and exporting. It relies on trade, not FDI.

Motivations for foreign direct investment

Foreign investment takes place for a handful of specific reasons or motivations.

Natural resource seeking

One of the oldest motivations for foreign investment is to secure natural resources found abroad, such as petroleum, minerals or agricultural products. Often these products can be procured by trade, but if the company undertakes activities that call for ownership and management of assets, such as oil exploration, copper mining or processing rubber, then the activity is considered to be direct investment.

Market seeking

Perhaps the common motivation for foreign investment is to seek revenues from new markets. Often new markets can be reached by exports, but many forces may push for local production: transportation costs, trade barriers, factor costs and more. Very many examples of international growth, ranging from Nestlé foods to Sony televisions to McDonald's restaurants, are all examples of market seeking. In each instance, companies locate some or all of their business model in a host market in order to generate revenues from that country.

A variant of market seeking is foreign investment to provide goods and services to other multinationals already present in the local market. Manufacturing firms demand that their suppliers establish businesses locally, often with consistent product quality and pricing. McDonald's enters new markets to sell its products to local customers, but may then ask its suppliers to locate there, as well. Amcor Rentsch, which supplies packaging for major cigarette and food companies, understands that serving major accounts depends on being able to supply them globally with efficient delivery at consistent prices and quality. The same holds for service firms that provide key activities for businesses. Banks, consulting firms, accounting firms, package delivery companies and more have expanded abroad, not according to their timetable, but in a rapid fashion to serve their rapidly expanding clients.

At first glance this may seem like another form of market seeking, and even a less risky one at that, since the company enters the new country with assurance of revenues from its customer base. But in other respects this form of expansion can be very problematic, since firms don't have the luxury to expand abroad when they're ready, or at the scale they wish. Rather, they have to follow the timetable and scope requirements of their customers, which may call for speed and flexibility in managing international growth.

Cost seeking

The purpose of cost seeking is to locate activities in one country to incur lower costs, then export those products for sale elsewhere. Cost seeking is a relatively recent phenomenon, as it relies on efficient shipping and the ability to manage a far-flung business model, with close coordination among activities in various countries. Some examples date back to the 1970s, when semiconductor factories performed design and capital-intensive steps in the United States, but labour-intensive activities such as bonding and assembly in low-wage countries in Asia. At about the same time, Phil Knight had the insight to assemble athletic shoes in what were then low-wage countries of Korea and Taiwan. Today, of course, Nike still performs design and marketing in the United States, but looks to Indonesia, Vietnam and other low-wage countries for labour-intensive activities. More broadly, the numbers of *maquiladoras* along the US–Mexico border and the rapid growth of factories in Shenzen, China, are examples of foreign investment for cost seeking.

Knowledge seeking

Thanks to the growing importance of knowledge or intellectual capital in a wide range of industries, a most recent motivation for foreign investment is to tap leading know-how, wherever it may be found. The motivation isn't necessarily to sell in that particular market, and it certainly isn't to lower costs. Eli Lilly's planned investments in research and development, mentioned above, are a good example. Microsoft offers another example: Microsoft performed all of its software development at Redmond, Washington, until 1997, when it announced plans to develop software in Cambridge, England, in Hyderabad, India, and in China. Why these locations? Not for cost reasons, or even the size of the local markets, but to harness some of the best brains in the world.

Global network optimizers

A final motivation for foreign investment is *network optimization*. The benefit isn't found in any one country, but is achieved by adding value by optimizing the entire network. One example is provided in the energy industry, where national deregulation in electricity is a major trend in many European countries, as well as in the United States. Firms like Enron, PowerGen, Texas Utilities and Scottish Power aren't looking to earn a profit by matching electricity generation and distribution in a given country, or even to match generation and delivery across countries, but aim to balance their upstream and downstream positions across a portfolio of countries. Their business model manages risk and optimizes long and short positions among countries, something possible only for firms with an array of these assets in multiple markets.

Can a company have more than one motivation for foreign investment? Of course. Take Mercedes-Benz. Until the 1990s, its luxury cars were a symbol of prestige and fine engineering recognized on all continents, yet product design, procurement of parts and manufacturing all took place in Germany. Mercedes had a *global strategy* – but didn't need to locate activities abroad, other than a dealership network to sell and service imported cars. By 1992, that strategy was untenable. Japanese automakers – Toyota, Nissan, Honda – had moved up-market. Germany's high costs, combined with the strong Deutsche Mark, made exports uncompetitive. As a result, Mercedes followed a two-pronged strategy, shifting to a full line of vehicles, away from exclusive reliance on luxury cars, and also locating production abroad.

Shifting motivations for foreign investment

A study undertaken in 1997, shown in Figure 2.2, gives an idea of how motivations for foreign investment are shifting. Managers in a sample of companies were asked to rate the frequency with which they undertook three kinds of international growth: (1) *trade*; (2) foreign investment for export elsewhere – that is, *cost seeking*; and (3) foreign investment for sale in the local market – that is, *market seeking*. For the years just completed, 1992–1996, *exports* rated 2.1, *market seeking* 2.2, and *cost seeking* at 1.1 For the next four years, the same companies predicted a slightly lower importance for *trade* (from 2.1 to 1.8), but greater importance for *market seeking* (2.2 to

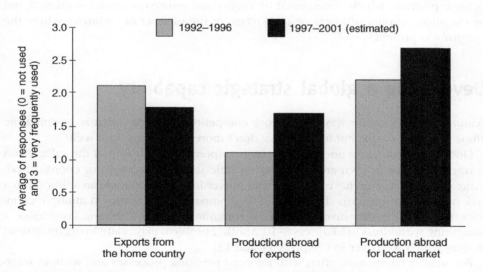

Figure 2.2: *Changing motivations for FDI, 1992-96 and 1997-2001*

Reproduced by permission of UNCTAD, Invest in France Mission and Arthur Andersen, in collaboration with DATAR (1997).

2.7) and *cost seeking* (1.1 to 1.7). These companies expected market seeking to continue to be more important than cost seeking, although the gap was narrowing. The greatest growth was expected for *cost seeking*, as companies planned to spread their value chain across national lines.

Global strategy: the second stage

So far we've thought about global strategy from the vantage point of a local firm, which is just beginning to identify opportunities on a worldwide basis. But what if a company is already operating in several countries? The question remains the same: *How can we identify and take advantage of global opportunities?* But the answers may take us in very different directions.

If a company is at the beginning of its international growth, pursuing a global strategy means identifying opportunities around the world for sourcing inputs, markets for exports or locations for cost-efficient manufacturing. They show how competitive advantage can be improved by optimizing activities globally.

If a company has already set up activities around the world, the next frontier in pursuing a global strategy might be to better integrate activities across countries. For example, improvements in coordination and communication might enable it to consolidate several factories across adjacent countries into a single regional factory, or to replace procurement in each country with coordinated procurement on a regional or global level.

The result may be a *reduction* of assets and employees in some countries – seemingly the opposite of international growth. But the objective is always a superior competitive position, which is measured by profits and return on capital employed, not by the sheer amount of assets or employees, or the number of countries where the company is present.

Developing a global strategic capability

Scanning worldwide for ways to improve competitive position – that is, grasping the globe – sounds simple enough. So why don't more companies do it well?

One answer is that no one in particular is responsible. Each step of the value chain is responsible for its own area, but there is little strategic oversight or coordination. Large companies often have the analytical power in each functional area, but often a lack of coordination across functions. If the company has activities in multiple countries, the problem may involve a lack of communication and sharing knowledge – something we address in Chapters 8–10. Another problem may relate to organizational design, which we cover in Chapters 11 and 12.

For smaller companies, often with informal planning processes and without international experience, undertaking global strategic thinking for the first time is a new and daunting challenge. What's the first step? Is it to form a department of global strategy?

Absolutely not. Grasping the global is too important, too pervasive, to be marginalized in a silo. It needs to be recognized as everyone's business, and linked with all key areas.

A good first step is to convene managers from key functions, and brainstorm ways the company can improve its competitive position by capturing global opportunities at each stage. One approach is to depict the value chain and ask, for each stage, two questions: first, the extent to which worldwide opportunities in procurement, manufacturing, marketing, and so on, could improve the company's competitive position; and second, the extent to which the company is already taking advantage of these opportunities. Comparing the potential gains to the present gains reveals the most important gaps, and identifies priorities for action.

 # SUMMARY

Companies pursue a global strategy when they *identify and take advantage of opportunities on a worldwide basis.* The place to begin is by understanding the value chain, that is, the sequence of steps that contribute to value for the customer. At each stage of the chain, companies should ask how they can benefit from global opportunities, whether in terms of sourcing inputs or exporting output. Common questions include where to conduct R&D, where to procure inputs, where to manufacture, where to find customers, how to market products, where to raise capital and/or where to recruit employees.

This global approach to value-chain analysis highlights the similarities and differences among industries when it comes to exploiting opportunities outside the home market. In some industries, for example, there are benefits to a global strategy at almost all steps of the value chain, resulting in a strong need for a global position. In other industries, a global strategy is rewarded in some steps but not others. And in still other industries, the benefits of a global strategy are few and far between, which means that those companies find little or no advantage to a global approach.

For many companies, a global strategy leads to FDI. The leading motivations for FDI include market seeking and cost seeking, with resource seeking and knowledge seeking important in many industries. Many firms undertake FDI for a combination of these reasons.

Companies just embarking on a global strategy should actively identify opportunities around the world. For companies that already have strong global positions, the next frontier in pursuing a global strategy might be to better integrate activities across countries. Finally, grasping the global is too important, too pervasive, to be marginalized in a silo. It needs to be recognized as everyone's business, and linked with all key areas.

LEARNING POINTS

- Analyse each stage of your value chain to identify potential global opportunities for each one, whether in terms of lowering costs, higher productivity or reaching new markets.
- Examine whether your industry *rewards* or *requires* a global position.
- Identify whether grasping the globe leads toward global sourcing, exporting or FDI – or perhaps all three.
- Know your motivation for FDI. Is it natural resource seeking, market seeking, cost seeking, knowledge seeking, network optimization or a combination of motives?
- If you are already operating in several countries, ask yourself how you can identify and take fuller advantage of global opportunities, perhaps by optimizing your worldwide network.
- Don't allocate responsibility for global strategy to one department. Encourage and involve all managers in the search to take full advantage of global opportunities.

References

David, D. (1997) Dossier on Globalization, *The Courier*, 164 (July–August).

Michaels, A. (2000) Lilly Eyes Expansion Abroad, *Financial Times*, 7 December 2000.

Perlmutter, H. (1969) The Tortuous Evolution of the Global Corporation, *Columbia Journal of World Business*.

Skapinker, M. (2000) A Whole World Away from Johannesburg, *Financial Times*, 23 November 2000, p. 12.

Thornhill, J. (2000) Interbrew Still Thirsting for Fresh Acquisitions in its Quest to Consolidate the World's Beers, *Financial Times*, 27 September 2000.

3

Crafting an International Growth Strategy

Developing an international growth strategy has to bear in mind impediments to growth, both internal and external to the firm. Other critical elements include choices about what activities will be performed, and in what markets. **Philip Rosenzweig** outlines the questions to ask and approaches to follow.

Overview

Identifying opportunities worldwide – *grasping the globe* – is an essential capability for any company today. Examining each step in the value chain, and asking how global opportunities can improve performance, is the first step toward building a strong global position.

The next questions are about action: *How do we get from our present position to our desired global position? And how can we reach that position quickly and successfully?*

It's tempting to seek a broad global position as fast as possible – tempting, but often unwise. There are, of course, examples of companies that are "born global", that from their birth locate specific activities in more than one country. But for companies already up and running, with activities in a home market, or with a small international position, rushing to build a broad global position is unwise. Remember the cautionary tale of Lincoln Electric in Chapter 1. Rather than rushing, it's better to craft a strategy – a series of steps – that will develop the desired global position over time.

Know your impediments to growth

Devising a strategy of international growth calls for an understanding of constraints. Some are internal to the company, others external.

Internal resources

The most obvious impediment to rapid growth are financial resources, or the funding needed to finance new investments abroad. The importance of financial resources to fuel international growth is obvious. Goldman Sachs recently ran an advertisement that pictured a couple of young managers in a small business. The caption read: "Inside every risky under-capitalized company is a blue chip multinational struggling to get out." It continued: "It's the size of your idea that counts, we can help you secure financing." The message was clear: capital is the key to international growth, and we can help you secure financing.

Financial resources are the most obvious impediment to growth, but they're often not the most important. In fact, it's easy to over-estimate their importance. Other resources prove more elusive. Managerial talent is often a serious resource constraint, especially for small and rapidly growing companies that can hardly find enough talented employees for their core domestic business. Freeing up staff for foreign assignments – a topic we'll address more fully in Chapter 6 – is a major barrier. Expertise on managing foreign activities in general, and on specific host markets in particular, is a major challenge. We'll have more to say about leveraging knowledge in Chapters 8 to 10. For the time being, the key point is for companies to identify and recognize fully the internal constraints they face regarding international growth.

External constraints

Companies also face a series of external constraints as they expand towards a desired global position. In a word, even if you've been successful at home, and even if you have abundant resources to expand abroad, what makes you think you'll be successful in a new country?

Leading the list is the strength of competitors in the host market, including both domestic firms and multinationals already in place. What competitive positions do they enjoy? Do they have successful business models? Have they tailored their offerings to local tastes? Do they have a loyal installed base? The key is to ask, sceptically, how a new entrant will compete successfully against existing competitors.

Some companies try to answer the question of existing competition by stating that their product is new and different – that they have no local competitors. Far from a point of encouragement, the lack of any local competition raises the possibility that the product or service is unsuited to local customers. Will they be receptive to your offering? Do they have the financial resources to afford your goods or services?

Finally, companies have to explore the availability of needed complements: suppliers and channels of distribution. Can the new entrant secure inputs at the right specifications, quantity, quality, price and reliability of supply? If not, it may be unable to move from exporting to local production, and may remain uncompetitive with local firms. Securing access to distribution channels can be even more daunting.

Basic strategic choices: what activities, what markets?

Moving from analysis to action means examining internal resource constraints and, at the same time, making clear-headed assessments of external impediments. Based on this analysis, companies have to marshal scarce resources in a focused way to ensure success. They need to address two questions: *what activities have to be performed, and what markets should be entered?* Of course, these questions are closely linked. They bring us back to the motivations for foreign expansion, as discussed in Chapter 2.

For *cost seekers* and *knowledge seekers*, international growth is about entering new markets in order to perform specific value-added activities, with the objective of eventual sales in other markets. They begin by identifying the activities they wish to perform, and then ask: where in the world shall we perform this activity? Where is the combination of cost, skills and productivity most desirable?

Market seekers, on the other hand, identify new markets where they can sell existing products; their focus is on market opportunities, customers, spending power, tastes and so on. Some *market seekers* are single-business companies, and roll out their business model in each country. Take McDonald's. Its strength is precisely the standard format restaurant with a similar menu. Precise product offerings will vary a bit, but standardization is by far more important and helpful to capture the essence. These companies have a fairly simple task: determining where to enter. They are less concerned with issues of what product lines to enter in, or what activities to perform, much less how these shift over time.

Market seekers with multiple products face a greater challenge. Not only must they decide where to enter, but they have to determine what product lines to begin with, and which to add over time. Some firms, in an attempt to replicate a successful home market formula, enter new markets with a full range of products. A better approach, given internal resource constraints, but also as a way to learn about local competitors and customers, is to begin with a limited range of products. In a sentence: *stay focused and do what's likely to succeed.*

A wide body of research suggests that companies do better when they enter new markets with product lines where they enjoy the greatest competitive advantage over local firms. By moving sequentially from greatest strength to lesser strength, companies build their capabilities rather than gamble all at once.

SEQUENTIAL MARKET ENTRY: STARTING WITH THE STRONGEST PRODUCT LINES

An insightful study of Japanese electronics firms entering the United States from 1976 to 1989, conducted by Professor Sea-Jin Chang of Korea University, revealed a clear sequential pattern of entry. These companies began by competing in their strongest line of business – that is, the one where they enjoyed the greatest advantage over local firms. That way, they offset the disadvantages they faced due to lack of familiarity with the local market and its competitive environment. As the subsidiary gained experience in doing business locally, it added lines of business that offered it a lower competitive advantage. Finally, when it learned to compete effectively in the local environment, it could add lines of business that offered little or no competitive advantage, and could learn from technologically superior US firms. Several subsidiaries of Japanese electronics firms added lines of business in precisely this fashion, adding new lines of business only when confident of success.

This pattern of incremental evolution may appear typical of Japanese firms, which are often thought to take a gradual and long-term perspective. Recent evidence, however, has shown that an evolutionary approach to the addition of lines of business describes the behaviour of many multinational companies, not just Japanese multinational companies. Data from European electronics firms entering the United States show largely the same pattern. Some European chemicals firms also exhibit a sequential approach to business entry, as exemplified by the French firm Rhône-Poulenc, which first entered the United States in areas of traditional strength such as agrochemicals and basic chemicals, and later acquired positions in surfactants and pharmaceuticals to tap local expertise and leverage it around the world.

CASE STUDY: SEQUENTIAL MARKET ENTRY AT SONY

Sony's global expansion provides a good example of sequential line of business entry. Until 1972, Sony manufactured all of its products in Japan and relied on exports. Its first investment abroad – foreign direct investment – came with a television assembly plant in San Diego, California, US. For Sony, televisions represented a core line of business, in which it enjoyed a strong competitive advantage over US firms. Two years later it expanded its US activities with a second line of business, audio equipment, and shortly thereafter in a third, magnetic tape.

In both of these, as well, Sony had a strong advantage over local firms. Sony's diversification resumed in the mid-1980s when a shift in the yen–dollar exchange rate stimulated further foreign investment. At that time, with a strong US country organization and substantial experience, Sony entered lines of business with a different motivation. Rather than exploit its existing advantages, it now entered in businesses where it sought to tap US technological leadership, such as data storage systems and personal telecommunications. Related to entry by line of business is the choice of entry mode, where once again Sony's experience was consistent with existing theory. At first Sony relied on small-scale greenfield investments as a way to ensure careful replication of its home country advantage; later, as it gained confidence in its ability to manage in the United States and as it sought to capture host country capabilities, it began to make acquisitions.

One of the most informative studies about international expansion was conducted by Andersen Consulting. The study focused on financial services companies that had expanded globally (Andersen, 2000). Financial services firms are *market seekers* – they sometimes tap the local market, and at other times they tap existing customers that had moved to those markets. The most common reasons for global expansion cited by financial services firms were: (a) to serve important customers in foreign markets; (b) to gain perceived advantage in foreign markets; and (c) to break out of a low-growth domestic market.

Andersen Consulting identified 31 financial services firms, many large and well-known companies from a variety of home countries. Interestingly – although perhaps not surprisingly – global expansion doesn't always lead to superior performance. In fact, only 14 of the 31 achieved superior return to shareholders over a ten-year period, defined as exceeding the local market average. Another five achieved superior revenue growth but not return to shareholders, and twelve of the 31 – fully 40% – underperformed the local market average.

What did the successful companies have in common? The best companies didn't try to replicate their home market business model, no matter how successful it may have been, in new markets. Rather, they started with a single line of business where they had the best chance of success. As Andersen Consulting explained: "They start their globalization push with a single line of business, such as credit cards, personal loans, re-insurance or investment brokerage. By taking this line-of-business approach to globalization, financial service companies can focus on activities in which they have unique or distinct competitive advantages."

Andersen Consulting found a consistent approach: "In every new country entered, each company had a clear competitive advantage of skill or scale and leveraged it effectively." What kinds of skills did they leverage? The list included brand management, distinctive go-to-market approaches including sales and marketing, superior distribution and customer management. The most successful firms also made use of shared systems to achieve scale economies in back office processing, and in addition leveraged their administrative services in human resources, finance, and purchasing both for best practices and for scale economies. In other words, they knew what they were good at, why their skills or scale might bestow them with a competitive advantage over local firms, and had the focused execution to leverage that benefit.

By contrast, almost half of the sample failed to achieve superior returns. Their motivations for foreign expansion weren't misguided – they were seeking new markets and were following existing customers abroad – but they had no compelling value proposition for local customers, or failed to exploit it.

There's a simple lesson: *lead with your strength*. The most successful firms led their international expansion with a narrowly targeted strategy, rather than trying to replicate their full-service business model in a new country. Leveraging their business know-how, technological expertise and scale leads to lower costs and more efficient customer service, which leads to further success – a virtuous cycle that leads to a broader position in time.

Evaluating new markets

The choice of new markets is a related, but just as complex, dimension of crafting a growth strategy. For years, multinational companies expanded into new markets slowly and incrementally, based on three criteria: *geographic proximity*, that is, to neighbouring countries first, and over time to most distant countries; *cultural similarity*, first to countries that were similar in habits, customs and language, and gradually toward more different cultures; and *similarity of economic development*, first to countries with similar standards of living and consumer buying power, and over time toward less developed markets.

CASE STUDY: GEOGRAPHIC EXPANSION AT COLGATE-PALMOLIVE

Colgate-Palmolive, the American consumer products firm, provides a good example of steady geographic expansion. It first entered Canada, a neighbour that was similar to the United States both in culture and economic development. By the 1940s, Colgate-Palmolive had established subsidiaries in 20 countries, virtually all of which were either geographically close to the United States (Canada and Mexico), shared an Anglo-Saxon culture and English language (Canada, United Kingdom, Australia and New Zealand), or were similar to the United States in economic development

(Canada, several countries in western Europe, Scandinavia, Australia and New Zealand). By restricting itself to these countries, Colgate-Palmolive needed to make only modest adaptations in product formulation and in its marketing approach; it refrained from entering countries where it would have faced sharp differences in culture and economic development.

Colgate-Palmolive then set its sights on more distant markets. In the 1950s and 1960s it expanded into Central America, a region close to the United States but less similar in culture or economic development. More recently, the firm expanded to several Asian and African nations, as well as to the newly opened markets in eastern European countries that were far from the United States, culturally dissimilar, and often sharply different in economic development. By the mid-1990s, Colgate-Palmolive managed subsidiaries in 75 countries on six continents. Its broad geographic position hadn't been achieved in one or even a few steps, but was the result of a gradual process of geographic expansion.

Many companies, including Colgate-Palmolive, expanded geographically over the course of several decades, beginning with countries that were similar and nearby, and eventually toward countries that were further and more distant.

Yet, as we stated in Chapter 1, the possibilities for new market entry have exploded. Companies can realistically enter scores of countries. In fact, they may need to develop a broad position for competitive survival. The capabilities needed for international growth in years past are no longer sufficient for today's competitive context. Colgate's steady approach, successful in past decades, is too slow in today's climate.

But in the face of all these possibilities, companies face a bewildering set of decisions and are often at a loss to evaluate them coherently. Many companies select countries for entry in a haphazard manner. Surprisingly, the decision process can be informal. Sometimes decisions are based on personal experiences by key managers – a visit long ago, an acquaintance in the country.

CASE STUDY: WHAT'S THE RIGHT UNIT? COUNTRIES, REGIONS, STATES

For purposes of simplicity we focus on the country as the unit of analysis – but companies must also question whether it's best to think in terms of countries, or a unit smaller than a country, like a province or state, or a unit larger than a country, such as a region. In large countries such as China or India, deciding to enter the country isn't the end of the story, but the beginning. Hyderabad or Bangalore, Uttar Pradesh or Mumbai, Shanghai or Shenzen?

In many instances, entry choices involve all three levels. Take the entry to Poland of Rentsch, the Swiss-based packaging company. At a first level, Rentsch wished to set up a plant in eastern Europe in 1993. Entry to the region was the first decision. Within eastern Europe, Rentsch evaluated countries and for reasons of geography, economics and demand for its product, chose Poland. But entry decisions didn't end there. Where in a large country like Poland should Rentsch set up manufacturing? Here it considered distance to existing customers, as well as universities and skill centres. The result of all these analyses was to locate in Lodz.

Mercedes Benz's entry to the United States in 1992 was a surprise to many: of all the places it could locate, Mercedes chose Vance, Alabama – a small town in a relatively poor state. Many observers noted that Alabama made sense for its low costs and traditional antipathy to unions, but other states in the American south looked at least as good, especially when it came to suppliers, skilled labour and infrastructure, including the nearby states of North Carolina and South Carolina. Cynics suggested that the deciding factor was an enormous investment subsidy. Mercedes executives countered that the commitment of local government officials was a deciding factor, and the ability to develop a greenfield site in a remote location was a plus.

Four categories for evaluating markets

Successful international growth depends on a systematic way to evaluate countries for entry. We suggest that an analysis of host markets should include four categories: *country factors*, which describe conditions that affect any company entering that country; *commercial factors*, which pertain to the specific industry; *competitive factors*, which address the size and strength of competitors, both local firms and other multinationals investing in the country; and finally, *network factors*, which recognize how the company's existing activities may help, or be helped by, any new entry.

Of course, before assessing potential markets, companies have to be clear about their goals. The first question isn't "Where shall I enter?" but "What are my motivations for international growth? What do I want to do abroad?" *Market seekers* will place a great deal of emphasis on the size of the market, disposable income, consumer habits and the strength of competitors. *Cost seekers* will care less about local consumers, and more about their ability to produce high-quality goods at low prices, and the laws permitting them to export. *Knowledge seekers* will, similarly, be more interested in the qualities of people it wishes to employ than local customers.

Country factors

Country factors pertain to the country as a whole, regardless of our particular industry or competitive position. They include geographic, demographic, economic and political factors.

One of the most comprehensive methods to evaluate host countries is *The World Competitiveness Yearbook*, published annually by IMD, our home institute, in collaboration with the University of Lausanne, Switzerland (IMD, 2000). *The World Competitiveness Yearbook* ranks countries on their ability to create an environment for companies to compete successfully. For any company contemplating entry to a new market, the factors included in the measures of country competitiveness are vital.

Variables are grouped into eight categories:

- *Domestic economy*, defined as the overall strength of the domestic economy at the macro level.

- *Internationalization*, defined as the extent to which the country participates in international trade and investment flows.
- *Government*, defined as the extent to which government policies are conducive to competitiveness.
- *Finance*, measured by the performance of capital markets and the quality of financial services.
- *Infrastructure*, measured as the extent to which resources and systems are adequate to serve the basic needs of business.
- *Management*, defined as the extent to which enterprises are managed in innovative, profitable and responsible manners.
- *Science and technology*, which measures the scientific and technological capability together with the success of basic and applied research.
- *People*, defined as the availability and qualifications of human resources.

These variables are scored and represented on an eight-dimensional spider diagram, as shown on Figure 3.1 for four sample countries, Australia, Belgium, Brazil and Canada. The better the environment for competitiveness of enterprises, the further the point from the origin, and the greater the area included.

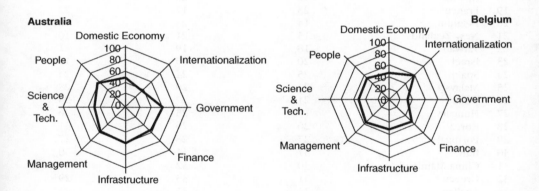

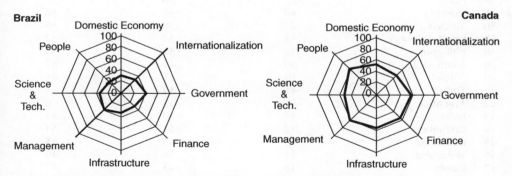

Figure 3.1: *Country competitiveness structure. Index values of the eight input factors*

Reproduced by permission of IMD from *The World Competiveness Yearbook 2000*.

Table 3.1: *Location attractiveness rankings*

Overall Ranking		Manufacturing	Research and development	Services and management
1	USA	1	1	1
2	Singapore	2	8	3
3	Finland	4	2	2
4	Netherlands	3	5	4
5	Switzerland	7	3	5
6	Luxembourg	–	18	8
7	Ireland	5	13	10
8	Germany	13	4	14
9	Sweden	8	7	13
10	Iceland	–	11	12
11	Canada	10	9	9
12	Denmark	9	12	11
13	Australia	11	10	7
14	China Hong Kong	6	22	6
15	United Kingdom	16	14	15
16	Norway	17	16	17
17	Japan	22	6	25
18	Austria	12	20	18
19	France	23	17	22
20	Belgium	14	23	20
21	New Zealand	15	21	16
22	Taiwan	18	19	21
23	Israel	20	15	19
24	Spain	25	24	24
25	Malaysia	24	29	28
26	Chile	21	27	23
27	Hungary	19	25	26
28	Korea	26	26	31
29	Portugal	27	28	27
30	Italy	37	31	30
31	China Mainland	30	32	39
32	Greece	31	33	29
33	Thailand	33	35	34
34	Brazil	29	30	32
35	Slovenia	40	41	38
36	Mexico	28	38	36
37	Czech Republic	34	34	42
38	Philippines	32	36	35
39	South Africa	36	42	37
40	Poland	39	37	41
41	Turkey	41	39	33
42	Argentina	35	43	40
43	India	38	40	43
44	Colombia	42	44	44
45	Indonesia	43	47	45
46	Venezuela	44	46	46
47	Russia	45	45	47

Reproduced by permission of IMD from *The World Competitiveness Yearbook 2000.*

In 1999, *The World Competitiveness Yearbook* added a new feature. In addition to the overall competitiveness of the country, it gave explicit attention to the country's attractiveness as a location for doing business. As described, "Attractiveness should not only be considered as a means to lure foreign investments, but as a prerequisite to retaining domestic firms' investments." Moreover, it recognized that attractiveness is related to motivation: one country may be very attractive as a site for low-cost manufacturing but hardly the place for high-tech research, whereas another country might be attractive for the opposite reason.

Accordingly, *The World Competitiveness Yearbook* composed three categories of *location attractiveness*: *manufacturing, research and development*, and *service and management*. The 2000 ranking for all countries in *The World Competitiveness Yearbook* by each category of location attractiveness is shown in Table 3.1. In large part, they draw on a similar set of variables about doing business in the host country, and therefore are highly correlated.

Yet there are interesting differences; a country may be highly attractive for one activity, but less so for others. For instance, Japan scores high for research and development (6) but much lower for manufacturing (22) and services (25); China Hong Kong shows the reverse, being attractive for manufacturing (6) and services (6) but lower for research and development (22).

The European Bank for Reconstruction and Development offers a similar scoring system (EBRD, 1999), gathering data on ten variables, and using a similar spider diagram to represent attractiveness. The EBRD scores countries in three categories: macro, micro, and law and order Each category has component variables, as follows.

- Macro: (1) political instability; (2) inflation; (3) exchange rates.
- Micro: (4) finance; (5) taxes and regulations; (6) infrastructure.
- Law and order: (7) functioning of the judiciary; (8) corruption; (9) street crime, theft and disorder; (10) organized crime.

The scores on each category are depicted on a spider web diagram, with highest scores closest to the origin, and lowest scores farthest out. The smaller the area within the spider web, the more attractive the country for inward investment. (Figure 3.2).

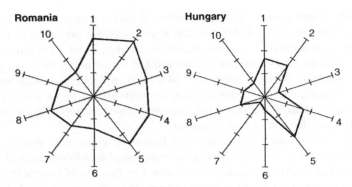

Figure 3.2: *Assessment of the investment climate. Examples are given for Romania and Hungary. Macro: (1) political instability; (2) inflation; (3) exchange rates. Micro: (4) finance; (5) taxes and regulations; (6) infrastructure. Law and order: (7) functioning of the judiciary; (8) corruption; (9) street crime, theft and disorder; (10) organized crime. Note that the extremity of each axis represents a score of 4, indicating a less favourable investment climate. The fuller the circle for a country, the more challenging is its investment climate*
Reproduced by permission of EBRD from the *Transition Report 1999.*

The great advantage of *The World Competitiveness Yearbook* and the EBRD study is the ability to compare easily across countries. On the other hand, for all of their wealth of data, neither is designed to provide in-depth narrative information about any single country. For that, a variety of other sources of information are available, including:

- *Economist Intelligence Unit* country reports;
- *Financial Times* country reports;
- public organizations in your country dedicated to foreign expansion;
- host country chambers of commerce;
- host country investment development agencies;
- your embassy or commercial officers in potential host countries.

Commercial factors

Country analysis pertains broadly to all companies considering entry, but doesn't differentiate among industries. Any company, of course, is interested in entry in a particular industry, not entry full-stop. It is interested in the factors that will allow it to compete in a range of commercial activities. And depending on the industry involved, a given host country may be more or less attractive.

The factors that should be evaluated are specific to a given industry and are included under commercial factors. They can be grouped into a few broad categories: customers, suppliers, workforce, infrastructure and channels of distribution.

Customers. It is not enough to have a general sense of the country's consumption patterns and disposable income. How, we must ask, will customers greet our particular product or service? Do they have a demonstrated taste for our product, or are we introducing something entirely new? Do local consumers have the ability to pay for our product – will it be affordable or a luxury? Will our product, bearing a foreign brand, have a special advantage or face additional obstacles?

Suppliers. If we hope to manufacture our product locally, will we find suppliers available locally? Will their quality and price meet our needs? If not, can we import supplies in sufficient quantity, or are there barriers to import, either regulatory (quotas, tariffs) or in terms of transportation costs? The more we must rely on imported supplies, of course, the more our costs will be linked to foreign currencies, imposing a currency exposure risk.

Workforce. In addition to general country factors regarding the local workforce – wages, education, work ethic and so on – we need to ask about the specific skills needed for the business we're in. Knowledge seekers begin with this issue, because if there isn't a local workforce with the skills needed, then entry is pointless. For cost seekers, too, the attraction of entry is often linked to employees with a particular productivity (output per cost) profile.

Infrastructure. Does our business require specific infrastructure, such as abundant water, inexpensive energy or rapid internal transportation? Are we specially reliant on advanced telecommunications? Beyond a general assessment of infrastructure, we need to identify the specific requirements for our business.

Channels of distribution. For some businesses, success depends on a given set of distribution channels, such as distributors or retail channels. Even if a company is satisfied that it can build local production, find suppliers and hire employees, it may find that the lack of complementary companies to handle commercial activities such as distribution is a major barrier to success. Similarly, are there channels of communication, including mass media, that allow us to succeed at our business model?

CASE STUDY: HEINEKEN'S ENTRY TO VIETNAM: BALANCING COUNTRY AND COMMERCIAL FACTORS

Heineken entered Vietnam in 1991 with a joint venture to form Vietnam Brewery Limited in Ho Chi Minh City. In terms of country factors, Vietnam's size and population made it highly attractive. As for competitor factors, Heineken was to be the first western brewer entering after the fall of the South Vietnam government in 1975, and it looked forward to substantial first-mover advantages.

More daunting were commercial factors. Heineken could look to no local suppliers of packaging – cans, bottles or even labels. There were no established channels of distribution for beverages – just many road-side stands. The Vietnamese, while literate and intelligent as a people, had little training in commercial skills and had suffered from 15 years of communist rule in the south. Infrastructure for transportation and refrigerated delivery were low. As Heineken's first country managing director put it, the greatest challenges weren't related to building the brewery, something Heineken knew how to do, or even selecting and training its local workforce. The greatest challenge was commercial – building a distribution network, building brand awareness and getting the product to market.

Competitive factors

Strategy is never crafted in a vacuum – it's always about competition. The competitive dimension is also key when evaluating host markets. Even if country and commercial factors seem attractive, the possible moves and countermoves of rival companies may dissuade us from entry.

But exactly what competitors should we consider? It's not as simple as identifying other companies in our industry. For market seekers, competitors are those companies that offer the same kind of product or service. But for cost seekers, competitors aren't necessarily from the same industry. More likely, they're companies looking to perform the same activities as you are, whether in your industry or not. They're rivals for the resources you want – and if you're not seeking final customers, then the basis of competition is something else. For a cost seeker, competitors may be other cost-seeking companies that are attracting the same employees – that is, the same skill set at comparable wages. For knowledge seekers, once again competitors are companies looking to hire similar talented people, such as scientists or engineers, whether in your industry or not.

This line of thinking suggests that finding a host market where we face little in the way of competition is, other things being equal, desirable. But not so fast. The presence of some competitors may mean the ground has been prepared for our entry. It may be easier to enter into a setting where labour laws have been tested, where suppliers have been developed, and where infrastructure is in place, perhaps thanks to a first competitor. As Michael Porter described in *The Competitive Advantage of Nations* (Porter, 1990), clusters of companies competing in the same industry create healthy environments for education, for suppliers, for customers and as magnets for skilled labour. Far from seeking to avoid countries where our competitors are operating, we may find that they have built on strengths in the local economy and have created a ripe setting for our success. So again, be careful how you think about competitors. In some circumstances they may be a deterrent, but in others an attraction.

Finally, strong competitors may be helpful to us in a paradoxical way: they force us to raise our level of competitiveness. We have to learn when confronted with strong local companies – and the fruits of this learning can be applied elsewhere in the world.

CASE STUDY: JOLLIBEE'S EVALUATION OF NEW MARKETS

After growing successfully in its home market of the Philippines during the 1980s, Jollibee Foods Corporation turned its attention to international growth. Initial expansion to Singapore, Taiwan and Indonesia all came about through family friends who asked Jollibee to open franchises, not because of any careful analysis. Like many companies, it was reactive and haphazard and met with mixed success.

In the next few years, Jollibee followed an international growth strategy of "planting the flag" – that is, building at least some presence in several different countries that were either nearby or where Filipino expatriates lived. By 1996, there were 24 Jollibee stores spread among 10 countries: Brunei (6), Saudi Arabia (4), Indonesia (3), Kuwait (3), United Arab Emirates (2), Hong Kong (2), Bahrain, Guam, Malaysia and Vietnam (1 each). But the result was a dispersion that spread resources thin: there wasn't enough critical mass to succeed anywhere.

By 1998, Jollibee retrenched some of its losing operations and took a focused approach to international growth. Choice of which countries to enter was critical. Scarce resources – financial, managerial – didn't permit Jollibee to enter multiple markets at once; it needed to evaluate among very different options. There were three major contenders: Papua New Guinea, a moderate-sized market but one where Jollibee could have a strong first-mover advantage; Hong Kong, where a large Filipino expatriate community beckoned, and which might serve as a springboard to China, but where competition was intense; and the United States, specifically California, which offered a large market but which was already crowded with local competitors.

To the surprise of many, Jollibee decided against Papua New Guinea – which could be profitable in the short term, but offered less in the way of long-term success – and decided to enter Hong Kong and California. Both had sizeable Filipino expatriate communities that offered immediate returns, and both held a promise for future growth. Both would also push Jollibee to sharpen its skills by competing with strong local players. The former strategy of "plant-the-flag", with its dispersion of resources, was replaced by a clear focus on two large markets. In this sense, Jollibee combined all aspects of new market evaluation: country, commercial, competitive and network.

Network factors

Country, commercial and competitive factors are vital, but they're insufficient. International growth isn't a series of isolated decisions; it's a process of extending a business model worldwide. Opportunities can't be appraised one at a time. They only take on their full meaning and value when seen in the context of the entire company, meaning all its activities around the world, and its plans for future growth.

For many companies, the obvious question – *Is this an attractive country to enter?* – has to be rephrased – *Is this an attractive country to enter given where I already am, and given where I'd like to eventually go?*

There are three second-order questions that follow:

- How can my existing position – that is, activities in countries where I'm already present – help me compete effectively in this new market?
- How can activities in the new market contribute to help me with my existing activities?
- How can entry in this new market lead to further entries? That is, can it serve as a platform for further entries?

Answers to these questions call, in turn, for a systematic analysis of each stage of the value chain. For example:

- In *purchasing*, can adjacent markets combine purchases to lower their input costs?
- In *manufacturing*, can adjacent markets help each other in sharing capability? On one hand, can we export to the new market by drawing on existing manufacturing capacity in adjacent markets? On the other hand, can the additional customers in the new market let existing plants in adjacent countries operate at greater capacity and thereby achieve lower unit costs of production?
- In *marketing*, can neighbouring countries share media advertising, use the same language and a common set of channels?
- In *technical or customer support*, can adjacent countries share resources and operate more efficiently?
- Are our *customers* mobile across countries, in which case offering the same product or service may enable us to serve their needs better?

These are just some of the questions to pose. The key is to examine new markets not in isolation, one at a time, but as they relate to our ongoing activities. International growth is a process of building and extending a network, and the benefits or risks of any single country must be considered in this broader context.

 # SUMMARY

Crafting a global strategy demands a series of steps, not a single leap. It means understanding internal resource constraints, as well as external impediments including competitors, to identify products and markets.

Regarding the choice of products, successful companies lead with their strength, ensuring success in the early phase of international growth, and building capabilities for subsequent expansion. When it comes to evaluating countries for entry, successful firms use a systematic approach that takes into account country, commercial, competitive and network factors.

Yet even this series of decisions about what to do, and where to do it, only addresses the strategic capabilities needed for accelerated international growth. Implementing a successful growth strategy calls for a variety of other capabilities: working with partners, rapid staff deployment, leveraging expertise globally and adapting the organization design. We turn our attention to those capabilities in the subsequent chapters.

 **LEARNING POINTS**

- International growth is a *process* – it requires a series of steps, not a single leap.
- Know your impediments to rapid growth: both internal resources and external market factors.
- Focus on your strength: what will allow you to compete successfully against local firms?
- When entering new markets, don't offer your full line of products or services. Rather, *lead with your strength*.
- Take a systematic approach to evaluating new markets: country, commercial, and competitive factors.
- Consider network implications of any new entry: how will presence in a new market take advantage of our existing position, or else set the stage for further entries?

References

Andersen, A. (2000) Globalization in Financial Services, *Global Thought Leadership Special Report*, Andersen Consulting, 2000.

ERBD (1999) *Transition Report 1999*, European Bank for Reconstruction and Development.

IMD (2000) *The World Competitiveness Yearbook 2000*, Institute for Management Development, Lausanne.

Porter, ME (1990) *The Competitive Advantage of Nations*, Free Press, New York.

Part Two

Managing Global Partnerships

4

Competing through Alliances and Joint Ventures

Alliances are becoming an integral part of international growth. Companies are forming partnerships for a wide variety of reasons, from exploiting new opportunities in expanding markets, to dealing with technological change, to coping with economic and political uncertainties. But they are anything but an easy option. **Vladimir Pucik** examines the range of issues companies should consider when it comes to alliances.

Overview

More and more firms are entering into alliances in their quest to speed up their international growth. Initially considered only as a means of securing market entry, alliances today are an integral part of global strategies in all aspects of the value chain. There are many reasons why alliances are created, and it is important to consider the "why" of an alliance, before looking for the "who".

Alliances are anything but an easy option and demand a lot of management time and resources. They involve a complex process that is full of ambiguities and contradictions reflecting the complexities of international competition. There are the tensions between competition and collaboration, between global and local interests, between the venture and its parents, between leveraging and developing competencies. Nor are they immutable: alliances evolve.

There are a range of issues that companies seeking alliances have to consider, including the selection of partner, the type of link and the question of control. Contracts are important, but ultimately they serve only as frameworks for a long-term relationship. Learning from the alliances should be a key objective, not only to prevent the erosion of a firm's competitive position, but as a building block for the future.

Why form a strategic alliance?

Alliance-based organizations constitute a significant share of new business ventures today. They are important and commonly used tools of international growth. In the superheated environment of global competition, where the emphasis is on exploiting new opportunities from expanding markets and rapid technological change while coping with economic and political risks and uncertainties, seeking partners for cross-border alliances of many different forms is an increasingly popular strategy.

Some alliances are created to cut the cost of market entry; others are geared to exploit economies of scale or scope. Some alliances aim to leverage existing capabilities; others are set up to create new knowledge. Some alliances seek to achieve an "insider" status; others to extend global reach. What alliances are not about are companies being nice to each other.

A "win–win" strategy is only a tool to create a healthy alliance; it should not be seen as the goal in itself. Obviously, for an alliance to be sustainable, it must benefit all partners: respect for the partner's needs and mutual value creation are prerequisites for a successful relationship. But this does not imply that value creation must be equal or that all alliances should be sustainable for an indefinite period. Most are transitory in nature, reflecting a competitive situation at a particular point in time. When the situation changes, so does the need for the alliance. The definition of a "win" may change as the company strategy evolves, as will the role that the alliance is expected to perform.

Contrary to a popular metaphor, an alliance is *not* like a marriage – longer alliances are not necessarily better. The success of an alliance should not be measured by its longevity. The only valid measure of alliance success is the degree to which an international alliance helps the firm to improve its ability to compete in global markets. Problematic alliances drain away management energy and resources, but they often are allowed to limp on for too long, since shutting them down would imply "failure".

Alliance is a process, not a deal

Although the number of international alliances is on the rise, the alliance fever is often a symptom of a competitive problem, not its solution. Many alliances do not live up to expectations and they show persistently high rates of failure. This occurs mostly when alliances are conceived as defensive tools, when firms participate in alliances primarily to save resources, or simply to supplement what they lack. However, defensive alliances seldom work, as the focus on "taking" from the alliance will usually be accompanied by little investment in learning, particularly if the primary objective has been to minimize capability development costs. As a result, the firm's competitive position, both in the market and *vis-à-vis* the partner, deteriorates.

By contrast, cross-border alliances are most effective when they are part of an offensive strategy, when they emphasize building a common competitive and learning culture. Successful collaborations partners embark on a "race to learn", they see the alliance as a tool for faster and broader gains in competitive capability, for example, in market penetration or technology acquisition. Rather than reducing investment in competency development, these firms increase their organization-wide learning skills because they recognize that the investment will be recovered through the growth of their business.

However, an alliance is not just a deal between two or more partners; it is a complex process that is full of the ambiguities and contradictions that reflect the tensions of international competition. The process starts with establishing the strategy for the business, then selecting the partner, negotiating the specific contract and managing the implementation. The result should be improved competitive advantage. It requires continued attention to detail as well as a longer-term view. It also implies an emphasis on organizational learning and accumulation of "invisible assets": new competencies that improve competitive advantage. But alliances are not forever. Most alliances either die early or evolve, just as any other business venture. Alliance stability is a contradiction in terms.

Finally, alliances are always much harder to implement than most companies expect, and they can take up enormous amounts of management time. Before they embark on alliances, companies should take a hard look at why they are doing it. If it is because everyone else is, or because a competitor might do it first, then the best strategy is to think again.

Developing strategic framework: What kind of alliance?

There is a wide range of inter-firm links that companies engage in, from creating a jointly owned business unit, usually called a joint venture, to a much less formal collaboration. Figure 4.1 (based on the work of Yoshino and Rangan, 1995) shows the breadth and depth of possible alliance relationships.

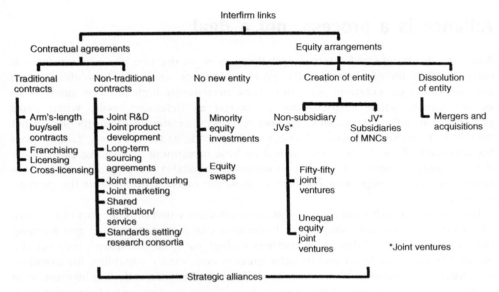

Figure 4.1: *Classification of strategic alliances*

Reprinted by permission of Harvard Business School Press. From *Strategic Alliances* by Yoshino & Rangan. Boston, MA 1995. Copyright © 1995 by the President and Fellows of Harvard College, all rights reserved.

The management challenges obviously increase as companies move through the spectrum of alliances, from "simple" marketing agreements with foreign distributors, or "original equipment manufacturers" manufacturing agreements, to stand-alone ventures. However, alliances by their nature are dynamic, and change over time with shifts in the relative bargaining power of the partners and their expectations about alliance objectives. This needs to be kept in mind from the outset.

There are two dimensions of alliance relationships that require a careful consideration: the strategic intent of the partners, and the expected contribution of the venture to the creation of new knowledge. With respect to strategic intent, alliances among firms with *competitive* strategic interests may require different management approaches than those where interests are *complementary*. With respect to knowledge creation, while all alliances involve learning, some are actually formed with the main purpose of generating new knowledge. This *learning/knowledge creation*

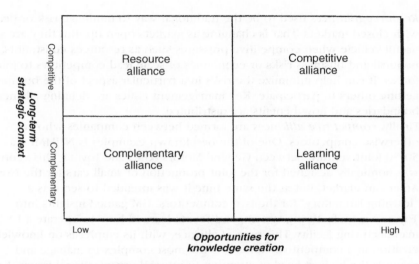

Figure 4.2: *Strategic framework for international alliances*

aspect of alliances has major implications for how the alliance should be organized. Both of these dimensions can change over time.

Figure 4.2 shows the four archetypes of alliance strategies based on their strategic and knowledge-creation contexts: complementary, learning, resource and competitive alliances.

- A *complementary alliance* is formed when two (or more) partners with complementary strategic intent join forces to exploit their existing resources or competencies – by linking different elements of the value chain, for instance – and where knowledge creation is not a prime objective. A typical complementary alliance is the traditional joint venture where one partner contributes technology and the other facilitates entry into a local market. Or two partners may contribute complementary products that may lead to a new product stream. Key management issues are long-term synergy and resources commitment. There are elements of this type of alliance in all alliances.
- A *learning alliance* can develop from a complementary alliance when both partners share an interest in enhancing their individual competencies, whether through an exchange of existing knowledge, or the development of new knowledge where the partners jointly participate in the same value chain activities. An example of the learning alliances is the Fuji-Xerox joint venture in Japan. Originally set up to facilitate Xerox's penetration of the Japanese market, it now serves as a critical source of competency development for the Xerox Corporation worldwide. Compared to complementary alliances, learning alliances can be more long term and require much more interaction, shared work and interface management. Key management issues are the acceleration of learning and knowledge diffusion.

- *Resource alliances* used to be the traditional way to minimize risk or deal with closed markets. That is changing as markets open up. But they are still a useful vehicle when competitive pressures such as resources constraints, political and business risks or economies of scale lead competitors to join forces. It can help minimize the risks in a particular aspect of the business by getting others to participate. Key management issues are defining alliance boundaries and how benefits are distributed.
- Finally, *competitive alliances* are formed between companies who are otherwise competitors. One of the best-known examples is NUMMI – a 50/50 joint venture between General Motors (GM) and Toyota. This venture was nominally designed for the joint production of small cars for the North American market, but at the same time it was intended to serve as a "learning laboratory" for the two competitors. GM gained insights into Toyota's manufacturing system, and Toyota learned how to operate a US-based manufacturing facility. This type of alliance, with its emphasis on knowledge creation in a competitive context, is the most complex to manage and requires the highest level of attention to internal organizational issues. Key management issues are maintaining learning parity, and balancing trust and vigilance.

Alliances in all four quadrants can enhance a firm's competitive advantage. However, the management challenges associated with each alliance scenario are fundamentally different. Problems occur when the company does not know what kind of alliance it has entered, or when it does not read and respond appropriately to early signals that the nature of an alliance is changing.

For example, in a complementary alliance it might be possible to rely on the local partner to recruit and train the alliance workforce since the loyalty factor may not be an issue, at least in the short run. However, in a competitive alliance such an approach could prove costly in the event of subsequent conflict between the partners. In a complementary alliance it may make sense to set up the venture as a stand-alone entity to promote internal entrepreneurship. In a resources partnership, there are also benefits in creating an entity with clear boundaries so that the competitive strategic context does not inhibit the performance of the alliance. However, in learning alliances the boundaries between the venture and the parent should be thin to maximize the opportunities for fast knowledge sharing. In a competitive alliance, it is not just fast learning that matters but also its speed and effectiveness relative to the partner – maintaining learning parity is the key to sustaining such as relationship. The knowledge-creation strategies have to be clearly calibrated, with measures of the learning outcomes integrated into the performance management process.

There are no generic alliances, and none of these types of alliance is "better" than another. One cannot argue that one strategy should be pursued and another avoided. The point to remember is that alliances do not always fit neatly into conceptual boxes. Some partnerships are complementary in parts of the value chain and competitive in others. Also, alliance strategies are not set in stone. Not only can they display elements of several or even all of the above types, but they also may shift in focus over time as strategic intent changes. So what began as a complementary alliance, for example, can eventually become a competitive alliance, or a resource alliance can turn into a learning alliance.

That is fine if this is well understood by both sides. But partners can get upset when the other's strategic intent does change, even though it is naïve to expect the original assumptions to hold forever. To put it another way, you cannot control other people's dreams. Monitoring the direction of the alliance is thus essential. And, rather than put boundaries on alliances, think instead about how to manage the evolution. It will depend on any number of factors, internal and external to the firm. However, once interests diverge there is really no going back to the good old days.

It is also important to keep in mind that alliance positioning is not a unilateral decision. There are two sides, each of which has its own views and strategies. So the management process should match the strategic position. This is about the relationship as a whole, across the spectrum from strategy through to psychology. With an acquisition a closure of sorts can be reached, although sorting out post-merger integration brings its own challenges. But alliances are ambiguous because there is no sole owner, and therefore even well-designed alliances are often difficult to manage.

CASE STUDY: WHIRLPOOL CORPORATION ENTERING SLOVAKIA

In May 1992, Whirlpool Europe, the European subsidiary of Whirlpool Corporation, one of the world's leading manufacturers of large home appliances, formed a joint venture with Tatramat, the leading manufacturer of washing machines in what was then Czechoslovakia. It was situated in the town of Poprad, not far from the Tatra mountains. The Slovak company offered many of the ingredients Whirlpool was looking for in a potential partner in the region: it had the expertise in washing machines with an annual output of about 200 000 units, a skilled labour force, lower costs in comparison with western Europe and a good location for exports to eastern Europe.

The plan for the venture was both to introduce the Whirlpool brand into the region, and to use the factory as alternative capacity for western Europe. Whirlpool's long-term intention was to have 100% ownership, as a part of its European strategy of creating "focused" factories that could produce single product lines for multiple markets. On its part, Tatramat's managing director, Martin Ciran, knew that to survive his company needed modern technology, and access to markets and capital. He had already begun a radical rationalization of the manufacturing process in the Poprad factory, cutting down the Tatramat workforce from 2300 in 1989 to 1300 in 1991.

Negotiations had proved complex and drawn out but concluded in the fall of 1991 with an agreement to set up a joint venture. The new company, called Whirlpool-Tatramat, provided Whirlpool with the initial equity stake set at 44%, representing the cash value of shares in the venture purchased from Tatramat and Whirlpool's contribution of know-how in technology, manufacturing and marketing. The agreement stipulated that the new company, staffed by half of the Tatramat's workforce, would produce only top-loading washing machines, popular in the East. Whirlpool guaranteed the employment level and the integration of the joint venture into its sales network. Ciran was made managing director of the new venture. Only one expatriate joined the Poprad team.

Over the next few years the venture was plagued with difficulties. With less than 100000 units produced in 1993, the productivity and quality lagged significantly below original estimates. The overall economic situation in the region was also deteriorating. Losses were mounting, even with employee numbers cut down to just over 200 in spite of the original guarantees. By early 1994 Whirlpool was faced with a difficult decision: to invest additional money and become a majority owner, or cut the losses and leave.

Whirlpool decided to go ahead because it trusted the local management team and its ability to move the situation around. Its decision to stick it out proved to be the right one. In October 1996 the Slovak venture became a 100% subsidiary of Whirlpool Europe. By the year 2000, 700 plus employees were producing over one million units a year, with 80% of exports outside the country. It also boasted the highest plant productivity among Whirlpool's factories in Europe.

There are a number of lessons that can be taken from this experience. First of all, alliances evolve, and much of what was initially negotiated had been proven irrelevant (employment guarantees, market protection). Also, Whirlpool was willing to give its Slovak partner the time and opportunities to learn. For example, Whirlpool agreed to carry on making an older model for longer than it should have, until the locals themselves were ready to move on. Perhaps most critical was the leadership factor – the role of Martin Ciran, who acted as the champion for the alliance even during the most difficult days.

Partner selection logic

Before commencing negotiations, it is important to remember that an alliance is a complex and often messy journey. This is not about the money involved as much as the enormous amount of management time alliances demand. There are three questions that should be answered at the start:

* What is my long-term goal?
* Is an alliance really necessary?
* How long it is likely to last?

Companies need to be able to articulate the business objective of the proposed alliance, and what is the value added of engaging in a business relationship that will inevitably consume significant resources before yielding results. And mapping scenarios for exit should be part of the initial planning.

There are a number of factors to consider when it comes to selecting partners. Chief among these is to make sure you start with a strategy, not a partner. This may seem an obvious statement, but it is not always followed in practice. Companies, or more precisely their chief executives, sometimes "fall in love". Notwithstanding the importance of personal relationships at the top, there is a danger in selecting the partner before the strategic purpose is clarified.

There is no magic in the selection criteria. Look first for complementarity of benefits. Make sure that the partners can contribute in a meaningful fashion to competitive advantage and that the goals are compatible within a desired time horizon. Is there a potential for long-term synergy? Potential conflicts have to be critically examined. What would you do in your partner's shoes? And check if your strategic intent is matched by credible and sustainable leverage.

Dominant competitors are better avoided as alliance partners, or at least one has to be very realistic about obstacles in such relationships. On the other hand, sometimes it makes a lot of sense to ally against a common enemy. Take the case of three companies – one was Japanese, one American and one a family-owned German firm – who were third, fourth and fifth in the market and who formed a marketing alliance against the two dominant competitors. Meetings tended to be fraught with tension and arguments until one marketer had a simple but effective idea. In the meeting "war room" he stuck the logos of the two leading companies on the wall and when the arguments became too territorial, anyone in the room could push an under-the-table button which would make the logos flash. This made it abundantly clear just who the enemy was.

In terms of commitment to the alliance, it is always easy to get the chief executives to shake hands. But the truth is that some companies will never make good partners because they lack a collaborative culture and/or a complementarity of interests as partners does not exist. Check the partner's reputation in this respect; learn as much as you can before you sign the deal.

Controlling the alliance

In most negotiations, alliance governance is very close to the top of the agenda. However, control and influence are difficult to negotiate, as which partner controls the alliance depends mainly on its relevance to the business. One partner might have the majority equity stake, but that can have limited real value. Even if you have a contract that gives you "control", what is your actual leverage? There are many paths leading to exercise of control. The important point is that selecting a good partner and a careful management strategy to secure influence can be less costly and more effective than focusing on formal control.

In "joint-venture" type of alliances, equity and control are not always correlated. In the absence of other supporting mechanisms, equity control is no guarantee that the venture will evolve in line with the intended strategy. There is nothing wrong with attempting to gain a majority position, which may for example provide a tax or financial reporting advantage. However, it is a fallacy to assume that equity control equals management control. A minority equity position, coupled with effective representation on the venture management team and an influence over the flow of know-how, may have more real impact on how the venture operates than a nominal majority exercised from a distance.

From an accounting perspective, 51% of the shares may entitle the owner to 51% of the dividends, but these are often the last piece of the cash pie to be distributed. Internal transfer pricing, purchasing decisions, the cost of services provided by a local partner and payroll determined by compensation levels, all have an impact on cash flow long before any dividends are declared. At the same time, "the last two per cent" (going from a 49% share to 51%) is the most expensive piece of equity. While intangible contributions may substitute for capital in a minority position (the infusion of technical or market know-how, transfer of depreciated assets, brand equity), a majority position usually requires cash.

Another frequent mistake is to bargain for control by negotiating respective valuations of intangible or ill-defined inputs: know-how, brand, land, etc. This is usually a frustrating exercise; the only winners are the consultants. So first agree on the strategic direction, and then bring in the accountants to help make sense of the balance sheet, always bearing in mind that valuation of inputs is by its very nature arbitrary.

Sometimes, the quest for control is justified by the need to have a voting majority. But in fact, alliance boards seldom vote. Pushing through a majority vote, in most circumstances constitutes the first step in dissolving the alliance. If the partners have a common interest in maintaining the relationship, disputes are resolved in private, and boards act only after a consensus is reached. In addition, protection of strategic interests can be achieved by other means, such as shareholder agreements or articles of incorporation that stipulate what actions require unanimous or qualified majority consent of the shareholder.

Compare it to water polo: what you see above the water's surface are the elegant passes. But beneath the surface there is a lot of pushing and kicking. In alliances also, fights tend to happen on the ground floor. That is where more strength may be needed, as the partner who controls the operating decisions usually has most influence.

Ultimately, equity distribution should match the strategic context. Some companies will say they always have to have a majority stake. Others will say they never do. But what they should do is take each alliance case by case. Saying "always" or "never" can lead to trouble because alliances have more "motion" than might normally be anticipated. Alliances evolve; so will the equity position.

Think beyond contracts

Here are some useful points to bear in mind during negotiations:

- everything will take longer than expected;
- cultural differences are important, but common sense, open mind and respect for others can help;
- be realistic about your leverage, do not demand what you cannot enforce;
- you will never be too well prepared.

Negotation do's and don'ts

During the negotiating process, there are some critical things *to do*:

- prepare well
- develop personal relationships
- watch carefully and compare observations

- take time to analyse responses
- avoid intimidation
- stick with agreed-on team strategy
- caucus when you need to discuss matters privately
- make time for informal talk
- end meeting on a positive note.

Here are some critical things *not to do*:

- compromise your principles
- lose your temper
- be pressured; if you have doubts, delay
- rush the other side
- escalate demands
- surprise the other side
- wait to convey bad news
- argue among yourselves; save it for the caucus
- make promises you cannot meet
- underestimate the other side.

When negotiations are completed, a contract is signed. This might be the formal expression of intentions and can provide a framework for expected behaviour. But no matter in how much detail they are drawn up, there will always be another twist. So on the whole it is probably more advantageous to have the contract set an outline of how to proceed rather than try and predict in detail all the permutations that might arise.

Drawing contracts is a good discipline, since it brings into open the key issues that should be agreed on. But the focus of alliances should be not on the contracts, which are vital only until they are actually signed. As we discussed before, the strategic context of the alliance is most likely to shift over time and synergy cannot be protected by legal clauses. The best leverage is when the deal makes sense for both parties.

It is helpful when there is an understanding about the "end-game" from early on. Alliances do not last forever. The issue is: does one partner share this exit strategy with the other? It is a sensitive decision to make. With some partners it is possible. With others, it will destroy the deal because partners will wonder why they should enter into this process at all, if their prospective partner is already discussing the exit strategy.

Key alliance management challenges

Think of the management of alliances as a three-way process that takes place not only between partners, but also within each partner. Managers involved with the alliance should make sure all this is in alignment by continuously evaluating strategic synergy between the partners, monitoring compliance with commitment made, and at the same time promoting mutual learning. There is only one way to do it – maintaining trust and keeping up personal networks and relationships.

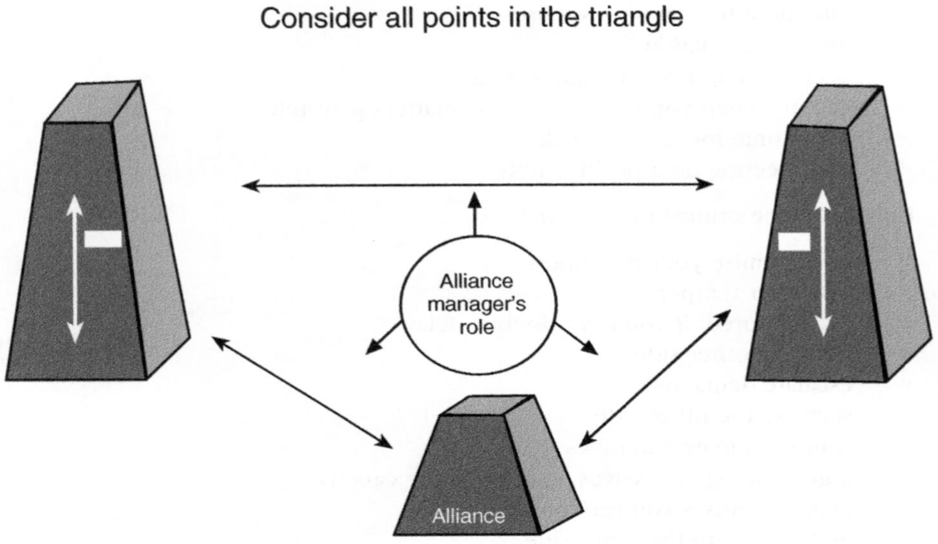

Consider all points in the triangle

Figure 4.3: *Alliance management process*
Reproduced with permission of Peter Killing, IMD.

The job of alliance managers is demanding (Figure 4.3). They might have a lot of accountability, but few resources. So what are the characteristics of successful alliance managers? To build trust and manage the relationships they must have professional credibility, the skills to exert lateral influence, show adaptability and flexibility, and most importantly a high tolerance for ambiguity and frustration.

The nomination of the venture manager can generate intense debate. One can argue that the venture manager must have the goodwill of both parents in order to operate effectively. If the ongoing commitment and support of both partners are needed for the venture to succeed, then installing somebody as venture managing director who overwhelmingly represents the interest of one partner may be counterproductive. And special care is needed when the joint entity is essentially independent of the parents' operations, as in the case of many complementary or resource alliances.

However, if the venture activities need to be integrated with that of the parent, then an arm's-length relationship may not be appropriate. There is a fine line between representing the best interests of the venture *and* that of the parent company, one of the many dualities that must be faced in alliance management. If an insider from one firm seems the logical choice as venture manager – because of his/her know-ledge of the business or geographical area – it is important to minimize incentives that show favouritism. It should be clear that the manager's future career depends on the success of the venture rather than on securing the ticket to come back home.

An alliance succeeds because managers and employees believe in the promise of the concept and are willing to invest personal effort to make it happen. Alliances without champions do not survive for long. The ambiguity and the uncertainty of the relationship impair the capacity to deal with the complex issues embedded in most partnerships. To prosper, alliances require champions, business leaders who believe in the purpose and who work hard to make it succeed.

The critical role of alliance learning

Alliance partners have to manage numerous ambiguities in the relationship, and figure out the borderline between competition and cooperation – although this will most likely be fuzzy at best. There is no right answer to how to manage an alliance. Nevertheless, it is better to work together from a platform of mutual strength rather than one of mutual weakness. Therefore, learning and capability development should be the ultimate aim.

Some alliances are formed with learning as the primary objective, in others, learning and knowledge creation complement more traditional business objectives. Of course, all alliances include some learning aspects, the least of which is how to work effectively with partners. However, in learning and competitive alliances, knowledge acquisition and assimilation become the focal point and the ability to learn becomes the key source of competitive advantage.

Effective alliance learning is important not only to prevent the erosion of a firm's competitive position, but also as a building block for the future. A well-known example of a successful learning alliance is Fuji-Xerox, a joint venture between Fuji Photo and Xerox Corporation that is now more than 30 years old. The venture was started to facilitate Xerox's entry into the Japanese market. In the late 1980s, other Japanese companies such as Canon and Ricoh aggressively attacked Xerox in its home US market with innovative products, competing on price and quality. Initially, Xerox was not able to respond and lost significant market share. However, recognizing that Fuji-Xerox competed successfully against the same players in Japan, the company launched a massive "learning from Japan" campaign aimed at transferring Fuji-Xerox's capabilities back to the mother firm. Because of this "reverse technology transfer", Xerox was able to stem the market erosion and began to recapture the lost share.

The success of Fuji-Xerox illustrates that strong strategic alliances focus on mutual learning. The trust between the partners allows them to concentrate on managing the business rather than on monitoring and control, and their mutual learning strengthens their position in the markets worldwide. Healthy alliances are based on mutual strength, while mutual weaknesses lead to paranoia and fear. Indeed, selecting partners who are known to be poor learners so as to guard against competency leaks is short-sighted. Weak learning capability is a sign of poor management, and poorly managed firms make poor partners.

Many of the difficulties with the implementation of long-term alliance strategies can be traced to the quality of the learning process and the underlying management practices. The ability to learn is especially important in competitive alliances where asymmetry in learning can result in an uneven distribution of benefits. Some alliances are born competitive; others migrate into a competitive alliance zone over time. This is not a strategic failure, but rather a positive indication that the partners have learned so much from each other that the original need to collaborate may have disappeared.

Obstacles to alliance learning

Within many firms are stubborn, interconnected obstacles to learning, and these will impede efforts to build and profit from the alliance. Some of the most common obstacles include:

- *Short-term planning horizon*. Alliance-planning is often driven by short-term contingencies that fail to take into account longer-term effects on the firm's competitive advantage. This logic assumes, for example, that the balance of competencies between partners and within the firm will not change with time. Similarly, there may be few incentives to invest in activities with longer-term payoffs.

- *Low priority on learning activities*. Business planning traditionally focuses on returns from tangible assets. Since it is difficult to assign a financial value to learning, activities like accumulating invisible assets – competencies for improving competitiveness – are often not funded. The result is that learning from the alliance fails to receive support.

- *Resource-poor staffing strategy*. Many firms cut costs by limiting both the size and quality of staff assigned to the alliance, particularly in offshore locations. Learning, however, depends on staff being able to influence the management process within the alliance, on credibility for alliance-dedicated training and development inside the partners' organizations, and on having some "slack resources" for planning ahead.

- *Tolerance for cross-cultural illiteracy*. Many executives assigned to cross-border alliances have never been required to develop sufficient intercultural skills. If they are, moreover, also struggling daily with obstacles like those on this list, their chances of maintaining a longer-term horizon, of active participation in new-knowledge acquisition, are minimal.

- *Career mobility clashes with learning*. Personnel transfer into an alliance-based organization can positively affect learning and the "home" firm only if acquired know-how is effectively transferred and disseminated consistently. The combination of a short-term perspective and fast upward mobility among high-potential executives will clearly impede know-how transfer.

- *Poor climate for know-how transfer*. Similarly, when learning from the "outside" is deemed an admission of weakness, knowledge acquisition will be poorly received. Further, many reward systems encourage the hoarding of critical information: someone's "market value" is based on maintaining knowledge gaps – not on an ability to diffuse learning.

- *Responsibility for learning unclear*. Even in firms where learning is valued, if the organization is complex, the stakes for learning may vary by group, unit or function. Thus, the actual value from learning activities may be perceived differently, as will be the commitment to provide support for them. One result is conflicting signals about learning support, acquisition and consistent dissemination of knowledge – within the alliance and at "home".

Core principles for alliance learning

- Build learning into the alliance agreement.
- Communicate the learning intent inside the parent.
- Assign responsibility for alliance learning.
- Secure early human resource involvement.
- Maintain human resource influence inside the alliance.
- Staff must be able to learn.
- Support learning-driven careers.
- Stimulate learning through training.
- Reward learning activities.
- Monitor your partner's learning.
- Pay attention to the alliance process.

Alliances as drivers for internationalization

An alliance is not just a deal between two or more partners; it is a complex process that is full of ambiguities and contradictions reflecting the complexities of international competition. There are the tensions between competition and collaboration, between global and local interests, between the venture and its parents, between leveraging and developing competencies.

In fact, companies often learn to manage the contradictions embedded in an international organization through their alliance experiences by having to learn to deal with the alliance paradoxes and dualities:

- There is no one model for an alliance. Each one has different aims and strategic objectives, implying different courses of management. This is similar to a growing international firm that has to differentiate the roles of its units and subsidiaries, managing them in different ways.
- How to "manage the future in the present" – because the strategic aims of tomorrow may be quite different from those of today.
- How to balance the fundamental tension between short-term performance and long-term collaboration and learning.
- How to recognize and deal with trade-offs where if one extreme is pushed too far, pathology can be created. There are many examples in alliances where if either the interests of the venture itself or the interests of the parent are pushed too far, it can irreparably damage the achievement of alliance aims.
- How to take important but "soft" aims such as learning and convert them into "hard" objectives through measurement, accountability and staffing.

Individual managers can also benefit from the alliance experience. In an alliance, people learn how to manage boundaries, how to deal with ambiguity and conflicting interests, and how to balance the tensions between managing for short-term operating results and building the long-term capabilities through continuous learning.

 # SUMMARY

Alliances are mostly transitional entities; therefore longevity is a poor measure of success. The aim is not to preserve the alliance at all costs but to contribute to the parent's competitive position. Alliances are dynamic; very few remain complementary for long. Alliances among competitors are increasingly frequent, but they are also the most complex.

Be flexible in negotiations and remember that management control and equity stake are not always correlated. Using equity to gain control is costly and often ineffective, compared to careful partner selection, operational leverage and people management. The decision about who should manage the venture depends on the strategic context.

Conflicting loyalties and complex relationships, coupled with uncertainty and instability, are characteristic of most alliances. The failings of an alliance are too easily attributed to cultural differences when the real culprit may be the lack of attention to people issues. Because of the underlying complexity, alliances without champions do not survive for long.

Using alliances to access and generate knowledge is increasingly important, but alliance learning is neither automatic nor free. There must be clear learning targets, sufficient investment in people and a tight alignment of management practices with learning objectives.

The key point to remember is that an alliance is a process not a deal. Success requires a long-term perspective, competitive focus and the ability to manage complexity.

 ## LEARNING POINTS

- Have a clear strategy *before* you seek an alliance partner.
- As alliance partners, you should share a common strategic vision.
- Alliances evolve; a contract is only a framework.

- Management control comes from relevance to the business.
- People issues can make or break alliances. Conflicting cultures are likely to be fatal to an alliance.
- Identify alliance champions early on.
- If you cannot tolerate ambiguity, do not enter a business alliance.
- You cannot stop your partner from learning; your own learning is your best defence.
- Always have an exit strategy in mind; most alliances do not last.
- An alliance is a process, not a deal.

Reference

Yoshino, M.Y. and Rangan, S. (1995) *Strategic Alliances: An Entrepreneurial Approach to Globalization*, Harvard Business School Press, Cambridge, Mass, p. 8.

5

Mergers and Acquisitions

The rise in the number of mergers and acquisitions in the global market continues at a relentless pace among companies of all sizes. The problem is these deals, particularly those done across borders, are increasingly complex and hard to get right. As **Vladimir Pucik** explains, there are a number of essential elements that have to be in place for mergers and acquisitions to achieve their promised objectives.

Overview

Mergers and acquisitions are an increasingly popular alternative to greenfield invest-ments and strategic alliances as a vehicle for accelerating international growth. Today, mergers and acquisitions (M&As) are utilized not only by large multinationals, but medium-sized and even small firms worldwide are exploring how to use them effectively.

The starting condition for a successful acquisition is articulation of the shared vision for the new organization. Some acquisitions are "mergers of equals"; in others one firm is set to prevail. The strategic logic behind each alternative determines the nature of the acquisition process, from due diligence, the role of the integration manager, to the human resource implications. In any kind of acquisition, and especially within an international context, it is important to pay attention to the cultural and people aspects. Retention of talent should always be the top priority.

The success of a number of companies that grew globally through acquisitions has shown that with a well-designed strategy, due diligence in preparation, attention to soft factors and speedy implementation, acquisitions can work.

The merger wave

The rise in the number of mergers and acquisitions in the global marketplace is relent-less, with more deals in the last two years of the century than ever before – 10 000 plus per year and growing. Also, the deals are no longer a mainly American phenom-enon, as companies in other parts of the world such as Europe, Japan, South-east Asia and South America join in the game. In fact, the fastest growing type of deal is a cross-border acquisition. The value of acquisitions outside of the home country reached over 750 billion dollars in 1999, covering about half of all the deals announced. And, even when merging companies are domiciled in the same country, often a significant part of their operations involves affiliates in different parts of the world.

While the global mega-deals continue to grab the headlines, more and more M&A activities take place among rapidly growing small and medium-sized firms – a phe-nomenon most likely to dominate the discussions on M&As in the forthcoming decade. There are a number of reasons why companies pursue cross-border mergers and acquisitions:

- Advantage of market dominance, economies of scale and channel control
- Extending geographical reach through rapid market entry
- Inability to adapt organically to changes in competitive conditions
- Financial leverage through improved credit, debt and tax management
- Resource acquisition, both tangible and intangible
- Access to talent and knowledge.

The ultimate driver is, of course, the increase in global competition and the cor-responding erosion of national boundaries. As both trends are likely to continue, so will the increase in cross-border M&As. In this context, the obvious question to ask is to what extent all these corporate marriages have worked. Research seems to point to the fact that only a few of these deals in the 1990s achieved the promised financial results:

- A study by the American Management Association has found that only about 15% of M&As in the US during the early 1990s achieved the stated financial objectives.
- According to the 1999 study of cross-border acquisitions sponsored by KPMG, 17% of deals increased shareholder value, 30% left it unchanged and 53% decreased it.
- A similar study conducted by A.T. Kearney put the failure rate at 58% and concluded "on balance, mergers hurt shareholders".
- A joint 1997 Mercer Consulting/*Economist* study reported said that two out of three deals have not worked as planned, and according to *Fortune Magazine*, only 23% of US acquisitions earned their cost of capital.

THE ACQUISITION PARADOX

Research on acquisitions highlighted numerous paradoxes. Here are a few examples.

- *A study of US banks showed that merged banks cut costs more slowly than banks that did not merge. In other words, merged banks were too busy merging to cut costs, while those that didn't got the message about the need for more efficiencies and looked for ways to improve their operations.*
- *In another survey, increasing revenues by 1% has five times greater impact than decreasing operating expenses, yet managers in most acquisitions spend the bulk of their time searching for ways to reduce expenses. In acquisitions and mergers, companies talk a lot about creating synergies and the lower costs of the combined operation. But, there may be a greater impact on shareholder value if merged companies focus on increasing revenues rather than reducing cost.*
- *According to one management scholar, nearly half the time top management spends on M&As goes into creating the deal, in contrast to 8% of time devoted to implementation. Far too much management time is spent on the deal itself rather than making it work.*

Why do acquisitions fail?

There is little doubt that acquisitions, particularly those that reach across borders, are complex and difficult to get right. The business press is full of stories of international acquisitions that failed to meet the original objectives; after all, many of these deals are highly visible, thus they provide a good story. And with hindsight, many of the factors that cause these acquisitions to under-perform may seem obvious.

One of the major reasons why acquisitions fail, even when on the surface they should enjoy great benefits of synergy, is the *difference in the vision* about where the two sides want the combined entity to go. For the sake of the deal, this difference is often glossed over, but if firms do not start with a common and *specific* understanding of where they want to take the new organization and how they want to get there, reaching a successful end point is very difficult.

The acquisition can fail because of *attrition of talent and capabilities*, most likely when companies are not clear about their talent priorities or the right methods to retain key staff. Yet another reason for failure is the *loss of intangible assets*. Customers are not asked their opinion of a merger and might feel disgruntled about being passed on to another entity. That can lead to a loss of potential value almost overnight. Relationships with vendors, community and government can also suffer when the new owner is perceived, rightly or wrongly, as insensitive to local interests.

International mergers can also suffer from underestimation of the *high transition and coordination costs* linking the new entities due to time and physical distance, negating some of the advantages of the potential synergies. Related to that is the danger of "*synergy*" *gridlock*, a situation when management so desperately searches for ways to deliver the savings it promised to the stock market, while the costs are going up, that it loses track of the business. The larger the merger, the more difficulties in operational integration can be expected.

Finally, the frequent failures of international M&A deals may be linked to the *lack of "cultural fit"* between the two organizations. It is inevitable that merging organizations with differing history, environment and national cultures that amplify the variations in management style, will create challenges, and it is often said that companies should not entertain deals where a significant cultural mismatch might be a problem.

However, companies do not have the option of avoiding potential opportunities because of cultural issues as they seek to accelerate their international growth – the forces of market competition are unrelenting. This does not mean that cultural differences, and other soft factors should now be ignored. To the contrary, because they are so critical, they have to be well defined and managed.

What is the desired end-state?

In successful mergers and acquisitions, partners share the purpose and accept the terms of their relationship. However, the reality is that corporate marriages are often based on unattainable assumptions. Here, carefully defining and making explicit the end-state is the first step in making the new relationship work. Managers and employees in the new entity are then able to focus on the business and let go of any wishful thinking that may run counter to the reality of the deal.

There are a number of options (Figure 5.1), based on the direction and degree of anticipated integration, each with its own logic and set of guiding principles for implementation.

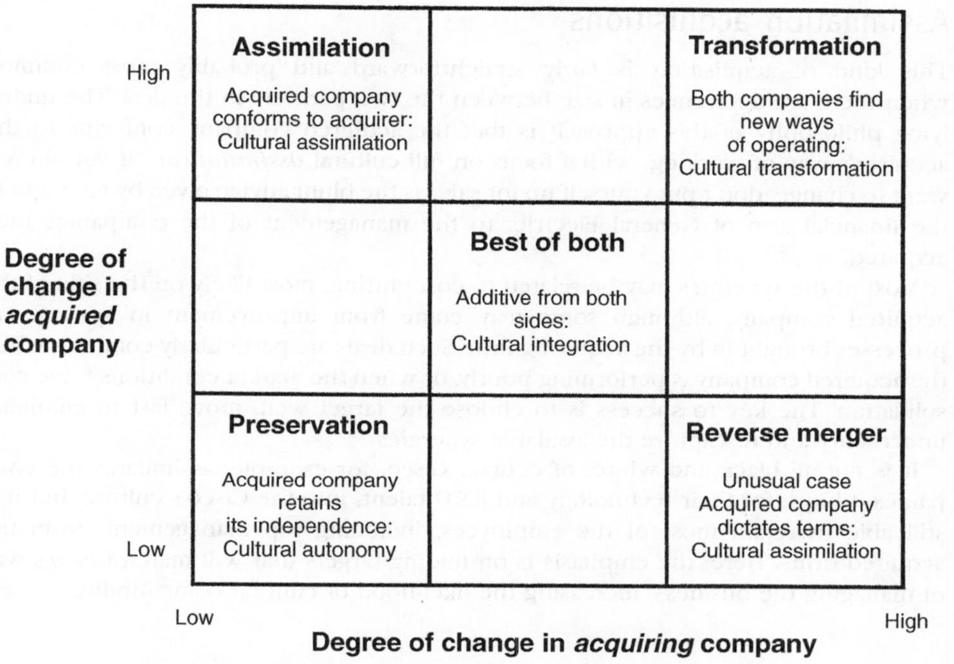

Assimilation Acquired company conforms to acquirer: Cultural assimilation		**Transformation** Both companies find new ways of operating: Cultural transformation
	Best of both Additive from both sides: Cultural integration	
Preservation Acquired company retains its independence: Cultural autonomy		**Reverse merger** Unusual case Acquired company dictates terms: Cultural assimilation

High — Low (Degree of change in *acquired* company)

Low — High (**Degree of change in *acquiring* company**)

Figure 5.1: *Strategies for post-merger outcomes*

Reproduced with permission of Prentice-Hall (part of the Pearson Education Group) from P.H. Mirvis and M.L. Marks (1994) *Managing the Merger: Making it Work*.

Stand-alone acquisitions

When a deal is announced, it often contains a reference that the acquired company will *preserve* its independence and cultural autonomy. This often occurs when one of the rationales of the merger is to get hold of talented management, or other soft skills (such as speed of product development) and retain them, and when conformance to the acquiring company rules and systems could be detrimental to the acquired company's competitive advantage.

The key to success here is to protect the boundary of the new subsidiary from unwarranted and disruptive intrusions from the parent, but this is hard to achieve. Even with the best intentions, there can be a form of creeping assimilation as the acquiring company encourages the acquired one to begin to work in the same way and develop systems and processes which match those of the parent organization.

Because of operational pressures, most stand-alone acquisitions do not last. More likely, while the acquired company may still appear independent to the outside world, internally, the acquired company, or at least some parts of it, is merged with the rest of the organization. Or, "stand-alone" is a temporary phenomenon, until other dimensions of the deal come through, such as additional acquisitions.

Assimilation acquisitions

This kind of acquisition is fairly straightforward and probably most common when there are differences in size between the two partners in the deal. The underlying philosophy of this approach is that the acquired company conforms to the acquirer's way of working, with a focus on full cultural *assimilation*. "If you do not want to change, don't put yourself up for sale," is the blunt advice given by GE Capital, the financial arm of General Electric, to the management of the companies they acquired.

Most of the synergies may be related to cost cutting, most likely on the side of the acquired company, although some may come from improvement in system and processes brought in by the acquiring firm. Such deals are particularly common when the acquired company is performing poorly, or when the market conditions force consolidation. The key to success is to choose the target well, move fast to eliminate uncertainty and to capture the available synergies.

It is not all black and white, of course. Cisco, for example, assimilates the companies it buys, for their technology and R&D talent, into the Cisco's culture, but it is still able to retain most of the employees, including top management, from the acquired firms. Here, the emphasis is on finding targets that will match Cisco's way of managing the business, increasing the likelihood of cultural compatibility.

Reverse merger

This is a mirror image of assimilation, although it does not happen very often. Usually, the organization that buys hopes to gain capabilities from the one bought. It typically involves an acquired business unit absorbing the operations of a parallel unit in the acquirer. When Nokia, for instance, bought a high-tech firm in California for its R&D knowledge, it gave the new unit global responsibilities, which meant that part of the business in Finland now reports to California.

Sometimes, the reverse merger is unintended. A few years ago, a French metal product company acquired its smaller British competitor. Today, to the surprise of many, the management style and systems of the new company resemble the culture of the acquired firm. What has happened? When the two companie merged, it was easier for everyone to adapt the explicit and transparent systems of the British firm, more suitable for cross-border business, than to emulate more ambiguous and subtle rules embedded in the old French organization.

Best of both

The intriguing option is the "*best of both*", often described as a "merger of equals". This holds out the promise of "no pain" since in theory it takes the best practices from both sides and integrates them. There are, however, very few examples of those that have truly succeeded since it is very difficult to do so. The danger in the "best of both" integration process is that it may become too political and time-consuming. Who decides what is "best"?

The process of just making the decisions can be very complex, even to the extent of defining the terms. Also, if two companies declare that the merger is one of equals, does that mean top management is split 50/50 even if in terms of excellence the real split is 80/20? The controversy surrounding the Daimler Chrysler merger is only the most visible example. Without shared respect for the knowledge and skills of each company this kind of strategy will not work.

The key to success is the fairness of the process. The test of the "best of both" approach may be the ability to keep the people who do not get the top jobs. Having similar cultures helps. The AstraZeneca or Exxon/Mobil merger has proceeded relatively smoothly because the similarities were more pronounced than the differences, and the new group has been relatively successful at identifying the best practices from each side, as well as having a balance of top management from the two firms.

Transformation acquisition

With *transformation*, both companies are hoping to use the merger to transform themselves in a sharp break from the past. Merger or acquisition can be the catalyst for trying to do things differently, because it forces companies to review their past as a way of looking forward to new ways of operating as a combined entity. This can involve the way the company is run, or what business it is in, or both.

An example of transformation is Nortel, a telecom equipment manufacturer. Several years ago it bought Bay Networks in California to spearhead its shift away from voice to digital and optical networks. It also moved its headquarters to California – though retaining Canada as its legal base – with the aim of benefiting from Bay Networks' culture of speed and entrepreneurship. This was a case of the parent company changing its culture by incorporating learning from the junior partner. It also led to a new name, new management style and new business strategy.

This kind of merger is usually most complex and most difficult to implement. It requires a full commitment, focus and strong leadership at the top (e.g., Percy Barnevik at ABB) to avoid getting trapped in endless debates, while ongoing business suffers. If change is what is desired, there may be easier ways to achieve it than through an acquisition.

What kind of culture do you want?

The new organization will have a culture, whether it is by default or design. The motives for the merger, the industry dynamics, coordination needs, management style, implementation skills, all will influence what kind of organization and culture will emerge from the deal.

In the case of a hostile takeover, or when a company is put up for sale due to its poor performance, it may be argued that the vision for the end-state is very clear: one company wants to take another over and assimilate it into its culture. In most international acquisitions, the reality is more complex. While hostile takeovers are increasing (Vodafone's acquisition of Mannesmann being the landmark event), most cross-border deals are still done through direct negotiations between the parties, not by solicitation of shareholder votes.

In such a case, articulating and sharing the vision of the desired end-state in terms of strategy, organization and management style are critical. It eliminates misconceptions about how the new organization will operate, and avoid misinterpretation of what people hear or may want to believe. It is also the first step in communication of the plan to the employees, assuring them that the management knows where it is going. When reality is different from the espoused strategy, the people on the front line are usually the first ones to know.

Clarity in communication gets rid of ambiguities. When BP took over Amoco, it did so for the oil reserves owned by Amoco. If you were a manager in Amoco with 25 years' experience you might not be very happy about that, but you would probably have a good idea where you stood: you either go along with being absorbed into the BP way of working or leave. In contrast, when top executives speak about a "merger of equals", as in the case of DaimlerChrysler, but actually mean absorption, the lack a shared purpose and the resulting conflicts lead to loss of valuable time, attrition of talent and, ultimately, to poor business results.

Just as bad is a lack of consistency in what top management is saying. In the failed Deutsche-Dresdner banking merger, mixed signals from the leadership about the future of the combined organization's investment banking operations created opposition in both camps, ultimately forcing a cancellation of a deal that on paper looked very promising.

A complicating factor is that often there will be parts of each organization where a particular approach to the merger makes sense and others where it does not. There are very few M&As which achieve a perfect fit across the whole organization. For some parts of the business, a full assimilation may be the best approach; in others, a reverse merger could be a more appropriate strategy. It very much depends on the condition of the business, and the skills and competencies of people in it. Time and competitive environment are also important influences; the direction chosen may not be ideal, but one cannot search for a perfect partner forever.

Due diligence process

Getting the strategy right depends very much on doing the homework. Good planning is not possible without good data. Due diligence in an acquisition has two aspects to it. One is, of course, clarifying the legal, financial and business picture. The infrastructure to get this kind of information is well developed, as is the methodology for the analysis. The other, equally important, but often neglected, is about the culture and people in the organization to be acquired. It is important to understand the "soft" side of the deal before proceeding, so cultural and human issues can be addressed already in the early stages of the acquisition. In fact there is ample evidence (see Table 5.1) that the "soft" issues are among the most critical factors determining acquisition success.

Table 5.1: *Critical issues for M&A success*

Issue	% of companies who felt that this issue was critical
Retention of key talent	76
Communication	71
Retention of key managers	67
Integration of corporate cultures	51

This exhibit is taken from Ira T. Kay & Mike Shelton, "The people problem in mergers," The McKinsey Quarterly, 2000 Number 4, and can be found on the publication's Web site, www.mckinseyquarterly.com. Used by permission. The full article from which this chart is excerpted can be viewed online at http://mckinseyquarterly.com/login.asp? ArtID=934.

Often companies believe that this kind of information is not available, especially during the initial planning stage where secrecy and confidentiality are important. However, in most cases there is a large amount of information accessible about companies, their cultural strengths and weaknesses, their management and people. What is usually lacking is not information, but the discipline and rigour in collecting and analysing the data. Two methodologies can be especially useful here: cultural assessment and human capital audit.

Cultural assessment

The purpose of cultural assessment is to evaluate factors that may influence the organizational fit, to understand the future cultural dynamics, and prepare a plan of how the cultural issues should be addressed if the deal goes forward. Depending on the stage of the negotiations and the resources available, cultural assessment can be formal or informal, using market intelligence, external data sources, surveys or interviews. What is important is to have at least a rudimentary framework that helps in organizing the issues and arriving at the proper conclusions.

Some assessment questions should look at the leadership of the target company and its view of the business environment, its attitude towards competition, customer and change:

- What are their core beliefs about what it takes to win?
- What drives business strategy: innovation and change or tradition?
- Is the company long- or short-term oriented?
- How much risk is the company used to accepting?
- What is its approach to external partners: competition or collaboration?
- Who are the important stakeholders in the organization?

Other questions may examine leadership principles and how the company manages internal systems:

- Is the company result-oriented or process-oriented?
- Where is power: concentrated on the top/in certain functions or diffused?
- How are decisions made: by consensus, consultation or by authority?
- How does the company manage information: is the flow of information wide or narrow?
- What counts as being a valuable employee: values, skills and competencies, getting results?
- What is the value of teamwork versus individual performance?

Some companies use cultural assessment as an input to a stop/go decision concerning the acquisition. For example, Cisco avoids buying companies with cultures that are substantially different from its own, as it recognizes that it would be difficult to tackle differences in expectations of how a business should be run and still retain the key staff, which it wants to do. On the other hand, GE Capital, with less concern about retention, is more aggressive in its approach to cultural differences. For GE, cultural assessment is also a "must" but mainly as a tool to plan integration. One cannot say that one approach is better than the other, but both companies are clear in where they want to go and how they want to get there.

The challenge in conducting a cultural assessment is to approach the subject with a proper perspective. After all, most difficulties in cross-border acquisitions can at a certain level of generalization be traced to culture. Even a disagreement about the price of the deal can be blamed on cultural differences. Where some see cultural obstacles, other may simply observe poor management. "It was like two drunks trying to hold each other up," commented the *Wall Street Journal* on one case of spectacular cross-border merger fiasco attributed to cultural misunderstandings. At the same time, there may be a limit on how many cultural boundaries one can safely cross: every time a large Japanese "old-economy" company tried to buy a Silicon Valley start-up, the result was a failure.

Human capital audit

There are two dimensions to the human capital audit. One dimension is preventive, focused on liabilities such as pension plan obligations, outstanding grievances or employee litigation, or other employment-related constraints that may impact the acquisition – for example cost of anticipated restructuring. It also includes comparing the compensation policies, benefits and labour contracts of both firms.

The other dimension, and in the long run probably more critical to the success of the acquisition, is focused on talent identification. It is essential to confirm that the target company has the talent necessary to execute the acquisition strategy; to identify which individuals are key to sustaining the value of the deal; and to assess any potential weaknesses in the management cadre. It is also important to understand the motivation and incentive structure, and highlight any differences that may impact retention. Finally, understanding the structure of the organization helps to clarify who is who.

Some examples of questions to consider:

- What unique skills do the employees have?
- How does the target's talent compare to ours?
- What is the background of the management team?
- What will happen if some of them leave?
- What is the compensation philosophy?
- How much pay is at risk at various levels of the firm?
- What are the reporting relationships?
- How are decisions made?

Where does this information come from? Former employees, consultants, executive search firms and customers knowledgeable about the company are usually the best source. Some data are already in the public domain, and web-based search engines can speed up the process of finding the information.

Still, many companies ignore the talent question early in the M&A process. They do not take the time to define the type of talent critical to the success of the deal, relying instead on financial performance data as a proxy for talent. However, without early talent assessments, companies may acquire targets with weaker than expected talent or talent that has a high likelihood of departure. Early talent assessment helps to pinpoint the potential risk factors so that the acquiring company can begin developing strategies to address anticipated problems as early as possible. It also helps in speeding up the eventual decision about who should stay and who should leave.

Implementing acquisitions

A systematic and explicit integration process is at the heart of most successful acquisitions – people often talk about the importance of the "first 100 days" when it comes to post-M&A integration. All acquisitions require some degree of integration, but it is important to tailor what is integrated and how it is to be done – based on the purpose of the acquisition and the characteristics of the companies involved. Maintaining the focus on the key areas that create value is the critical part of the integration process.

To do this well, a number of elements must be put in place:

- Agree on the business model logic and strategic goals, creating a shared vision. Present a clear vision of how the acquisition/merger will create value and ensure that the employees understand the logic. Having a well-articulated message can also help deal with any potential political and/or competitive issues which can arise once the deal is announced.
- Identify key priorities that have the potential to impact significantly the performance of the new acquisition. These should be done very early in the integration planning process and integration projects launched immediately after the deal is closed.

- Develop understanding of each other's capabilities, assist businesses to take advantage of existing resources, and identify and implement opportunities for business synergy, especially where results can be achieved quickly.
- Define value and norms for leadership behaviours. Clarify performance standards and rewards and recognition principles. Establish common ground for corporate governance, and spell out how decisions are made.
- Surface hidden issues and concerns that may create conflict in the new organization. This is an area that is often neglected, but which should be tackled as early as possible. Some companies today use the intranet to monitor online how people in the acquired company really feel so something can be done before unhappy staff walk away.
- Specify next steps for integration and post-integration planning, starting with feedback to speed up the integration, and capturing the learning from the process to enhance the capability of the organization to execute future acquisitions.
- Deliver and celebrate quick wins: nothing can be more motivating to the employees of the new company because it offers proof that the merger/acquisition was the right way to go.

The critical role of the integration manager

Integration of the acquired company with the new parent is a delicate and complicated process, but who should be responsible for making it happen? After closing, the due-diligence team with a deep knowledge of the acquired company disbands or goes on after another deal. At the same time, a new management team is not yet fully in place. This is why companies are increasingly turning to an integration manager to guide the process, to make sure the time-lines and targets are met, and that the people on both sides quickly learn to work with each other.

What is expected of this role? First, integration managers should facilitate and manage integration activities, making sure that time-lines are followed and critical decisions are made according to the agreed-on schedule, removing the bottlenecks and making sure that the speed of integration is maintained. They help engineer short-term successes that produce business results essential for creating positive energy around the merger. They should also act as the champions for behaviours and norms consistent with new standards, communicating key messages across the new organization.

An important aspect of the job is forging social connections and helping the acquired company understand how the new owner operates and what it can offer in terms of capabilities. The integration manager can help the new company take advantage of existing resources, educate the new management team about common processes, and help with essential but intangible aspects such as interpreting the new language, culture and customers. New companies often have little knowledge about the way things work in the business they are now part of. Equally important for the integration manager is the role of information "gatekeeper" between the two sides to protect the new business from the embrace of an owner eager to help but who could end up destroying what makes the business work. The integration manager can thus help the new owner understand the acquired business and what it can bring.

What combination of skills is required of the integration manager? First of all, a deep knowledge of the acquiring company is a must; where to get information, whom to talk to about various subjects, how does the informal system work. The integration manager must be tough about deadlines or about coming to a decision, but he also should be a good listener, able to relate to different levels of authority; thus flexible leadership style is another requirement. Comfort with chaos and ambiguity, emotional and cultural intelligence and willingness to take risk and make independent decisions are some of the traits expected in this role.

Retaining the talent

People problems are a major cause of failed mergers. Many acquired businesses lose key employees soon after the acquisition. When there is not sufficient communication, and especially if staff cuts are expected – employees will leave, and the best will exit first – they have other choices. And it can be taken for granted that after a deal is announced, and well before the actual closing, the headhunters move in immediately to pick off any promising managers unsure about their career opportunities in the new organization. For talented employees waiting to see what will happen to them in the new company, a concrete job offer from another company looks very attractive.

Retention of the key employees is therefore crucial to achieving acquisition goals. That means knowing exactly who they are, particularly if they are lower down in the acquired organization, building on the talent identification effort in the due diligence stage. Companies may offer stock options, retention bonuses, or other incentives to employees who stay through a merger or until a specific merger-related project is completed. What will ultimately work, however, depends on employees' expectations as well as the labour and tax legislation in countries involved.

The key to success in retaining talent is fast and open communication. In Cisco, on day one of the acquisition, the integration team holds small group sessions with all acquired employees to discuss expectations and answer questions. Often, the key members of the integration team were themselves brought into Cisco by acquisition, so they not only understand well what the newly joined employees are going through, but their messages are received with additional credibility.

At the same time, even the most elaborate retention incentives cannot substitute for a one-on-one relationship of trust with executives of the acquiring firm. In communication with top talent, senior management involvement is critical to successful retention. High-potential employees at most companies are used to senior-level attention. Without the same treatment from the acquiring company, these employees may doubt their future and will be more likely to depart. Here, distance may be a hindrance, but it cannot be an excuse. Meetings and informal workshops in the early days of the acquisition, if not already before closing, can go a long way to build a foundation for a long-term relationship.

Yet, retention success cannot be taken for granted. In acquisitions involving knowledge-intensive firms, it is also important to protect the value of the deal from competitive implications of employee defection. When trade secrets and confidential information are important assets of the acquired companies, then it is wise to tie the closing to no-competion, no-disclosure agreements with key employees. It is also essential to clarify who has rights to technology, the acquired company or individual employees.

Moving with speed

When companies are asked what they have learned from their past M&A experiences, they *always* say: "We should have moved faster, and we should have done in nine months what it took us a year to do." GE Capital, for example, has cut down the 100-day process to 60–75 both because it has learned how to move faster and because it has developed the tools to do so. And that is essential, because if a company is taking two to three years to integrate, not enough attention is being spent where it really counts – with the customers. According to GE:

Decisions about management structure, key roles, reporting relationships, layoffs, restructuring and other career-affecting aspects of the integration should be made, announced, and implemented as soon as possible after the deal is signed, within days, if possible. Creeping changes, uncertainty and anxiety that last for months are debilitating and immediately start to drain value from an acquisition.

Analysis should not be confused with indecision. There are very few occasions when the answer is unanimous – there is always another way to do things. If a company waits until there is total consensus it will take too long to do anything.

There will be a number of systems and processes that must be integrated quickly in order to attain synergies. Examples are IT, sales reporting systems, logistics and procurement. Once these key areas are identified, it may help to make sure that each one of these value drivers has a team of people associated with it, having a clear mandate, performance targets and accountability. At the same time, while such teams can smooth the path to integration, there is a limit to how many there should be, since too many committees can slow things down. Prioritization is critical. As stated by one experienced M&A manager: "We only attack things that would bring benefits to the business. We did not integrate just for the sake of integrating."

Often, restructuring is an essential step to get to the necessary synergies. Restructuring should not be confused with integrating, but here the rule is similar: it should be done *early, fast and once*, minimizing the uncertainty of "waiting for the other shoe to drop". A problem jeopardizing the success of many acquisitions has been a tendency to restructure slowly, with the best intentions not to upset the old culture, and give people the time to adjust. Meanwhile, of course, while time, effort and resources are being spent on reaching the consensus and negotiating the details of implementation, competitors come along and take away the business.

There is no doubt that the pressure of work caused by the need to manage integration as well as "doing the day job" can be formidable. Add to that the tendency for people to resist change and the shortage of appropriately qualified management talent and you have a recipe for an over-stressed, under-performing work environment. Managing this involves preparing the employees for the change, involving them to ensure understanding, preparing a schedule for the changes, implementing them, and then putting in place all the structures, policies and practices to support the new organization. Acquisition is a change process. Not surprisingly, companies that do well in managing change are also good in managing acquisitions.

Measuring M&A success

A well-thought integration plan should detail how progress is going to be measured. What gets measured gets done; without measurements, there is no accountability. Some of the ways to measure success include:

- retention of key contributors
- goals met in terms of schedule, revenue and cost
- integration of key systems and technologies
- best practices shared and adopted
- employee morale survey results
- creation of shareholder value.

However, in the long term, the only valid measure of success is the satisfied customer. Does the acquisition create customer value? From a customer's point of view, has it made sense? If it has not, then there is not much chance for long-term growth. When short-term synergies are exhausted, deals that do not create customer value have not much chance of being sustained.

Strong focus on the customer can also help generate the energy to push through the required changes. It cuts down on internal politics and conflicts that divert management attention away from the business. And bear in mind that creating customer value occurs only *after* the deal is done, which makes post-merger integration a critical success factor.

M&As as an organizational capability

There is little doubt that companies that master the art of international acquisitions will gain significant market advantage. When there is a sound strategy behind the merger and when the acquisition process is well managed, M&As can become a major tool for international growth. For some companies, such as GE Capital or Cisco, expanding through acquisitions is already a well-proven part of their business strategies. They understand well that the capability to execute acquisitions is one of the core competitive capabilities for the future, and that the intangible aspects of an acquisition are just as important as its financial dimensions.

To capture its M&A capabilities, GE Capital has developed a tightly controlled process for acquisitions, as shown in Figure 5.2. It is a "live document" – as the company accumulates more experience, it is continuously fine-tuned. What this

Figure 5.2: *The wheel of fortune at GE Capital*
Reprinted by permission of *Harvard Business Review.* From *Making the Deal Real* by Ashkenas,
DeMonaco & Francis, p. 167, January–February 1998. Copyright © 1998 by the President and Fellows of
Harvard College, all rights reserved.

detailed process does is give guidance about what needs to be done, highlights the
key issues and decision points, provides the methodology and resources; however, it
also lets the GE staff involved in the process find the right answers for themselves.
Flexibility in reaching solutions is important, because all deals are different. In acquisitions, learning never stops.

GE CAPITAL'S WHEEL OF FORTUNE

The work starts at the pre-acquisition stage, where the framework for integration is set:

- *Begin cultural assessment*
- *Identify cultural barriers to integration success*
- *Select integration manager*

- *Assess strengths and weaknesses of business and function leaders*
- *Develop communication strategy*

The next stage focuses on the integration process:

- *Formally introduce integration manager*
- *Orient new executive to GE Capital*
- *Jointly formulate integration plan, including 100-day and communication plans*
- *Visibly involve senior management*
- *Provide sufficient resources and assign accountability*

Integration is done rapidly:

- *Use process tools to accelerate integration*
- *Use audit staff to audit key processes*
- *Use feedback and learning to adapt integration plan continually*
- *Initiate short-term management exchange*

The final stage is assimilation:

- *Continue developing common tools, practices, processes and language*
- *Continue long-term management exchanges*
- *Utilize corporate education resources*
- *Use audit staff for integration audit*

SUMMARY

The acquisition process starts with the creation of vision and strategy for the combined organization. There are a number of options, based on the direction and degree of anticipated integration, each with its own logic and set of guiding principles for implementation. Clarity in communication about the strategy is an essential foundation for success.

The "soft" part of the due diligence process is just as important as the financial analysis. Most M&A failures are linked to post-merger integration, and cultural and people issues consistently rank as one of the key causes of difficulties in executing acquisitions. A well-structured cultural assessment and human capital audit can help focus management attention on potential problems.

In any acquisition, retention of top talent should be on the list of key priorities. The retention efforts start during the due diligence process that should spotlight top talent. Retention incentives can help during transition, but in the long run, retention requires commitment from senior management to build personal relationships with top talent from the newly acquired organization.

After the deal is closed, it is imperative to move with speed. Key decisions about management structure, senior appointments and about anything related to people's careers should be made as soon as possible. Uncertainty and anxiety after the acquisition drain energy from the business. Ability to manage post-merger integration can become a major source of competitive advantage.

 **LEARNING POINTS**

- Do your homework: mergers and acquisitions are always more complicated than at first glance.
- Think about the end-state before you start.
- Be clear about your intentions.
- Do not underestimate cross-cultural differences, but do not confuse culture with poor management.
- Make talent assessment an integral part of due diligence.
- Appoint an integration manager to speed up the process.
- Identify points of resistance and address them early.
- Secure and celebrate quick wins.
- Measure M&A outcomes and assign accountability.
- Capture the learning to improve future acquisitions.
- Keep in mind that the deal must make sense for the customer.

Part Three

Staffing the Global Company

6

Managing Expatriation

Expatriates have long been one of the mainstays of international growth. Dispatching company representatives to foreign posts is usually one of the first steps when companies decide to expand abroad. But managing the process of expatriation is becoming increasingly challenging. **Vladimir Pucik** offers insights into the expatriate cycle, from selection and preparation through to support and repatriation.

Overview

Reliance on the expatriation of managers for guiding international growth is a natural first step in building a multinational company. But expatriation is anything but straightforward. Getting enough of the right employees to dispatch to foreign postings, providing them with the support necessary to succeed, and bringing them home without derailing their careers, has proven to be a challenging task.

Expatriates may fulfil many different roles. A starting point for understanding expatriation is the recognition that it is a *process*, not an event, and no single factor can guarantee success. Getting it wrong on any dimension – personal or organizational – significantly increases the likelihood of failure, which is costly to everyone.

Making an expatriate assignment a success for the individual, the family and the firm requires a focused attention from everyone involved in the process, from the initial selection until repatriation. Developing an effective approach to the issues and problems of expatriation is therefore one of the building blocks for rapid international growth.

Why use expatriates?

Chapter 1 described how foreign direct investment (FDI) has grown substantially over the last few years, leading to a substantial rise in the number of companies, large and small, embarking on international expansion. Because it is often hard to find qualified local employees to lead this process, very few firms launch their international expansion without at least a small core of expatriates. And even for companies that have a long tradition of operating abroad, because of the changing role of the expatriate assignments, the number of employees in international assignments is expected to increase (Table 6.1).

Table 6.1: *The onward march of expatriates. Responses to the question: Are you sending more or fewer people on international assignments to these regions?*

	Europe	North America	Asia
More	44%	41%	63%
Same	42%	45%	31%
Fewer	14%	14%	6%

Source: *1997/1998 Worldwide Survey of International Assignments Policies and Practices*, based on 650 companies with 70 000 expatriates. Copyright © 1998 by Organization Resources Counselors, Inc., New York. All rights reserved. Reprinted with permission.

Traditionally most expatriates were sent abroad for two main reasons. The first was to act as overseers for the parent firm, focusing on control and/or knowledge transfer in what could be called a "*corporate agency*" role. The typical assignment would last for three years or longer. The second reason was to deal with short-term *start up or problem solving* needs. When these were sorted out, the expatriates returned. In both cases the expatriates were seen to possess knowledge and competencies not available locally. When companies began their international expansion most expatriates were sent abroad to fulfil one of these two roles.

In later stages of internationalization, and with the development of local management and professional capabilities, there is less demand for expatriate assignments geared to "teaching skills to the locals". At the same time, companies face an increasing need to develop international coordinating capabilities. Mobility across borders is the key tool in this regard, but the "learning" character of assignments when the primary role is *competence development* is radically different from the expatriation "controlling" roles dominant in the past.

Finally, a rapidly growing category of expatriation today is the short-term learning assignments of young high-potential professionals who move across borders primarily for *personal development*. During the 1990s, the proportion of assignees on short-term transfers of less than 12 months increased from 5 to nearly 20 per cent of all US expatriates, and these often involve rotation in several countries, even regions. In a number of international firms, such assignments are becoming an integral part of career development planning for young professionals and managers.

In reality, of course, the distinctions in expatriate roles are not so clear-cut, with many expatriates playing multiple roles. Most employees in learning assignments should also create value, since learning by doing is often the best way to learn, and

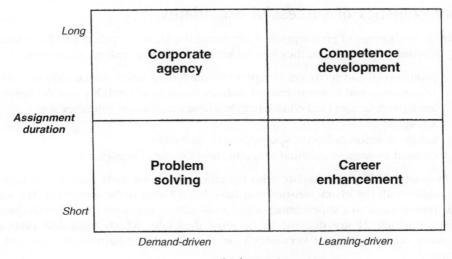

Figure 6.1: *The purpose of expatriation*

thus respond to "demand". On the other hand, there is an expectation that employees in "agency" positions implicitly learn from the context of their jobs, enlarging personal skills as well organizational competencies.

Therefore, even in companies in the early stages of international expansion and with only a handful of expatriates, it is worthwhile to think ahead and develop a set of practices that will be sustainable in the long term. Experience has shown that retrofitting the system later on will be an expensive exercise.

Selecting expatriates

A successful assignment starts with an appropriate selection. However, this is too often focused mainly on technical and managerial competence and fails to take into consideration "softer" factors, such as the executive's cross-cultural ability or the family's disposition to live abroad.

Why are "soft" factors important? A number of studies have pointed out that the expatriate's poor performance can be caused by personal attributes. The personality profile and psychological traits, such as the inability to deal with stressful situations, or a lack of the right attitudes and skills (including language competence) to communicate with people from different cultures can all hamper a successful assignment.

Just as important are family issues. In fact, the inability of the spouse and/or the family to adjust to the new country is probably the main reason for expatriate failure. Dual career couples – and there are more and more of them – may also experience stress in international assignments because of the expected negative effects of a career interruption.

Characteristics of successful expatriates

There is no shortage of prescriptions concerning the ideal competencies of an expatriate. In broad generalization, they can be grouped into five distinct categories:

- professional and technical competence (including international experience)
- relationship and communication abilities (such as adaptability and flexibility)
- leadership factors (self-confidence, learning orientation, tolerance for ambiguity)
- family situation (adaptive spouse, stable marriage)
- cultural awareness (cultural empathy, host-country language).

Obviously, finding a candidate who fits all of the above traits may not be easy. If one adds up all the characteristics that have been found to be important, the ideal expatriate is close to a superhuman! One cross-cultural textbook identified 68 dimensions, of which 21 are deemed to be most desirable. Which traits and skills are the most relevant depend very much on the role the expatriate is expected to assume.

For agency-type assignments, clear managerial qualifications together with the relevant professional skills are the essential foundation. Expatriates in such roles should also be able to improvise and find new solutions in the face of unexpected changes, impart confidence in their own ability to solve problems in difficult situations, and most of all, motivate all members of the organization to cooperate. In contrast, for learning-oriented assignments, relationship abilities and cultural awareness may be more important than traditional professional skills since they are the keys that open access to new knowledge.

How should companies respond to these recommendations? The starting point is to enlarge the pool of potential candidates for cross-border assignments, and make sure that the international track attracts those with the best potential to succeed in the firm. As a consequence, while expatriation used to be an exclusive domain of senior male executives from the headquarter country, today's expatriates are an increasingly heterogeneous group – with much broader gender and cultural diversity.

Assessment tools and techniques

While only a minority of firms relies on any kind of standardized tests and evaluations, there is no shortage of expatriate selection tools for those companies interested in formal assessment methods. Certainly, some desirable expatriate traits such as inter-cultural adaptability, conflict-resolution style or willingness to communicate can be assessed using psychometric tests.

When a formal assessment is used, it is important to consider that:

- It should not serve to screen out unsuitable candidates but to enable the potential expatriate or even the whole family to consider carefully all factors that may influence the success of the future assignment.
- In consultation with experts, it can be used to design an approach to problematic areas. An appropriate assessment can help to find the right structure (duration, role, cultural context, etc.) to increase the likelihood of success.

Some companies test only candidates after they have been identified for an international assignment. Others, such as Nestlé, screen all professional hires for future success as "global managers".

Still, by far the most common assessment method is simply to interview the potential candidate. The obvious way to enhance the quality of expatriate selection is therefore to improve the quality of the interview processes. Experience shows that individuals responsible for selecting expatriates should have international experience. Input from the host country can also improve the odds of getting it right.

A number of experienced international firms send potential expatriates on a pre-assignment orientation visit. In some cases, this is done to help the local hosts evaluate the candidate's fit with the new environment, or for the candidate to have a good look at the location before agreeing to the task, to avoid any costly surprises later.

> **CASE STUDY: AN ORIENTATION PROGRAMME COULD HAVE PREVENTED THIS**
>
> *Recently, a Swiss-based multinational, after an extensive internal search, assigned an expatriate to a senior position in Moscow. The newly appointed executive – with no previous experience outside western Europe – flew in, got into an argument at customs, with a taxi driver, and at the hotel reception. Moscow was certainly not what he imagined it to be. The next day he took a flight back and resigned. One career was derailed and the company was back to square one.*

In principle, a strong case can be made that an individual should not be penalized for *not* being willing to take a particular job or move to a certain location, especially if there is a perceived hardship for one's family. Lack of commitment or desire to work internationally only increases the likelihood of failure and avoiding failure is obviously in everyone's best interest.

Family considerations have a critical impact on the outcome of the assignment. It makes a lot of sense to involve the candidate's spouse, if not the whole family, in the pre-departure assessment and counselling, or at least include them in cultural briefing. However, "buying-off" the family to gain acceptance can be shortsighted, as a temporary increase in the standards of living can make successful repatriation more difficult.

Best practices for expatriate staffing

- Recruit employees who have lived or were educated abroad.
- Give new international assignees realistic job and career previews.
- Interview the spouse of the expatriate as part of the selection process.
- Provide short-term assignments to increase the pool of employees with international experience.
- Make international assignment planning a part of a career development process.
- Communicate the value of international assignments to the company's mission.

Preparing for the assignment

A typical expatriate assignment means being immersed in a new job, a new role, and most importantly, a new culture, creating uncertainty and stress for the expatriate and his or her family. When employees work in a culturally unfamiliar environment they have to learn to adjust to new sets of rules regarding cultural norms, values and assumptions. These include:

- *Adjusting to a foreign workplace.* The first dimension of cross-cultural adjustment is to a foreign workplace. This may be the easiest dimension, because job adjustment is aided by similarities in procedures, policies and tasks inside the firm, although the foreign operation's culture could still be dramatically different from that inside the home office. Increasing job clarity by specifying job expectations, responsibilities and objectives, allowing greater job discretion and freedom, and lessening role conflict by eliminating, or at least reducing conflicting demands (usually of the global/local variety) can help. Some companies schedule an overlap with the job incumbent to ease some of the strains in dealing with the less transparent obstacles.
- *Adjusting to the general environment.* The second dimension is adjustment to the general environment; this is perceived as more difficult than adjustment to the job. This may include reaction to housing, safety, food, education, transportation and health conditions. Companies often provide expatriates with (generally very expensive) logistics support to minimize environmental differences, such as expatriate housing and educational allowances. But, notwithstanding the expense, there are limits to how much cultural stability money can buy. Previous international experience, the novelty of the culture, the quality of the orientation (including for the family) and time spent with other expatriates prior to the assignment are some of the other factors that can influence the adjustment process.
- *Adjusting to interacting with local nationals.* Adjusting to interactions with local nationals is generally the most difficult challenge. This is the case for both the expatriate and the spouse. Behavioural norms, patterns of communication, how conflicts are resolved, etc., may be different in the new culture. This can create frustration or even anger, as the ingrained cultural routines not only often do not work, but may even be counterproductive. Again the novelty, toughness and distance of the culture, time spent with other expatriates prior to the assignment, and especially the quality of support network inside the host country (including spousal assistance programme), as well as linkage with the home office, may influence how expatriates adjust and perform.

A good preparation and training can go a long way to reduce the time it takes to adjust to the new environment. There are four broad categories of issues for companies to consider with respect to pre-departure support: the content and timing of training, the need for language education, and inclusion of the family.

Training content

There is no shortage of available learning programmes and technologies ranging from simple cultural briefings, books and videos to case studies and complex cross-cultural simulations. Some training tools focus on providing information, others deal with the emotional and affective dimensions of operating in a new culture. Not all preparation must happen in a classroom. Pre-assignment visits, coaching by an experienced manager early in an assignment and "shadowing" the country in a previous job are all viable alternatives to formal training.

Obviously, no one training methodology will be universally useful. This is not only because different jobs, different roles and different cultures have all different requirements that may need mastering, as well as different competencies and therefore a different kind and amount of preparation. More importantly, expatriates each approach their assignments with a unique set of skills and experiences based on their personality, learning orientation, life stage, career history and expectations, and, critically, the nature of the expected assignment.

Timing of training

Leading global firms invest heavily in the training of their international managers. Obviously, the longer the time span from the selection to the start of the assignment, the easier it is to arrange for solid pre-departure training. While costs can be a serious obstacle for newcomers to the international scene, resources devoted to expatriate training are usually money well spent.

However, unless properly designed, pre-departure training can have unintended consequences. In one of the earliest studies on expatriate success in Japan, researchers observed that the level of pre-departure training was negatively correlated with expatriate adjustment to the local environment. The possible explanation is that the cultural stereotype of a homogeneous Japan presented in the standard pre-departure training "package" did not correspond to the multifaceted reality – the outcome was confusion in the minds of expatriates.

These kinds of experiences, and lack of resources for extensive pre-departure training, lead many to argue that effective cross-cultural training is best conducted after the start of the assignment and targeted to help the expatriates to continue learning about the host culture and improve their international skills during the stay abroad. The ultimate test of assimilation is the ability to recognize and understand differences *within* a culture and this comes only with experience.

Speaking the local language

Everyone would agree that knowledge of the local language is beneficial in any circumstances. However, is it a must, or it is just a "nice" feature to add to the portfolio of an expatriate's skills? The answer very much depends on the nature of the assignment and the required levels of communication within the local cultural context.

Some expatriate jobs are focused on internal cross-border control and coordination, not on interaction with local customers. For this purpose, in most international firms, English is rapidly becoming the "office" language of choice. On the other hand, when the assignment requires extensive communication outside of the firm boundaries, or with local employees who may not speak English or any other "office" language, a capacity to speak a local language may be essential.

For example, for expatriates expected to take over leadership positions in local affiliates, Nestlé offers language training over the 14 months period between acceptance of assignment and departure. Other companies may offer, or even demand, short-term intensive immersion training. However, conversation classes for the expatriate while on the assignment may be an investment of questionable value if it only involves a one-hour event once a week.

Preparing the family

Family well-being is seen as an increasingly important prerequisite of expatriate effectiveness. Therefore preparation and training for the family, or at least the spouse, deserve the same amount of attention and material support as that of the expatriate. This should not be seen as a benefit provided to entice the expatriate to accept the assignment; rather it is an essential investment increasing the likelihood that the assignment will be a success.

Because the expatriate's spouse is most likely more exposed to the local culture than the expatriate who spends most of his or her time on the job, learning the language may be an important step in facilitating adjustment to living abroad. Without at least some local language skills the spouse (and the family) will tend to remain isolated inside the expatriate "ghetto" which, while materially abundant, is known to generate high levels of stress and frustration.

Guidance and support after the arrival to the new location, for example by helping the expatriate to access a network of contacts to help in the relocation and cultural adaptation process, are critical – as first impressions matter. Also, additional "free" time upon arrival prior to starting the new job may be beneficial for many expatriates. This would minimize the need to divide their attention between family and work, so when the family is settled, they can turn their full focus on the job.

Best practices for expatriate training and development

- Provide the expatriate with an orientation programme before the assignment.
- Send the expatriate for a visit to the host country (provide a period of orientation abroad).
- Involve the family in the orientation programme.
- Offer language, cultural and business training during the assignment.
- Use international assignment as a leadership top-management development tool.
- For high-potential employees, provide a challenging international assignment within two to three years after entry.

However, keep in mind that while a number of steps can be made to improve adjustment, there are limits to what the organization can do. The secret to successful adjustment lies usually with the personality of the expatriate.

Appraising expatriate performance

Typically, the performance appraisals have two broad objectives: first to assess past performance (with the dual aims of feedback to the employee, and implications for pay and promotion decisions); and second to set development goals to improve performance in future. But, given the differentiated roles and responsibilities of expatriates identified above, performance evaluation should be carefully targeted to the specific role and responsibility expected from the expatriate. The challenge is that while conducting performance appraisals is not easy in any circumstances, the difficulties are compounded in the expatriate context.

What is the purpose of the appraisal?

Aside from the typical conflict in all appraisal situations between performance assessment and development, there are particular problems in the expatriate situation concerning pay and promotions. Traditional financial incentives are often distorted by the constraints of expatriate compensation schemes heavily tilted toward fixed income and benefit-rich packages. With respect to promotional incentives, research shows that relatively few international assignments lead to promotion after the return home, even though most expatriates expected them to. And what about the consequences for under-performance? The high cost of international mobility may lead to greater tolerance for under-performance. It does not make sense to put much effort into an appraisal exercise unless the issues of appraisal outcomes are addressed first.

The development aspect of the appraisal puts the onus on the careful choice of the appraisers, as only those who can observe the expatriates in action can have much to say about their developmental needs. But again, there are no "generic" expatriate development needs. An experienced plant manager sent repeatedly abroad to manage a start-up is in a very different developmental stage than a junior marketing representative learning the ropes of global account management. In fact, one may even argue that in learning-driven assignments, development equals performance.

What standards and criteria to use?

As for performance standards, there is no universal approach. The number of expatriates and their position in the affiliates impact the choice of criteria. Some companies compare expatriates with the parent company managers, some treat expatriates as they would a local employee in the same job, while others add specific criteria reflecting the nature of the expatriate's job (for example, in the parent company, interaction with top government officials and legislators is the role of the CEO and specialized staff in external relations. In foreign affiliates, the same task may fall on the shoulders of expatriates many layers below.)

The main reason why companies use expatriate-specific criteria is that for most expatriates, technical competence is a necessary, but not sufficient condition for successful performance. Cross-cultural and interpersonal skills, sensitivity to local norms and values, understanding of differences in labour practices or customer relations and ease of adaptation to unfamiliar environment are just a few of the traits that could be appraised, especially from the developmental perspective.

Another challenge is the definition of performance. Many environmental factors such as exchange rate fluctuations, local borrowing costs and changes in the tax regime have an impact on the performance of the subsidiary, which in turn typically will affect the performance evaluation of its expatriate managers. Other measurement challenges are internal, such as transfer pricing. Defining performance in multinational firms is therefore a complex issue, going well beyond accounting adjustments. How these challenges are operationally resolved can have a major impact on how expatriates act.

The time horizon of expatriates versus locals is also an issue – short-term success in the job versus accountability for the long-term performance of the business unit. Indeed, the short-term focus is one of the most frequent criticisms levelled at expatriate managers by their local subordinates. Rightly or wrongly, expatriates are often perceived as caring about results only within the time frame of their expected assignments. This is a generic problem when employees move across intra-organizational boundaries, but it has special significance in the cross-cultural context.

There is one long-term consideration that many consider a "must" criterion in expatriate appraisals, namely developing a local successor. This is obviously a desirable goal, but in practice not easy to implement. Sometimes the goal is conveniently forgotten as the limitations of local reality set in. At the other extreme, rigid adherence to such a visible target may lead to a situation where an unqualified local successor is appointed, and the returning expatriate can check off the objective – only to see the performance of the unit collapse in the long term. Finally, the local executive is removed (usually bought out at great expense) and another expatriate parachutes in with the order to fix the performance and groom a successor.

Who should perform the evaluation?

A frequent complaint about expatriate appraisal is the fact that many expatriates are evaluated mainly by superiors or human resource staff in the home office, who may not have much international experience. For example, a study of Finnish companies operating internationally reported that in 79% of the firms the expatriate performance evaluation was conducted by a superior located in Finland. Are such raters competent? Even having international experience may not necessarily provide the rater with all the understanding needed to evaluate the performance of a manager in a far-away international subsidiary. At the same time, knowing that performance is being judged only in the head office may also induce the expatriate to spend more effort in managing the centre rather than managing the business.

Another important issue is to what extent local managers can influence the performance appraisal of the expatriate. For example, in studies of Japanese companies abroad, only in a few cases did local executives provide meaningful input in the appraisal of their Japanese subordinates. Some local managers take it as inevitable due to the ownership structure and strategic orientation of the firm. Others see this as a major obstacle to their own effectiveness as managers, as without a role in the appraisal process, their impact on subordinate behaviours is seen as limited. The degree to which local executives have input into the performance appraisal of the expatriates is a good indication of the degree to which the company is following a meaningful localization strategy.

Part of the justification for excluding the input of local managers is that people from different cultures may often misinterpret one another's behaviour. This is indeed a valid concern. From this perspective, the utilization of 360° feedback in some form or another guarantees multiple points of view on expatriate performance, and this is probably the appropriate direction for resolving some of these dilemmas. However, this does not eliminate the risk of perverse results. In one major multinational, local staff was politely enthusiastic about an overtly incompetent expatriate. They knew that if they said anything negative, they would be saddled with the individual for a longer period of time!

Expatriate compensation strategies

Newcomers to internationalization have a wide array of choices when it comes to expatriate compensation. Pay consultants worldwide have developed rather elaborate systems for how to account for the cost-of-living differences between various countries, how to respond to variations in tax regimes, or how to provide incentives for employees to work in so-called hardship areas. However, developing an effective expatriate compensation system is a task that goes far beyond technical analysis. It is, in fact, linked closely to the company's internationalization strategy.

Historically, during the very early stages of internationalization, the expatriate pay package was usually a result of individual negotiations. Since many foreign assignments were not considered particularly desirable from the point of view of a traditional career progression, financial incentives such as relocation premiums were common – mostly dependent on the bargaining skills of the expatriate. However, as increased global presence led to an increase in the number of expatriates, the *ad hoc* negotiation-driven approach quickly outlived its usefulness.

The next generation of compensation plans attempted to provide at least a common base – usually the higher of home or host-country salary – plus an "expatriate premium" component, in many cases still negotiated on an individual basis. The net result was generally the high and continuously escalating expatriate cost and difficulty in repatriation after the completion of the assignment. As the expatriate population continued to increase, a number of methodologies have emerged to help companies select a more systematic approach that could facilitate this transition. The balance sheet approach to expatriate compensation is probably the most widespread.

Balance sheet approach

The term "balance sheet" refers to any compensation system that is designed to enable expatriates to maintain a standard of living roughly equivalent to the standard of living in their own country, irrespective of the location of their assignment. Home-country salary is proportionately divided in several components based on norms: a typical breakdown is goods and services, housing, taxes and a reserve. Home and host-country expenses for each component are compared and the expatriate is compensated for the increased cost.

However, while the balance sheet methodology is simple in concept, it is still complex in implementation. For example, what is the definition of the home country for the purpose of the balance sheet calculations? When expatriates all come from the same country or economic region, work abroad for a single two–three year assignment, and then are expected to return to their home country, there is no ambiguity about what is home. But if expatriates in one foreign location come from different countries with substantially different costs of living, the methodology may result in unacceptably wide discrepancies in compensation. On the other hand, if the company uses headquarter location as "home", then expatriates from countries with lower compensation standards will be difficult to repatriate. Some companies use a modified approach where the real "home" is the base for goods and services while headquarter standards are applied to housing (the most visible component of compensation).

The balance sheet methodology is popular, as it is perceived to maintain in a reasonably cost-effective manner the purchasing power of the expatriate, thus eliminating most of the financial obstacles to mobility. In reality, this methodology still tends to overcompensate – but probably less than the alternatives. It encourages expatriates to import their lifestyles, thereby creating barriers between expatriate and locals especially in countries with lower purchasing power. Also, as a sizeable part of compensation and lifestyle is protected, it is difficult to establish a clear connection between results and rewards.

Another weakness of the balance sheet approach (indeed of most compensation methodologies) is their reliance on norms tailored to the "average" expatriate. Again, the increased heterogeneity of the expatriate population is creating havoc with this assumption. For example, the balance sheet approach generally does not allow adjustments for expatriates whose spouses suspend their own careers. For some expatriates, support for children's education may top the list of essential benefits; while for others it may be long-term care for parents left behind. The cafeteria approach to benefits, pricing such benefits and permitting choice within a limit, is often essential. And for short-term assignments, it may be more convenient to provide simple lump-sum payments to cover the additional expenses and let the expatriates manage their finance the way they see fit. This avoids unnecessary entitlements or intruding too much into private financial circumstances.

In some firms, the vast majority of international assignments are confined to a specific region (e.g., the European Union or the Association of Southeast Asian Nations). In that case, it may be advisable to tailor the policy to the conditions within the region rather than applying a worldwide policy. Again, differences in treatment of "regional" and "global" expatriates have to be carefully monitored. Whenever employees in similar jobs are treated differently, morale and commitment are bound to suffer.

Designing effective compensation plans

Most pay methodologies make universal assumptions about where expatriates come from, what their role is and where they are going. But no system as such can be an obvious panacea to the multiple demands of expatriation.

It could be argued that if a firm's expatriate population consists of several categories (for example, senior executives, mid-level professionals and junior trainees), compensation packages should perhaps be tailored to their specific needs. After all, the motives for expatriation vary from one category to another. This may lead to a unified global compensation plan for the senior executives irrespective of their location, a balance sheet approach for most expatriate managers and professionals, and local pay systems for entry-level and junior assignees. Alternatively, the company may have one system for career expatriates and another for those on short assignments.

Best practices in expatriate appraisal and compensation

- Ensure a timely performance review.
- Modify the performance evaluation system to incorporate the distinctive conditions of local countries.
- Get multiple opinions concerning an expatriate's performance.
- Tailor the compensation plan to the expatriation strategy.
- Provide flexible benefits targeted to specific needs.
- Ensure equity and transparency.

When it comes to the choice of expatriate compensation strategy, the starting point is to clarify two key questions:

- What categories of expatriates the company has, or will have in future.
- Whether all categories of expatriates should be paid using the same method.

The selection of the specific expatriate compensation plan is then influenced primarily by three sets of considerations:

- Cost efficiency – making sure that the plan delivers intended benefits in the most cost-effective manner (including tax consequences).
- Equity issues – making sure that the plan is equitable irrespective of the assignment location or nationality of the expatriate.
- System maintenance – making sure that the plan is relatively transparent and easy to administer.

It is also important to bear in mind that compensation is only one of the factors contributing to an employee's desire to take an international assignment. Non-financial rewards such as learning opportunities and expectations of future career gains are also important motivators. When expatriation is a "ticket to nowhere", no amount of effort to fine-tune the pay will produce a committed and dedicated expatriate workforce.

Bringing expatriates home

Most expatriates eventually come home. But what could be seen as a routine move may in reality be a rather complex process of renegotiating one's own identity and culture, rebuilding the critical corporate networks, and re-anchoring one's career in the organization. In a world of nearly continuous restructuring, the safe harbour of international jobs becomes quickly only a distant memory. Combined with a frequent loss in social status – no more invitations to the Prime Minister's Christmas party – and a loss of financial benefits associated with expatriation, the cultural shock of "coming home" may be even larger than the shock associated with the initial expatriation.

On the job, many expatriates find it particularly difficult to unlearn the autonomy and freedom they have enjoyed in their international assignment. Even more difficult to cope with are "make-work" assignments, doled out to the returnees stuck in the holding pattern waiting for a "real" job opportunity to open up. It is therefore no surprise that the available data point to a relatively high turnover of employees after return from international assignments. High turnover is costly, and in addition, it may have a negative impact on the willingness of others to accept an international assignment. However, a lot can be done to improve the odds of a successful return, at relatively low cost.

The best repatriation practices focus on advance planning in order to provide meaningful opportunities upon return that create value for the employee as well as for the company, and on emotional and logistical support during the transition. An important objective of career discussions is to enhance the opportunities to utilize the knowledge and skills absorbed during the assignment.

The place to start is to maintain a continuous dialogue with the expatriate about events and opportunities at home through a formal or informal networking or mentoring programme. For example, the employee's mentor at Coca-Cola leads the repatriation job search. The employee is also provided with repatriation counselling and a "safety net" of one year to locate to another position within the company. At IBM and Lafarge, a "career manager" or "advisor" monitors the expatriate's development throughout the assignment, keeps him or her informed, serves as an advocate during the home country succession planning process and helps the expatriate's family relocate back home.

Best practices in repatriation

- Develop a network of contacts to keep the expatriate up-to-date on home-country operations.
- Establish mentor relationships between expatriates and executives from home location.

- Monitor career paths of international managers so that they are not relegated to the "slow track" because of their international assignments.
- Provide opportunities for the returning manager to use the knowledge and skills learned internationally.
- Assist the expatriate's spouse in finding a job abroad and upon return.
- Assign the repatriated family to a welcome group composed of other families who have lived abroad.

Some companies have pre-established an end-date to every assignment to help plan for repatriation well in advance of the candidate's return. Another frequently applied policy is to require the dispatching unit to take formal responsibility to find a comparable position to that from which the expatriate departed – although after being away for three–four years, this may actually result in a demotion – a fate experienced by a surprisingly large number of returnees.

And, just as in the case of the initial expatriation, it is not only the employee, but also the whole family that is coming back. Support with job-hunting for the spouse – often after an extended absence from the job market – counselling for teenage children, or simply setting up welcome programmes may go a long way in eliminating the stress and confusion often associated with the return home.

Finally, based on our experience with a number of multinational firms we can offer two observations on increasing the odds of a successful repatriation:

- First, the best predictor of successful repatriation is performance of the expatriate before the international assignment. The successful repatriation starts with careful selection.
- Second, seeing is believing. The international track record of top executives demonstrates the value of the expatriate experience and eases the worry about repatriation.

 **SUMMARY**

A number of key themes regarding the effective management of the expatriation process have emerged.

In the area of *staffing and selection*, the thrust is on making sure that the international track attracts those with the best potential to succeed in the firm. The assessment for international assignment is becoming increasingly rigorous and often involves the candidate's spouse. The structure of assignments is becoming more flexible and family well-being is now recognized as an important element of expatriate effectiveness.

From the *management development* perspective, international assignments are viewed as an intrinsic part of career progression, providing opportunities both for a transfer of know-how as well as learning of new competencies by the international manager. Leading global firms invest heavily in the training of their international managers. However, training is not only provided in the pre-departure stage, but the expatriates are expected to continue learning about the host culture and improve their international skills during the assignment.

The expatriate role, the duration of the assignment, the long-term implications and the nature of the business, all have a bearing on what kind of compensation approach is the most appropriate. Effective *reward systems* also look beyond salary and benefits. Access to career development and learning opportunities and even support for the spouse are some of the tools that companies can use to motivate and retain talented expatriates.

Finally, the *repatriation* stage of the international assignment is receiving growing attention in order to reduce the perceived high turnover of returning executives. Successful returns have a positive impact on the willingness of others to accept an international assignment. The best practices focus on advance planning in order to provide meaningful opportunities upon return that create value for the employee as well as for the company, and on emotional and logistical support during the transition.

 **LEARNING POINTS**

- The expatriate population is becoming increasingly diverse in age, nationality and purpose.
- As companies gain international experience, the role of expatriates is bound to change.
- For expatriate selection, "soft" factors are just as important as technical competence.
- Don't select a person, select a family.
- Expatriate training that facilitates adjustment is a very good investment.
- Ensure multiple points of view on expatriate performance.
- There is no perfect expatriate compensation system – but the trade-offs can be managed.
- Do not underestimate the cultural shock of coming home.
- Dead-end jobs for returning expatriates kill international initiatives.
- Successful expatriation builds commitment to the global culture.

7

Developing Local Talent

More multinationals are trying to reduce their dependence on expatriates for a variety of reasons, including the potential for discouraging promising local employees and the sheer expense. But overcoming barriers to the process known as localization demands that companies make a concerted effort to develop local managers.
Philip Rosenzweig reviews the steps that companies should follow to make localization work.

> **"To be a true global player, you need to have local talent in management positions who are given responsibilities in strategic decision-making as part of a global business unit."**
>
> **Marc Kalton, *Arthur D. Little***

Overview

Many companies rely on expatriates when they enter new markets. But relying too heavily on expatriates present problems, ranging from a lack of knowledge to high costs to discouragement of local managers. The answer is to replace expatriates with local managers, a process we call *localization*.

Most managers agree with the aims of localization but have a difficult time making it work. The reasons include a failure to develop local managers, a bias against different backgrounds in the promotion process, and the lack of an explicit imperative for promoting local managers. The best companies address these challenges by making an explicit effort to attract and retain superior local talent, by placing a priority on the development of local managers, and by adopting explicit goals for localization, backing them up with incentives and rewards.

The problem with relying on expatriates

As Chapter 6 showed, expatriates are critical for managing international growth. They jump-start the new subsidiary, transfer vital technical and commercial expertise, and impart company values to the local workforce. But continued reliance on expatriates raises a number of problems:

- Expatriates rarely know the host country as well as local nationals, who not only understand the culture and language, but are often well connected in the community. To adapt products or services for local needs, and to achieve the full potential in a host country, it's imperative to make full use of the talents of local managers.
- If top positions remain held by expatriates, local nationals will often become discouraged and leave for better opportunities elsewhere. The best local talent will remain if it sees that opportunities are open to all, not just reserved for expatriates.
- Reliance on expatriates can slow the pace of international growth. If every new entry requires a cohort of expatriates, it follows that growth is limited by the availability of managers for expatriate assignments. Yet many successful companies have a shortage, not a surplus, of available managers. This problem is especially acute for mid-sized or small companies who lack depth in their management ranks.

- Expatriates are expensive. Considering many of the features standard in expatriate packages, such as allowances for housing, children's education, tax equalization, and much more, the cost of an expatriate can range from 150% to 400% of the manager's cost in the home country. All else being equal, reducing reliance on expatriates is desirable for cost reasons alone.

For these reasons, many multinationals try to reduce their reliance on expatriates and bring local managers into positions of responsibility, a process known as *localization*. They know that in the short run it's easy to rely on expatriates; but in the long run, there's really no alternative to localization. Volker Büring, vice president of human resources at Accor, the world's leading hotel and business service company, puts it this way: "*You can win a battle with expatriates, but you cannot win a war.*"

Unfortunately, localization is easier in theory than in practice. Most companies find it hard to localize management as quickly and successfully as they'd like. They're stuck in a cycle of sending expatriates abroad, then replacing them with new expatriates, and so on in a continually revolving door. Several years later, local subsidiaries still have expatriates in most key positions, a situation that's expensive, demotivating for local nationals, and a missed opportunity in terms of new ideas and local adaptation.

CASE STUDY: A NOTE ON TERMINOLOGY: WHAT'S LOCALIZATION?

We define "localization" as the process of replacing expatriate managers with local nationals. But not everyone uses the terms this way, so a word of caution is warranted.

In some countries, the process is referred to as "nationalization", a term we've avoided as it is generally used to mean the shift from private ownership to ownership by the national government. In the context of multinational firms, localization may be a challenge, but nationalization is something entirely more dangerous.

But even the use of the word localization can differ. At one large Japanese company with global operations, where all key positions around the world were held by Japanese citizens, all managers claimed to favour localization – but with very different meanings. To Europeans, localization meant that local nationals should take over key management positions. To the Japanese, localization meant that decisions would be made locally, rather than in Tokyo, but of course the managers with decision-making authority would be Japanese. The result was a vicious cycle: the Europeans wouldn't stay long since they saw their careers limited, and the Japanese wouldn't promote any Europeans for fear they'd leave, so it kept on going on and on.

Finally, at times there is sensitivity about the word "local". To some people, referring to the citizen of the host nation as a "local" is one step above calling that person a "native". Images come to mind of racial stereotyping, colonial superiority and so on. It is better to use a reference to the specific country – as in Indianization, Emiratization, for example. Or, regarding the general practice, and not limited to a specific country, perhaps "local national" or "local citizen", is better, not just "local", which is an adjective and not a noun.

Why localization is difficult

Why is localization so difficult? The first reason given is usually a lack of sufficiently qualified local managers. We'd like to place more local managers into key positions, goes the argument, but they're just not available. In the short term there's often truth to this view, especially if a senior position calls for a high degree of technical or company-specific expertise. There's no denying that in many countries, experienced managers with high technical and managerial skills aren't in great abundance.

But in the longer term this argument is doubtful. The chronic inability to replace expatriate managers with local managers is rarely due to the lack of ability on the part of the local population, but more likely due to failures on the part of the company. Generally the failure to localize management can be traced to three underlying causes:

- a failure to develop local employees;
- a resistance – often unconscious – to promote people with different profiles and backgrounds into senior positions;
- a pre-occupation with narrow business objectives, at the expense of an emphasis on localization.

Failure to develop local employees

Simply put, many companies don't dedicate the time and resources to developing local managers. They don't place sufficient importance on hiring, on retention, or on skill development, and consequently never build a strong cadre of local nationals with the qualifications to take over key positions. In other instances, there is adequate attention to technical and commercial skill development, but little in the way of managerial or leadership skill-building, including taking on progressively important responsibilities. These formative experiences are critical to developing experience and demonstrating leadership ability.

Failure to promote local managers into senior positions

The most important single barrier to localization is often a resistance – unconscious and even unintended – to promote local employees into senior positions. Well-meaning multinationals may say all the right things regarding the importance of placing local nationals in key positions, but somehow always find a reason not to take the final step.

The main culprit is the way companies make promotion decisions. Often they're based on a candidate's resemblance to some ideal. We feel comfortable with a candidate who reminds us of successful managers; and we tend to avoid choosing managers who depart from the mould. In *Men and Women of the Corporation*, Rosabeth Moss Kanter described this practice as "homosocial reproduction" – an inelegant tag to describe a phenomenon that has kept women and ethnic minorities out of positions of power (Moss Kanter, 1977). In multinational companies, the same tendency to promote based on a fit with some preconception works to keep local nationals out of important positions. Managers may believe, with all sincerity that they don't discriminate based on nationality, but their natural tendency for continuity and fit makes it hard for local nationals to break through.

Curiously, the unwillingness to promote local managers may be more acute in companies with strong corporate cultures. In *Built to Last: Successful Habits of Visionary Companies*, James C. Collins and Jerry I. Porras identify a strong culture as one of the distinguishing features of outstanding companies. They compare these companies to close-knit societies where it's critical to fit in. Employees share the core tenets of a clear ideology, and display a "tightness of fit" where members feel they belong to something special. The result: a level of employee loyalty, commitment to organizational purpose, and personal dedication which leads to superior performance.

But there's a flip side. The stronger the corporate culture, the more resistant it may be to people who bring new and different qualities, something inevitable when expanding internationally. Thus the paradox: what is often a strength – firm cohesion and strength of culture – may pose an impediment to localization. Collins and Porras note that in many excellent companies, "It's binary: either you're in or you're out, and there seems to be no middle ground" (Collins and Porras, 1994). Unfortunately, many local nationals find themselves "outsiders", excluded from advancement to key positions.

A compounding factor is language: the sheer ability of local managers to speak the parent company's language, and to participate in decision-making discussions at a high level. Not only are local nationals "outsiders" in background and culture, but often also in language. Furthermore, expatriate managers often confuse language ability with intelligence. Excellent local managers may not always possess the best language skills, and may be overlooked in favour of colleagues whose language skills are outstanding. At one British company operating in South America, expatriates were quickly impressed with those local employees who spoke excellent English, and – at least as perceived by local nationals – inferred that they were the most capable, something not always true.

The combination of a strong corporate culture and a difficult language has provided a powerful barrier to localization in many Japanese and Korean firms. Emphasis on seniority, on language and on decision-making styles has made it difficult for any managers of other nationalities to reach the highest levels of management.

Failure to give explicit importance to localization

The final obstacle is one of priority. Many expatriate managers focus on business objectives: their goal is to meet revenue targets, develop a brand, build a commercial network and so on. Very likely they have made a career out of successfully pursuing conventional performance objectives from their home country experience, and find it natural to continue emphasizing these objectives in a new country. (They may indeed have been selected for the job specifically because of their abilities in these areas; so the cause of such problems can be traced back one step, to the selection criteria for expatriates.) The result, of course, is that by focusing on conventional targets, localization as an explicit objective is often overlooked. Little wonder, then, that many companies have a revolving door of expatriates.

A SHORT HISTORY OF "-IZATION"

The process of replacing expatriates with local nationals isn't new. Before the rise of multinational companies, invading armies and colonial governments sought, at various times, to staff their legions and armies with indigenous people – maintaining control while leveraging their scarce human resources.

One of the earliest references to localization dates back to the first decade of the 20th century. In 1907, just a few years after the Philippines became the first US territory overseas, the Americans were seeking to replace American officials with locals – a process called "Philippinization" (Karnow, 1989).

Perhaps the first multinational company to confront this challenge explicitly was Unilever. In the 1930s, Lever Brothers placed an Indian national in charge of the Indian subsidiary – something unheard of at the time. In time, Unilever referred simply to "ization" as the general process of placing local nationals in top positions. Today, in countless companies around the world, localization is a major priority.

WHEN NOT TO LOCALIZE MANAGEMENT

Localization of management positions makes sense as a general policy, but there are exceptions. Sometimes nationality is an intrinsic part of the perceived value. Take a Swiss private bank: customers go there because they want to see a Swiss, the embodiment of the service; otherwise customers would walk down the street and go to a local bank. Precisely what sets them apart is the expatriate, the embodiment of value-added. Similarly, the head of brewing at Heineken is always Dutch, which is part of the perceived value.

Another exception has to do with control. Many multinationals are quick to localize positions like corporate affairs and human resources, slower to localize production and marketing, and even slower to localize finance.

Finally, localization takes on a special function in partnerships, such as acquisitions and alliances. One company said that when it had a joint venture with a local firm, it wanted its lead manager to be of the parent nationality, not a second local manager.

Breaking the cycle: steps to localization

Overcoming barriers to localization requires a concerted effort. It won't happen on its own. Successful companies follow a three-step process:

- They make a conscious effort to recruit and retain superior local talent.
- They dedicate time and resources to developing local managers.
- They make explicit the goal to localize management, providing performance measures with incentives and rewards.

Recruiting and retaining local talent

Attracting talent is among the greatest challenges for any company. A recent report from McKinsey & Co, titled "The War for Talent", summed it up nicely: competition among leading companies is, above all, a competition to attract and retain the best people.

For foreign subsidiaries of multinational companies, recruiting takes on a special twist. In many countries, the best graduates, sensing greater possibilities for advancement, prefer careers with locally based companies. But in other countries, multinationals enjoy significant advantages when it comes to attracting local talent. Especially in emerging markets, they may be able to offer superior career opportunities, both in country and potentially abroad; they may offer better training opportunities; and they bring exposure to cutting-edge business practices.

Most of those advantages apply to large companies, which enjoy prestigious reputations and can offer excellent training programmes and career prospects. Small companies have few of these advantages, and often find hiring local talent to be daunting.

Regardless of their size, multinationals can focus on four ways to attract the best local candidates:

- *Make a clear commitment to the country.* The first challenge, especially for small companies, is to express clearly the company's commitment to the country. They need to state: "*We're here to stay*." Evidence of staying power in other countries, expressions of the amount of investment, explicit plans for growth in the country – and other means can help demonstrate a strong commitment for the future.
- *Offer superior development planning.* Companies should devise a clear development plan for each local manager – ideally in a collaborative way that not only draws on inputs from the manager, but also signals to him or her the company's commitment. Such a plan may include specific competence building or development opportunities. It may also involve training programmes, either offered locally or internationally.
- *Provide superior career opportunities.* The ability to offer career opportunities is a real plus for multinationals. One dimension, of course, pertains to positions in the local market, which is precisely the issue of localization. Successful localization creates a precedent and may attract strong applicants. A second dimension has to do with overseas opportunities, that is, potential expatriate careers. There's no reason why strong local candidates should be limited to rising in their home country; the best multinationals look to deploy their talent on a global basis.
- *Provide good financial compensation.* Salary and bonus are important – in many instances, they are the single most important factor for attracting local talent. Multinational firms often find their ability to pay world-standard salaries is a substantial edge over local competitors. Yet many leading companies try not to place too much emphasis on financial compensation because employees who come for top dollar may soon leave for a better offer

elsewhere. Far better is to build loyalty and commitment through a combination of factors.

Developing local hiring channels

The recruiting process itself is often a challenge. Established multinationals, with strong connections in the country, may have means to recruit young professionals and experienced managers on their own. They can advertise job openings, their human resources departments can process applications, they can interview applicants. They can create links with governmental agencies and industrial organizations to identify candidates. Proctor & Gamble, for instance, was able to attract a large number of young Chinese employees by recruiting actively at major universities across the country (Hsieh, Lavoie and Samek, 1999).

Mid-sized and small companies generally don't have the resources to conduct high-profile advertising or large-scale recruiting, nor do they have the staff to process hundreds of applications. The compensating good news is that their needs are often moderate, as they seek a smaller number of people, and at times a very few.

How can these companies identify and attract local talent quickly? One approach is to seek assistance from the human resource departments of local companies of partner firms, or of companies with the same parent country. In either event, new entrants may be able to leverage established human resource departments both in publicizing needs and in evaluating candidates. Especially if they compete in different industries, they may be receptive to providing guidance, or offering services in hiring local employees.

A more common approach is to work with local employment agencies and management search firms who are well connected and can guide the search process. Yet companies should be under no illusions that a local search firm is an answer by itself. Companies must never abdicate full authority to the local search firm, but must always play a role of guidance and oversight. Becoming dependent on a local search firm is dangerous, and resulting errors can take years to correct.

Some guidelines for working with local search firms include:

- To help identify a good local search firm, companies can begin by seeking recommendations. Ask other companies from your home country who they use.
- When beginning discussions with search firms, ask for references. What companies have they worked for, and with what results? Next, get to know specific individuals in the firm.
- Very often, especially for management level searches, the personal network and skills of the individual are critical. The company is often less important than the individual.
- Be clear about the skills you need. What skills or capabilities are truly required, and which are desirable? Without a very clear sense of these points, you won't be in a position to provide accurate direction.
- Where possible, work with more than one search firm. Avoid exclusive relations, and use the experience gained with one firm to help stimulate the quality of search undertaken by the other.

Developing management and leadership skills

As we showed in Chapter 1, many companies are expanding rapidly into emerging markets, where levels of education and technical skills are highly variable, and into countries only recently converted to market economies, where experience in business and commercial skills may be low. Successful localization of management depends not only on hiring bright and energetic people, but providing the necessary training and development to ensure their growth and ability to contribute at higher levels.

Most companies today, especially larger ones with established human resource functions, have quite sophisticated ways to identify and measure key competencies. For mid-sized or small companies, often with limited human resource capabilities, some explicit thought about categories of skills and competencies is helpful.

It's vital that companies be clear about the qualities needed for promotion into senior management. There's no point in saying that technical training is key, and then reject a candidate for not having managerial experience. What's necessary, and what's desirable? How important is language ability? Company knowledge? Specific technical skills? Probing should take place in an open dialogue among people, not just expatriates doing the thinking. Make sure you know the difference between quality and perceived quality.

When assessing the present capabilities of employees, and comparing them against desired capabilities, we can focus on four areas which lead to specific training and development:

- *technical skills*, including operations, manufacturing, logistics and information technology;
- *commercial skills*, including marketing, service delivery and customer relationship management;
- *analytical skills*, including strategy and competition, finance and cash management;
- *managerial skills*, including team building, decision making, delegation and coaching.

Some large companies have set up their own management schools, where sometimes hundreds of new hires are trained in a variety of commercial, analytical, and managerial fields. In large and strategically important countries, such as China, some leading multinationals have invested in company schools such as the Motorola University in Beijing and the ABB China Business School. Hundreds of employees have received technical and managerial instruction at these institutions. Other multinationals, including Nestlé, have adopted a tiered approach, with early training taking place in the host country; lower level management training on a regional basis; and higher level training handled on a global basis. In addition to imparting business skills, these programmes have the effect of building informal networks among managers across national lines.

For companies with a few hundred employees, a dedicated training department, let alone a company university, is out of the question. Yet the need to invest in the development of local employees is at least as great as for large firms. Not only are mid-sized and small firms more immediately dependent on local managers, and less able to rely on a deep bench of expatriates, but the willingness to invest in local managers is essential to retain the best talent. Rather than setting up permanent training centres, smaller companies can rely on managers from elsewhere in the world to visit and conduct training sessions. They can also send individual managers on management development programmes either in the country or abroad.

Promoting local nationals into key positions

Hiring strong local employees is a first step, and making concerted efforts for their development and training is a second step, but ensuring that local nationals achieve key positions of responsibility remains difficult in many companies. The problem, as explained above, is a combination of risk aversion and a preference for well-known profiles.

How can companies break through? There are a few ways. One tactic is to insist that any short list of possible successors includes local nationals as well as expatriates. Perhaps a local national won't be the chosen candidate at first, but over time, the very consideration of local nationals for these jobs may change perceptions about them, making them seem plausible.

Such an approach is a step in the right direction for many companies, but it addresses inputs, not outputs. A stronger approach is to set targets for outputs – that is, local managers who are promoted into key positions. Some companies are breaking the revolving-door by making local replacement a top priority. At BOC Gas's China subsidiary, expatriate performance evaluation is explicitly linked to localization: "*They must work themselves out of their jobs in 3 to 6 years – or be deemed incompetent*" (Hsieh, Lavoie and Samek, 1999).

Exhorting managers to replace themselves with local managers isn't enough. To help the process, companies can set up a plan to identify, train and provide developmental opportunities to candidates. The key is to begin the preparation sufficiently early so as not to fall short at the end, and to prepare enough managers so that unexpected departures don't create shortfalls. In addition to classroom experience, of course, it is important to develop one or more candidates. Clear training programmes, involving not only responsibilities on site, but also rotations and travel to elsewhere in the company can also play a role.

CASE STUDY: PLACING A LOCAL MANAGER IN CHARGE AT
HEWLETT PACKARD JAPAN

Putting local managers in charge isn't always difficult. Hewlett-Packard is known for its strong corporate culture and its practice of promoting from within, two factors that might be expected to impede localization of management. But Bill Hewlett and Dave Packard were open-minded and pragmatic managers, and not ones to stand on ceremony or tradition. They were also inclined to show confidence in people.

In the early 1960s Hewlett Packard (HP) set up a joint venture in Japan. Yokogawa Hewlett Packard had a factory and head office west of Tokyo, and employed almost entirely Japanese, but the general manager was an American sent by HP.

> *David Packard recalled:*
>
> *During the first few years of our Japanese joint venture, the [Yokogawa Hewlett-Packard] general manager, an American, came to the meetings and reported along with all of our other managers. . . .*
>
> *After this had gone on some years, a bright young Japanese manager, Kenzo Sasaoka, who was doing good work over there, cornered Bill Hewlett and me one day. He said,*
>
> *"Why don't you let me run YHP? We spend a lot of time – in fact, waste a lot of time – talking to [the American], and if something goes wrong, he's the fellow we blame. We really think we can do better." So we said, "Okay, you go ahead – you run the operation and we'll see how it goes" (Packard, 1995).*
>
> *Hewlett and Packard put Sasaoka in charge, and results remained excellent.*
>
> *Of course, the decision wasn't quite as informal and quick as described in Packard's memoirs. HP had a few factors in its favour: the presence of a strong local candidate, and the fact he was not just strong technically, but could behave in the open and direct manner consistent with HP's culture – unusual for a Japanese manager. In effect, Hewlett and Packard recognized that Sasaoka had the necessary traits of company culture: willingness to take risk, direct communication, pragmatism – combined with the many advantages of a local manager.*
>
> *For many companies, putting a local national in charge of an affiliate is one of the most difficult things imaginable, yet as seen in this example, for an open-minded and trusting company, it need not always be difficult.*

Review and intervention

Even with the steps above, companies must continually review their success and learn from shortfalls. If they've fallen short of meeting their targets for localization they must probe why. The analysis cannot only draw on the perceptions of expatriate managers, or headquarters at home, but must involve a cross-section of employees, local as well as expatriates. Exit interviews are an excellent means to understand the perspectives and experiences of managers who leave the company – possibly too late to change minds, but vital to redress biases.

One key point concerns the attrition rate of local managers at each level of the hierarchy. Some companies are good at hiring locally, but lose managers over the subsequent years at an alarming rate. Some loss is to be expected, of course, and multinationals may also be a target of poaching by local companies that value the initial training local nationals receive.

In one South American country, for instance, Nestlé estimated it needed to hire two entry-level professionals for every one it needed, since so many were hired away by other local companies. Far from becoming bitter, Nestlé accepted this situation and believed that, at least, it sowed good will throughout the economy by providing good entry-level training to so many managers. But if the rate of loss is greater than expected, and cutting into the talent pool needed for localization, then it's a real cause for worry. The only way to understand is to track, to inquire and to intervene.

Can we localize from the outset?

Some companies try to get around the difficult of replacing expatriates by going directly with local managers from the start. They try, in effect, to do without expatriates at all. To mid-sized and small companies, short on management resources and trying to economize while growing abroad, the appeal is great. As one manager put it, *"At the end of the day you have to give the business to the locals. So why bother with expats?"*

Can a company truly do without any expatriates? Yes and no – it depends on your definition. It may be impossible to do without the frequent visits and oversight of managers from the home country or at least neighbouring countries. But it may be possible to do without expatriates assigned on a full-time, multiyear basis. The experience of Rentsch, a Swiss-based packaging company, in Poland, provides an example as described below.

CASE STUDY: MANAGING WITHOUT EXPATRIATES: RENTSCH IN POLAND

Rentsch, a Swiss-based maker of packaging materials, opened a new subsidiary in Poland in 1994 without any full-time expatriates. At the time, Rentsch had 900 employees spread across plants in Switzerland, France, Germany, Portugal and Spain. Following the fall of communism, Rentsch decided to set up in eastern Europe, and acquired a bankrupt printing company in Lodz. A Swiss manager was project manager.

Staffing Rentsch Polska posed a serious challenge. A small company, without managers to spare, Rentsch wasn't in a position to send expatriates for long-term assignments. Instead, Rentsch named a Polish man, a member of the supervisory board, as Managing Director. For the first six months, the Swiss project manager spent three or four days each fortnight in Poland, helping to get the new plant up and running, and teaching the MD. In effect, they shared the job – the Swiss manager handled technical and commercial responsibilities, while the Polish manager built the organization and handled human resources. Over time, the Polish manager assumed more and more responsibility.

In parallel, some key engineers and functional specialists flew in from Rentsch's other sites to train Polish employees. Some Polish employees were also sent for brief apprenticeships to Rentsch factories. By relying on these visits, and through continuing support by the Swiss project manager, the new factory met or surpassed all performance targets, both for quality and timing, without any full-time expatriates. By the following year, the Polish MD was fully in charge, and communication with Switzerland remained close, but the plant was largely independent.

Looking back, the managing director of Rentsch Polska observed that the lack of any full-time expatriates sent a strong message to Polish employees: we believe in you and we'll support you, but success or failure is on your shoulders. This message inspired and motivated employees. For Rentsch, a company without managers to spare, the efficiency of foreign market entry without full-time expatriates was a huge plus.

For any company seeking to bypass full-time expatriates entirely, three elements are critical:

- hiring the "right" senior person;
- providing a mix of support and oversight;
- phasing in responsibility.

Hiring the "right" senior person

Attempting to do without expatriates places even more importance on the selection of the highest ranking local manager. The decision is hugely consequential, and unlike gradual phasing-in based on performance, you're making a major bet from the start. This person, for better or for worse, takes the lead in shaping the local organization, and the parent company's ability to monitor on-site is reduced. A mistake in hiring leads to problems that can multiply rapidly.

As noted above, many companies will look to management search firms to identify and select local managers. Especially in the absence of expatriates on the ground, the role of the search firm is even greater. Yet that underscores the importance of not relinquishing all decision-making to the search firm, but playing an active role.

The most important point to make is: be thorough and do your homework. If you let others make these decisions, it's your own fault. Successful companies know not to rely on first impressions. They know that their unfamiliarity in a new market makes them especially vulnerable. They also know, as we said earlier, not to confuse language ability with competence or integrity.

Next, a few points of admonition:

- *Check them out!* Don't be shy. Cross-reference, cross-check background information of all kinds, including educational and criminal records.
- *Look for track record.* What is the demonstrated interest? Is it in working for a western firm? How have they prepared themselves? This is perhaps more important than technical knowledge or direct experience.
- *Rely on multiple evaluations.* Screen using multiple people, from different functions, local and home office. Fly them to the home office, as a way to educate them about the company as well as a way to evaluate.

Support and monitoring

Once a lead local manager has been selected, there remain a number of key points to ensure smooth success.

- *Split the job.* Rather than hire the "CEO" or "MD," make two positions; fill one locally with modest responsibilities, and have an expatriate do the other. Reduce the dependence on any given person.
- *Establish clear ground rules.* Companies must not be shy about being clear regarding permissible and unpermissible behaviour. Issuing clear guidelines regarding hiring friends and relatives, giving contracts to friends

and relatives, and so forth, must be clear. Trust has to be won. Err on the
side of caution.

● *Provide remote support.* Frequent visits by senior managers from the home
  country or nearby countries are important, both to monitor local
  performance and to provide support. In addition, some companies appoint a
  dedicated contact with oversight responsibility, available at all times to the
  local manager.

● *Monitor performance closely.* Establish explicit performance targets and
  watch them closely. Err on the side of watching too closely. If that's a
  problem, you have the wrong local manager. Vigilant oversight is the cost of
  going with local managers from the start; you can't have it both ways.

Phasing in responsibility

As the local manager builds competencies, his or her responsibilities can be increased.
Jobs may no longer need to be split. The extent of remote oversight may diminish.
Erring on the side of caution is still a good idea, and performance must always be
monitored and audited, but over time the local manager can take on the full range of
responsibilities. At that time, transition is complete – without the presence of full-
time expatriates.

 # SUMMARY

Continual reliance on expatriates raises a number of problems, including ignorance
of the host country, discouragement of local nationals, shortage of supply and the
expense. Many multinationals try to reduce their reliance on expatriates and bring
local managers into positions of responsibility, a process known as *localization*. They
know that in the short run it's easy to rely on expatriates; but in the long run, there's
really no alternative to localization.

Generally the failure to localize management can be traced to three underlying
causes:

● a failure to develop local employees;
● a resistance – often unconscious – to promote people with different profiles
  and backgrounds into senior positions;
● a pre-occupation with narrow business objectives, at the expense of an
  emphasis on localization.

Overcoming barriers to localization requires a concerted effort. It won't happen
on its own. Successful companies can follow a three-step process: first, they make

a conscious effort to attract and retain superior local talent; second, they dedicate time and resources to developing local managers; and third, they make explicit the goal to localize management, providing performance measures with incentives and rewards.

Even with the steps above, companies must continually review their success and learn from shortfalls. If they've fallen short of meeting their targets for localization they must probe why. The analysis cannot only draw on the perceptions of expatriate managers, or headquarters at home, but must involve a cross-section of employees, local as well as expatriates.

 LEARNING POINTS

- Make a conscious effort to attract and retain superior local talent by making a clear commitment to the country, offering superior training and career opportunities, as well as good financial compensation.
- Ask partners for help in finding good people.
- Work with local employment agencies and management search firms to guide the search process.
- Provide the necessary training and development based on an assessment of candidates' technical, commercial, analytical and managerial skills.
- Promote local nationals to key positions to send a message to other potential managers. One tactic is to insist that any short list of possible candidates includes local nationals as well as expatriates.
- Set targets for the number of local managers to be promoted to certain positions within prescribed periods of time. Review successes and learn from failures.
- If the intention is to localize from the outset, do your homework thoroughly in terms of checking out potential candidates, and back them up with sufficient oversight and support from abroad.

References

CMR Focus Report, March 23 1998, p. 14.

Collins, James C. and Porras, Jerry I. (1994) *Built to Last: Successful Habits of Visionary Companies*, Harper Business, New York, p. 122.

Hsieh, T.-Y., Lavoie, J. and Samek, R.A.P. (1999) Think Global, Hire Local, *McKinsey Quarterly*, Number 4.

Karnow, Stanley (1989) *In our Image: America in the Philippines*, Random House, New York.

Moss Kanter, Rosabeth (1977) *Men and Women of the Corporation*, Basic Books, Inc, New York, p. 48.

Packard, David (1995) *The HP Way: How Bill Hewlett and I Built our Company*, Harper Business, New York, p. 123.

Part Four

Fostering Global Learning

8

The Global Learning Imperative

Learning is fast becoming one of the key strategic
capabilities that companies can use to stay ahead in the
competitive race. Replicating successful home strategies,
processes and approaches is no longer enough. Having a
learning mindset means being open to the richness and
diversity offered by the global "classroom". As **Xavier Gilbert**
explains, how firms learn and how they are able to manage
that learning on a global basis are critical elements in
accelerating successful international growth.

Overview

There is more to successful international growth than merely replicating, in new countries, a company's successful home strategies, processes and approaches. In fast-changing environments, copying past successful moves, even if done smartly, is bound to be inadequate. Increasingly, the emphasis has to be on learning quickly and continuously how to make the best out of a new local environment, and how to redeploy this learning globally. Seeing fast international growth as a means of ensuring rapid and effective learning will not only accelerate successful entry, but also produce a leading-edge global business model.

The world is not only a space to conquer, it also has many places to learn from: counting on its uniformity and consistency would support the idea of globally replicating one successful approach, but counting on its differences supports the view that what can be learned in one place will enrich our business model and make it more robust and effective globally.

To achieve this, a learning mindset is required, rather than a "missionary" mindset. A learning mindset sees action not just as getting things done, but also as a source of feedback that will continuously enrich the experience. This action–learning tension will obviously be richer in an international context than it can be at home. The experience gained previously will be challenged by the diverse information and the many places from which to learn; this will provide the opportunity for renewed learning all the time.

The world is a diverse and rich "classroom"; those companies that can learn from it faster have a competitive advantage. To support this learning mindset, the organization culture, the leadership style, the organization processes and the organization infrastructure provide important levers, as demonstrated by the attention successful companies give to these organization dimensions.

Managing and learning now look alike

The management literature and journalism generally focus on replicating successful strategies, processes, approaches, moves and methods when it comes to international growth. What did Jack Welch of General Electric (GE) do to energize a huge global organization? What did Microsoft do to retain its worldwide market domination? What did Nokia do to dominate the world mobile handset business? These are fascinating examples. But when it comes to doing it yourself, in your own context, you are essentially left to your own devices. The time seems to be gone when success was a great teacher.

The fact is that, in fast-changing environments, replication of past successful moves, even smart replication, is bound to be inadequate. Managing seems to have transformed itself from ensuring correct replication of proven methods to ensuring effective and rapid learning of new, work-in-progress approaches. To paraphrase a managerial cliché, doing two-thirds of the right things and learning from the outcome is better that doing one thing hundred per cent right and not knowing what to do next.

Seeing managing as a way of ensuring rapid and effective learning is the biggest mindset change required today. Successful companies have developed organizational capabilities that have allowed them to learn fast and effectively. *Formerly* successful companies are those that have stopped learning, often because they had focused too much on doing more of the same previously successful moves. *Continuously* successful companies are those that have been able to keep learning their way into new business models.

The learning imperative is, at the same time, a greater challenge and a greater opportunity for companies operating internationally. The challenge is generally well known. It is a fact that replication, in new geographical environments, of strategies that have been successful at home rarely works. This is not only because the markets and consumers are different. There is too much else that is different: managerial approaches, the way organizations function, the way people are motivated . . . The heart and soul of a company, what makes it tick, its DNA formula, are not easily transferable.

The learning opportunities are less well known and generally less appreciated. There is more to learn in a larger, more diverse "classroom". There are opportunities to develop new knowledge that other companies, focusing on making replication work, are missing. This new knowledge will, in turn, support further and faster international growth: a virtuous grow–learn–grow cycle.

DEFINING LEARNING IS LIKE DEFINING MANAGEMENT

Learning is developing and updating your models of the environment – or of a specific situation – to improve your effectiveness in, and your fitness for this environment.

When you learn, you use your past experience to interpret the feedback from the environment in relation to your own actions, and to draw from the feedback whatever you consider to be meaningful, appropriate consequences to sustain and improve your effectiveness or fitness.

The outcome of learning is fitness, an effective balance between feedback and behaviour. This is an unstable equilibrium that needs to be readjusted all the time. Fitness requires an effective coordination between feedback and behaviour.
Adapted from Doré and Mercier (1992).

How firms learn and how they are able to manage that learning on a global basis are thus critical elements in accelerating successful international growth. Effective exploitation of richer learning networks, more opportunities to experiment, the potential for new strategic directions, and a larger "classroom" in which to learn all give the firms which want to grow quickly internationally the edge over those who are less successful in managing knowledge on an international basis.

FAILURES OR LEARNING OPPORTUNITIES?

An IBM plant manager from the US was telling me of a situation in which he had been involved. Reviewing the ratios of plant performance across the world, someone in the corporate headquarters became alarmed that something was slipping sideways in several overseas manufacturing sites. Bizarrely, the ratios were saying that these plants were in havoc, although the machines still seemed to be delivering as if nothing was wrong. My friend was asked to go and find out what was going on; after all, there should not be two ways of making a computer, wherever it is in the world. But his enquiry showed that there indeed seemed to be many more than two ways. His question to me was this: is this situation the result of progressive deterioration that needs immediate and tough action? Given these plants' good output in spite of the ratios, wouldn't they have done much better if they had applied the same methods as the home plants? Or – and this is the important point – was there something to be learned that could be used elsewhere (perhaps even at home)?

The Swiss machine industry has traditionally – naturally – been obsessed with achieving the best possible quality. When Asian competition seemed to be making increasing inroads into many of its overseas markets; was this due to the impossibility of Swiss manufacturers matching Asian cost structures? Or was there something to be learned about real demand and real customer needs in these markets? Was there some knowledge that could be used preventively in other markets and something that the Swiss companies could actually learn and respond to as some eventually did?

Why do we need a larger classroom?
Building a knowledge advantage, globally

The learning agenda covers a lot more than learning how to do the same thing out there that we were already doing at home. There are several reasons for this. First, all markets do not evolve at the same pace; some are leading in some ways; others will follow soon after. Also, for historical and cultural reasons, some markets are more competitive than others, or are competitive in different ways. This enables learning about a wide range of different business models, which may have more potential for globalization than the home ones, because the home market may not be the best classroom. Finally, some activities in the business system may be more knowledge-intensive than others, providing more sustainable advantages globally – and these happen to be better developed in some other parts of the world.

In the same way as the Renaissance person travelled across Europe to learn philosophy, literature, architecture, sciences, astronomical navigation and business, so the modern corporation needs to learn globally:

- where the next product cycles can already be seen;
- where the incumbent business models will force thinking "out of the box";
- where new business-system activities are being shaped;
- where the strongest clusters of industry participants are found.

Learning about the next product cycle

Market demand characteristics evolve fast and travel across countries. If you look at the way the Japanese consumers have adopted and use NTT-DoCoMo's internet-compatible "i-mode" cell phones, you get an idea of what European consumers might eventually expect from 3-G (the European mobile-internet standard) services. The European promoters of WAP missed this learning opportunity, focusing on the technology only, and forgetting to learn about the consumers.

The competitive behaviour of large players is not deployed globally all at once. This means that observing something in the markets where it is first deployed allows others to pre-empt it in markets where it has not yet been deployed. For example, it is interesting that European retailers learned about mass retailing in the US and then developed very effective versions of this learning throughout Europe. US leaders like Wal-Mart now find it quite difficult to enter the European market.

Learning to think "out of the box" to differentiate from the incumbents

Entering markets where established leaders are already entrenched will force you to develop different business models to avoid or circumvent head-to-head competition. In many instances, this has allowed strategies that were more effective than those of the incumbents – who had, perhaps, lost their imagination.

In the early 90s, Nokia Networks had to develop internationally to sell its GSM network infrastructure beyond Finland in order to achieve the economies of scale necessary to survive in this business. Nokia was just a tiny, unknown entrant facing giants such as Ericsson, Alcatel, Siemens, Nortel, AT&T (which is now Lucent). There was no chance to confront successfully these old timers, who all had long-established relationships with the state-owned national telephone operators and whose share of market and share of mind dominated everywhere.

The only way to enter was to "learn together" with the "new operators" who were also striving to carve out a share of the newly deregulated national markets away from the old operators. In fact, it turned out that these new operators were quite happy to find in Nokia an alternative to the large equipment manufacturers who had entertained long, cosy relationships with the incumbent operators they had to fight. It also turned out that these new operators were the most entrepreneurial ones, often coming from businesses, like the media, where they had learned how to market services to consumers – Nokia Networks could benefit from this excellent knowledge faster than the other players who were focusing on the more traditional operators.

During the 90s, some non-European wine companies imagined that the way to enter the European market was to buy a French château. This was "inside the box" thinking! The few French châteaux with a global brand are unbelievably expensive. If you then buy a less well-known one, nobody knows it, especially 99.9% of the consumers who are not experts in the "good, less-known vineyards". Instead, as some New-World wine companies have found, developing reliable brands, offering a recognized name and image, producing a stable product year-in year-out, and, in short, delivering a rewarding consumer experience, has turned out to be a far more effective strategy. In addition, this strategy has had a global potential through, for example, global sourcing, multilocal packaging, global branding, umbrella branding, and so on, that the great French châteaux have not had, because their names are linked by law to a limited piece of land.

Learning to perform the business-system activities that will matter next

The business-system activities that contribute most to the customer's perceived value, and thus justify higher margins, also tend to be increasingly knowledge heavy. Outsourcing customer contact, for example to an agent or to a local partner, will deprive you from learning first-hand how to provide solutions to the local customer. This involves not only a product, but the associated services, the shopping experience, the complementary products and services, all that really creates customer value – and this is very knowledge intensive. A good example is the Danish toy company, LEGO, which started in the US in the early 60s using Samsonite as an agent. It quickly found that this prevented it from learning about the buying patterns and toy experience in one-third of the world market, and furthermore in a market that is generally ahead of Europe in its product life cycles. LEGO subsequently set up its own sales company in Connecticut in 1973.

The mobile phone handset sector provides another example of the importance of learning in advance what will matter. Manufacturing a handset will probably become like manufacturing a personal computer, i.e., it will not require a great deal of knowledge, since it has become a commodity activity and as such, is rewarded with minimal margins. Nokia's success is actually largely due to design and branding, rather than to unique technical performance. As mobile internet-access applications, mobile e-business, mobile entertainment and location-sensitive information develop, the "perceived value" created in the user interface, not only through design and branding, but through the whole usage experience, will take full precedence.

The corresponding activities will involve some combination of a friendly personal device – an extension of oneself, a "pet" object – and a preferred content supplier. As they allow systematic consumer profiling, these activities will be extremely knowledge heavy; however, they allow higher margins because of their perceived value. Everyone in this business is scrambling to be at this juncture point. For instance, Intel is moving into consumer devices, Microsoft is pushing its mobile operating system, applications and interface; AOL.com and other portals are building early-on a base of mobile users; there is mobile-Oracle, mobile-SAP, the successful i-mode of Japan's NTT-DoCoMo – the list goes on.

For the same reason, Nokia is involving itself in a wide range of ventures to test different combinations of devices and contents, alone or in alliances, to gain the knowledge that will be critical to justify margins in the mobile world. Having such ventures in every geographical market that matters, across the world, is obviously a requirement of this learning process. Perhaps with the temporary exception of Japan for consumer usage, there is not yet a lead market in this business.

The world wine business again provides a good example. Adopting an "out of the box" perspective, which activity in the wine value chain contributes most to the consumer's perceived value? For the vast majority of consumers, in all markets, it is the brand name. Many consumers know Château Margaux, but most of them do not know where the vineyard is, what the grapes are, what the soil is like or which steps from grape juice to wine really matter. If the brand name is recognized to signify a pleasant and reliable experience, the rest is really like assembling computers.

So, the key issue in the strategy of a wine company seeking to go international should be where can it best learn and practise the activities that support wine branding, not where the best soil exposure is. This thinking excludes entry points like France and Italy where brand names are attached by law to a tiny piece of land. In fact, one of the most objective places to learn about wine was the UK, as BRL-Hardy, the Australian wine company, learned (see the BRL-Hardy case study in Chapter 10).

Learning with the strongest clusters of industry participants

The activities that create most customer value in a business system could well be more developed in other markets. The fact that there is (a) little emotion attached to the local production of wine and thus the consumer is more objective in attaching value to taste; (b) the presence of a growing market of younger, affluent consumers seeking a lifestyle beverage somewhat more up-market than beer, and (c) the existence of a very powerful and sophisticated wine distribution system, make the UK an excellent place to develop wine branding know-how.

In the mobile handset business, Nokia, at an early stage, targeted as priority entry point the markets where it could learn most: the UK because, being a world leader in telecom deregulation, it had the most advanced telecom-service knowledge base and the US because this was where brand recognition would then make the biggest difference globally.

Most industry breakpoints have been triggered by outsiders to the industry sector where they occurred. Learning in other markets gives this outsider freshness and allows organizations to learn and develop right from the start a different perspective and a different mindset. This allows it to be more effective when competing globally, than a strategy extrapolated from the home base. Internationalization extrapolated from a home base strategy may have limitations inherent to that home base, which will tend to be replicated when moving internationally. An early exposure to a very different environment will correct these limitations, some of which can be in terms of hard resources (including financing) and some of which can be in terms of mindset and culture, requiring more advanced learning capabilities.

The French founder of the software company, Business Objects, which focuses on providing e-business-intelligence solutions for accessing, analysing and sharing corporate data, chose to be US-based right from the start. Expanding internationally from a French base would have had several disadvantages. For example, a French software company would find it harder to gain global credibility than a US one. Also, European corporations do not yet perceive real customer value in e-business-intelligence solutions. US corporations, on the other hand, with their higher e-business awareness, are the ideal customers to learn with when "making" this new market. Moving from outside-in was thus a better proposition than starting from Europe out. Concomitantly, the availability in the US of a venture capital sector that could see the value proposition certainly made the choice even clearer.

The global classroom is thus a very rich one. It is not a challenge to be overcome in order to expand internationally. It is a compelling opportunity for any company seeking to learn the new competitive advantages that are indispensable for its future.

Allowing global learning to take place: the foundations of fitness

As discussed earlier, learning is triggered by applying past experience to a new environment. This encounter will trigger feedback that will confirm or adapt the experience, and thus generate adaptive behaviour to maintain or enhance the fitness with the environment. The behaviour–feedback tension, which could also be described as the action–learning tension, is the foundation of *fitness*. Registering the feedback and debriefing it, so as to be able to improve one's response to it through improved experience, make action–learning possible. Without these four building blocks – *action, feedback, debriefing* and *experience building* – there is no sustained learning (Figure 8.1).

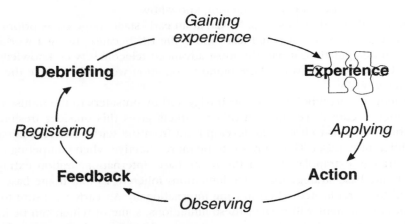

Figure 8.1: *Learning leads to new behaviour*

This may seem obvious, but, in fact, local learning is often discouraged because of the fear of not being able to control centrally the new adaptive behaviours that it will necessarily trigger locally, or because of an over-confidence in the local effectiveness of centrally enforced past successful behaviours. The managerial implications are important. The organization culture, the leadership style, the organization processes and the organization infrastructure will control the selection of "relevant" feedback and its comparison to previous experience. They will, in turn, control which initiatives are triggered by this feedback to enhance fitness to compete locally and/or to compete globally.

The organization culture, the leadership style, the organization processes and the organization infrastructure thus control which feedback gets integrated into the working business model, i.e., the game plan that embeds and stretches previous experience to decide its relevance, and to conceptualize the next action steps. These organization characteristics thus determine the flexibility, or lack thereof, of the business model – in a way, its learning potential. An explicit strategic intent, clearly communicated to the outpost teams, who are given clear reasons for being there, and a more or less extensive learning agenda, will influence feedback integration, the adaptive actions and the resulting fitness – global and local. A well-documented repertoire of processes, a widely available documentation of previous corporate experiences and best practices, will also influence the extent to which the business model can be enriched through successive rollouts, i.e., which balance will be struck, over time, between past successful models and new adaptive behaviours (Figure 8.2).

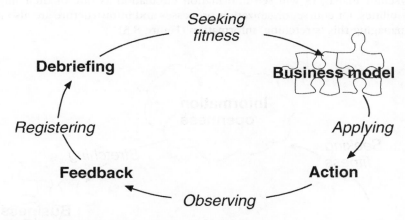

Figure 8.2: *Learning leads to new business models*

When the feedback becomes predictable, the unstable equilibrium between feedback and action becomes stable. The business model stabilizes and action becomes repetitive. Learning ceases. In particular, this is likely to happen when local fitness is more or less achieved. The results are achieved, the figures look good. But the learning machine is idle.

Sources of new information

New information can be used to maintain the equilibrium in an unstable state. First, new information can be generated by local intelligence, which is not directly generated by past actions and which is not feedback as such. The level of local entrepreneurship, the local curiosity and imagination, and the local ability to look for hidden information all play an important role in generating this disruptive information. These capabilities can also be managed through the various organization systems we have mentioned. The organization culture and the leadership style can play an particularly important role here.

New information can also be externally generated, injected into the local situation by the rest of the organization, senior management and corporate offices. To generate learning, this new information should not be top-down orders. Rather, it should consist of questions, pieces of information and stories from outside that generate more questions on the working business model.

The injection of new information is obviously manageable. It is a key management instrument – although often used without the appropriate learning agenda – in any organization, particularly in a global organization where distances can otherwise make information channels less effective. Organization systems will play a role in shaping this "disruptive", or at least "stretching" information. The organization culture will play a role, supporting transparency, informal information channels and non-hierarchical information channels, for example. The leadership style will also be important; leaders/senior managers will see information circulation as one of their important responsibilities. Of course, organization processes and infrastructure are also important in managing this "stretching" information (Figure 8.3).

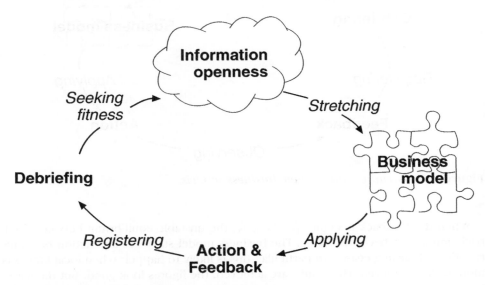

Figure 8.3: *Maintaining the fitness/learning tension*

Balancing between global and local fitness

In the context of a global organization, another dimension of the learning system is important as well. Since learning manifests itself as fitness, the balance struck between local fitness and global fitness is important. Global fitness is, of course, the ultimate purpose of the whole learning exercise: not only to introduce successfully the home business model locally, but, more importantly, to develop and deploy a business model that is globally fit and robust – a business model that leverages and mobilizes all the learning opportunities discussed above.

At the same time, if there is no local fitness, there is no global success. And nowhere else in the organization other than locally, can local fitness be enhanced – because local learning cannot take place anywhere else.

Yet, there are instances when one can be obtained without the other, at least in the short term. The challenge is ensuring that local learning, where the global-learning building blocks necessarily develop, also nurtures global learning. This challenge is to maintain a tension between global and local fitness in such a way that this happens.

As already discussed previously, the same four organization systems that shape the effectiveness of the learning tension, will also influence which balance is struck between global fitness and local fitness, or how local learning meshes with the evolving global business model:

- An organization culture that emphasizes a global vision and supports global success.
- A leadership style that circulates stretching information regarding contributions to the corporate global intent.
- Organization processes that emphasize global careers and circulate cross-organization benchmark information.
- An organization infrastructure that can provide the corporate-wide communication systems, the cross-organization accountability and the corporate-wide performance measures that keep the local mindset globally aware and maintain the local–global tension.

CASE STUDY: MAINTAINING THE GLOBAL–LOCAL TENSION AT ABB

Over the years, ABB is certainly a company where top management have paid a lot of attention to maintaining the adequate balance between global and local fitness. All CEOs, Percy Barnevik, Göran Lindahl and Jörgen Centerman have had it at the top of their minds. Percy Barnevik was famous for the set of slides he carried with him all the time to communicate his expectations on this matter. Göran Lindahl, who is still a member of ABB's board, emphasized in one of his last presentations as CEO how "ABB's global resources, local market know-how and technology, provide [the company] with a unique platform for building new value." Jörgen Centerman announced, in early 2001, a reorganization around four customer-centred business units: utilities; process industries; manufacturing and consumer industries; and oil, gas and petrochemicals, as the new centres of gravity for local fitness. Amongst other changes, a new corporate unit, Corporate Processes, was set up to ensure global fitness, because "highly flexible mass customization will require common business and management processes worldwide".

At a more micro level, ABB has managed the tension between local and global fitness, by making its local managers also accountable for global functions, a practice since emulated by many other global companies. ABB has also made itself famous for its fully transparent information process, ABACUS, to publicize the impact of local performance on global performance.

Applying the learning model

We now consider how this learning model can be applied and how it can help firms implement the necessary supporting organization systems, throughout the different stages of international growth, to accelerate international growth through smarter learning. These organization systems have already been discussed briefly in relation to the building blocks of learning and are outlined in more detail below and in Figure 8.4.

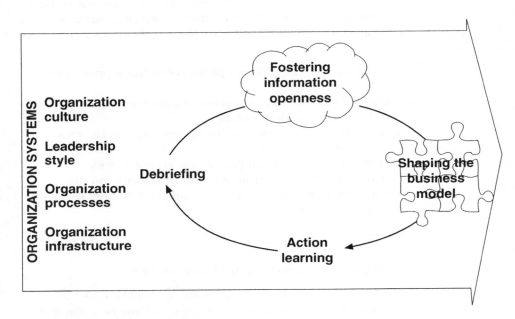

Figure 8.4: *How organization systems support learning and fitness*

The *organization culture* covers the generally accepted set of behaviour norms and guidelines that are often unconscious. The organization culture can be shaped and managed to trigger the desired behaviours. Some companies have managed to transform their culture quite fast, even internationally; IBM would be a good example of how a new global culture was introduced by an international virtual team of early internet zealots who shared the vision of developing web services. In an international context, where national cultures may challenge the organization culture, the latter appears to be generally surprisingly robust. Some organization cultures can be very attractive to the younger generations in more traditional national cultures, as Nokia, Oracle, or Cisco found as they were expanding internationally. These companies do pay a lot of attention to the way their organization cultures are deployed internationally.

The *leadership style* refers essentially to the role models established by senior management. The corresponding leadership behaviours communicate expectations, priorities and areas of accountability. Leadership styles can also be managed through a conscious effort of senior management and the awareness of the behaviours they explicitly or implicitly promote.

The French building materials company, Lafarge, is giving a lot of attention to the way its desired leadership style is internationally deployed. Traditionally, the company had promoted what was referred to as "participative management". In the late 60s, after a decade of very rapid international expansion, it found that the word "participative" could have very different interpretations in different cultures, from consensus based for some, to consultative, or hands-off, or even patronizing and pill-sweetening for others.

So a small international team was given the mission to propose a set of desirable leadership behaviours that would illustrate what was then called the "Lafarge way". After discussion and endorsement by senior management, these expectations were communicated personally by the CEO to all unit managers, worldwide, in the group. They were further reinforced regularly, in particular through the group's management development initiatives.

Organization processes consist of the formal policies regarding key areas such as objective setting and performance measurement, performance rewards, career management and decision processes. They are specifically designed to influence behaviour, although often in a mechanistic way, without taking into account the learning they can trigger indirectly in the longer term. In an international context, some processes may take a meaning that is quite different from the one it has in the home country. Expatriate policies designed to make foreign assignments more attractive, for example, may have undesirable local learning effects.

The *organization infrastructure*, finally, is both formal and informal. To a large extent, it supports and structures communication in the organization. The organization structure, the information systems (databases, access to databases, e-mail, etc.) and the physical infrastructure (layout of buildings, meeting areas, cafeterias, etc.) are known to play an important role in how people communicate. But more importantly, it is elements such as informal networks, the channels through which people really communicate, the contacts they have throughout the organization and the impromptu communication that have been found to have significantly more impact on learning and behaviour. Multicultural organizations offer many opportunities for informal communication networks, based on language, nationality, regional affinities, and so on. Because of geographical distance, they also tend to be a critical complement to the formal infrastructure.

SUMMARY

How firms learn and how they are able to manage that learning on a global basis are critical elements in accelerating successful international growth. Effective exploitation of richer learning networks, more opportunities to experiment, the potential for new strategic directions, and a larger "classroom" in which to learn all give the firm, which wants to grow internationally quickly, the edge over those who are less successful in managing knowledge on an international basis.

The learning agenda covers a lot more than learning how to do the same thing globally that a firm is already doing at home. There are several reasons for this. First, all markets do not evolve at the same pace; some are leading in some ways; others will follow soon after. Also, for historical and cultural reasons, some markets are more competitive than others, or are competitive in different ways. This enables learning about a wide range of different business models that may have more potential for globalization than the home ones, because the home market may not be the best classroom. Finally, some activities in the business system may be more knowledge intensive than others, providing more sustainable advantages globally.

However, several organization systems will control the selection of "relevant" feedback and its comparison to previous experience. They also will control which initiatives are triggered by this feedback to enhance fitness to compete locally and/or to compete globally. The goal should be to ensure that a tension is maintained between global and local fitness in such a way that the evolving global business model is continuously enriched through local learning, through:

- An organization culture that emphasizes a global vision.
- A leadership style that circulates stretching information.
- Organization processes that emphasize a global mindset.
- An organization infrastructure that can provide corporate-wide communication systems.

LEARNING POINTS

- When it comes to international expansion, do not focus only on the replication of strategies, processes and approaches that have worked successfully in the past because there is no guarantee they will work in new markets. In fact, operating in this way only could positively hamper the acceleration of international growth.
- Today management should encourage the collection, dissemination and exploitation of effective and rapid learning to serve as the basis of new and evolving business models.
- Trigger learning by applying past experience to a new environment. Firms which have access to richer learning networks, more opportunities to experiment, the potential for new strategic directions and a larger

"classroom" in which to learn will increasingly have the edge in international expansion.

- Be open to the new learning which new markets can offer, whether in terms of where they are in their evolutionary stage, their competitive environment or the knowledge-intensive developments.
- Be prepared to generate new learning by encouraging feedback which shows what works and what does not, and to use that new learning to generate adaptive behaviour to maintain or enhance fitness with the environment. This action–learning tension is the foundation of such fitness.
- Support this through the appropriate organization culture, the leadership style, the organization processes and the organization infrastructure. Injecting new information without the appropriate learning agenda will do little to improve the business model.
- Always bear in mind that, in the context of a global organization, the balance struck between local and global fitness is pivotal. The business model has to be not only globally fit and robust, but it must also exploit local learning, which in turn is the basis of global learning.

Reference

Doré, F.Y. and Mercier, P. (1992) *Les Fondements de l'Apprentissage et de la Cognition - The Foundations of Learning and Cognition*, Gäetan Morin Publisher, Canada.

CHAPTER 9

Deploying the Domestic Business Model Internationally: The Inside-out Approach

Companies entering new markets should be asking themselves this key question: how are we going to be better off after the move? Addressing this issue is instrumental in making sure that a learning agenda is embedded in the business model. **Xavier Gilbert** describes how this "inside-out" approach helps accelerate the internationalization process.

Overview

Many companies start their international expansion by deploying their domestic business model internationally. This is probably a normal first step for many of them, although this is by no means the only approach. However, this approach not only provides substantial and useful learning which helps accelerate international expansion as it unfolds, but it also helps to accelerate the subsequent steps in the internationalization process.

Stimulating local learning is critical for the business model to be optimized locally. For this learning to be effective, however, several prerequisites must be satisfied:

- a well-understood reason for going international;
- a well-documented and well-understood domestic business model;
- and a learning agenda that becomes the entry business model – the purpose is to learn, not to apply blindly past successful moves.

Deploying a business model in a new geographical context is learning in action. This local action learning must be supported by the company's culture, leadership style, processes and infrastructure. Underpinning these are four ingredients that activate and exploit the learning tension: fostering information openness, shaping the business model, action–learning and debriefing.

It is important to note – and accept – that this learning will not leave the company the same. As it gets redeployed across the company, the original domestic business model will necessarily be stretched and evolve.

Why go international?

Going international is often seen as extrapolating abroad what was already done successfully at home. Hence, it is easily taken for granted, and seen as just more of the same: selling across the border is just selling a little further away. Questioning why expanding internationally is being done at all and formulating the expected new competitive advantages from this move, rather than just more of the same advantages, are, in fact, rarely done. The key question, which is in fact an entire learning agenda, is *"How are we going to be better off after the move?"*

This is exemplified by a consumer goods company that had decided to compare its cost structure with that of a strong local competitor in one of the markets where it was present. The consumer goods company was already fairly international, while the competitor was essentially local. To its great disappointment, the consumer goods company discovered that its margins were lower than those of the local competitor. This sobering observation was shrugged off by some members of management who suggested that this was due to the fact that their company "had to pay for the extra cost of being international", as if being international was essentially the same as being domestic, except it was somewhat more expensive – an "extrapolation" that ignored the transformation that is likely to happen to a business model when it is deployed internationally.

Addressing the question "How are we going to be better off?" is critical in preparing the business model for the internationalization move. What do we need to learn for this improvement in our competitive position to happen? What needs to be adapted or are we embarking on a new direction all together? The answers to these questions need to be on everyone's mind. *A business model taken internationally is a learning agenda to be shared by all involved.*

Starting from what we know

Applying successful past experience is the first step in any learning process. As we discussed in Chapter 8, learning builds on past experience by challenging it in new contexts. For this to happen, however, the past experience must be sufficiently explicit, formalized and made available. As obvious as this may sound, in these first steps of international growth, this is not always the case for a number of reasons.

The past experience is not always there

For a number of different reasons, the past experience may not be available, or thought not to be available, or forgotten, or no longer available.

The experience in deploying the past competitive advantages may simply not be there because the company has been essentially active domestically and its only points of reference are related to its domestic strategies. In fact, in many instances, it simply did not realize that its experience in competing at home with international firms was valuable. It did not try to explore what were the advantages of these international players that it was missing itself by being only active domestically. A very successful small European materials research firm built a great reputation in helping medium-sized domestic firms develop new products. But all the best clients kept walking away at some point; they were expanding internationally and needed more global sources of know-how. The small materials firm had not realized that it was already competing internationally.

There are also situations where the outpost team forgets or is not aware of some of the company's knowledge that could, at least, serve as a starting point. When a European company in basic materials took over some denationalized companies in eastern Europe, the challenges that the teams found were so overwhelming that some of the corporate best practices were instantly forgotten. They were confronted with problems such as far too many workers, very low attention to quality and the total absence of a commercial orientation. They felt that they had to focus their immediate attention on these challenges.

In their desperation to prove that they could perform, they actually forgot some open-market basics that routinely existed in all the domestic plants, such as elementary measurement systems, normal finance and control tools, essential reporting mechanisms, common manufacturing yardsticks and basic training in resolving routine production hiccups. In one instance, an overheating piece of equipment, which would have been routinely dealt with in a domestic plant, resulted in a major crisis involving the headquarters' manufacturing director. The company rapidly established a checklist of basic proven processes to be implemented in any new acquisition, before anything else.

Past experience is hard to get

In that example, the attention of the frontline team was distracted from first applying the proven company basics due to the urgency of some other tasks. There are also instances when the available experience is not applied because nobody asks or wants to ask. Personal, informal networks are known to be the most effective tools for accessing knowledge and experience. They generally work better than the formal communication networks. In international contexts, where cultural differences, languages or simply distances can play an important role in communication, along with some organization processes like fast movements of people, these informal personal networks can easily lose their effectiveness. For cultural reasons, it may not be the right thing to do to ask for help. Poor language mastery may make it difficult. Getting hold of the people who have done it before may be quite difficult because they have moved on to some other job and country.

Also for cultural reasons, reinventing the wheel may be perceived as preferable to using proven approaches. Along this line of thought, some expatriates, or some local people alike, may overemphasize the "local differences" to protect themselves from central attempts to impose existing or common approaches. In 1999–2000, Oracle set out to deploy internally on a global basis its suite of e-business tools to prove that these tools could save one billion dollars. It found out that many of the arguments used previously, such as that human resources management was "so different and unique here", in fact had no substantial foundation. There was, in fact, nothing that could not be dealt with absolutely by the global e-human resource set of tools.

Past experience has not been seen to work or is not understood

Another situation when past experience easily gets forgotten is when some previous international moves were not successful. In such cases, it also very likely that those associated with them are not around any more. A large European company had had two failed attempts at entering the US market. But when it felt ready to try for a third time, those involved in gathering the international experience in the first two attempts had long been "fired" – the international knowledge had gone. In fact, it was later found that the reasons for the failures had been in the corporate office rather than with the people on the spot.

But even if previous moves were successful – perhaps especially if they were successful – the reasons for success have often not been analysed to consolidate the learning. There are rare cases when an international move was successful precisely for the reasons that the company was counting on. There are also cases when this is due to unexpected reasons: the old story comes to mind of the French sugar company penetrating successfully a not very developed overseas market because its sugar wrapping paper had been found to be effective in dyeing local fabrics when boiled with them.

Finally, there are also cases when international success can be best attributed to external factors. For example, the international presence of Microsoft is rather due to the efforts of the personal computer industry than to the global mindset of the company. It was only in the late 90s when it realized that the users of Microsoft Office could be using more than one language; still today, its centimetre measures strangely appear with odd decimals simply because they have been converted from inches. Not understanding the reasons for success, the company is unlikely to be able to repeat them.

The infrastructure is unable to document and communicate international experience

The reasons above are essentially "mindset" reasons why the available international experience is not tapped. There are also infrastructure reasons. Databases of past successful and unsuccessful experiences do not exist. Processes to be followed, covering the basics required in the course of any new entry, have not been established. Who has done what, who has had experience in a particular country, who has been involved in a particular international move has not been documented, for example through an internal "yellow pages". The information and communication infrastructure is simply not in place.

Developing five capabilities to help exploit experience

The four categories of organization systems that were discussed in Chapter 8 as supporting learning also play an important role in ensuring that the available experience can be easily tapped. In Table 9.1, we consider five capabilities that the organization systems must support for this experience to be available and tapped. The ability to *admit ignorance* is, of course, the starting point; as we have seen, it is not obvious in a multicultural context. The *initiative in searching information* is also important; again, in an international set-up, many obstacles can inhibit it and it needs to be supported. The *variety of information* sought and available also offers a richer and more adaptable experience that can be tapped. This is a capability that is naturally facilitated in a diverse international context. The *receptivity and absence of filters* address the "not invented here" syndrome, that is so frequent in preventing the redeployment of available experience. In international organizations, cultural barriers or the need to prove the local capabilities can easily make this worse. Finally, *willingness to share information* is also critical.

Table 9.1: *Ensuring that organization systems support the tapping of existing experience*

Tapping existing experience	Organization culture	Leadership style	Organization processes	Organization infrastructure
Admission of ignorance	It is OK to ask; no loss of face	Senior management asks naïve questions to local people	Career paths support cross-learning	Formal documentation and directories exist
Initiative in searching information	Direct communication across borders is possible; informal networks exist	Personal interest in local cultures and language capabilities	Available experience is easy to search	"Push" information is also distributed
Variety of information sought	Interest for what happens globally in the company is promoted	Frequent visits	Documentation is extensive, covering different aspects	Experience-rich intranet
Receptivity, absence of filters	New ideas are well accepted; no national pecking order	Senior management solicit local feedback on central issues	Experience is available to all; no "insider" treatment for some	Flat organization
Willingness to share information	Volunteering information across borders is frequent	Senior management routinely convey information across borders	Performance assessment looks at helping other countries	Information technology is deployed seamlessly

Applying the domestic business model – the inside-out approach

In this initial approach to internationalization, the company is stretching its domestic business model by implementing it in a new geographical context, or taking its "inside" business model, outside. This is already a learning agenda in itself, although companies are not always aware of this.

A road-map or a game plan?

The question "How internationally robust are the alleged advantages of the inside-out approach?" should be at the top of the learning agenda. Typically, however, this will not have been asked, nor will the organizational mindset be ready to test it first in an appropriate learning mode. In particular, this robustness will not have been questioned in a *dynamic* way, through a game plan simulating possible feedback responses arising from the context. The deployment of the expected advantages is rather seen as a linear road-map, with its risks, of course, and its binary outcome: it works – it does not. The "What if?" questions of a game plan have not been addressed, such as "Where are we exposed? What do we do if . . . ?"

But without this learning agenda, the resulting feedback will have little meaning and the next steps will probably not address it either. It is just random feedback, bad news of setback and failure, naturally leading to denial and ex-post rationalizations: the local markets are lagging behind and are not ready for our products, our local team is not good enough and they should try harder, the rest of the world is wrong and we are right. It then becomes difficult to imagine what the next steps could be.

One of these frequent road-maps, for example, is to invoke economies of scale as a justification for international expansion. But, internationally, these expected economies of scale will be challenged in new, often unexpected ways that were never experienced at home. Local volumes will be lower, resulting in higher transport and storage costs; the infrastructure support per unit will be more expensive; inventories will be higher. A dynamic game plan would have identified a number of working hypotheses to be confirmed for the expected economies of scale to materialize. If these working hypotheses have not been identified, the reasons for the eventual lack of results will be slow to identify, and the learning which encourages the development of new strategic moves will be slow to take place.

The replication of past successful business models is, understandably, a very frequent way to proceed into a new environment. You do not want to be reinventing the wheel all the time and, indeed, many companies have established fairly explicit strategic templates, based on past experience, to enter new territories. In surveys of how companies address the new-entry challenge of taking their business model internationally, we found that about half of them do have templates that the outpost teams are expected to apply. The other half prefer to remain flexible and adapt elements of their domestic business model on demand, in the new environment.

The need for a learning agenda

In both cases, however, these experience-based approaches require an explicit learning agenda of working hypotheses to be verified for the proposed international strategy to be effective. The required entry mindset must be a learning mindset – a mindset of stretching the business model, and soliciting feedback to adjust the behaviour, rather than an application or replication mindset.

Some of the key questions that need to be addressed in this learning agenda are given below.

- *Which specific competencies and know-how will be applied?*
- *How will they be transferred locally, to the market we are entering?*
- *How robust can we expect each of them to be?*
- *How will we test this robustness? How can we structure these tests (test variables, reference variables, place)?*
- *What local feedback can we expect?*
- *Which specific moves should we consider to "localize" them, to optimize them or to integrate them in the market we are entering?*

Allowing local learning to take place is critical for the business model to be optimized locally. Testing the robustness of its different building blocks can only be done locally; it requires local experimentation and local feedback. Enough room has to be left for this to be done. Expatriates who are given the mission to go and implement the domestic way know about the resulting tensions within the corporate offices. While they are supposed to be the experts in the corporate way, they will often know very little about the local context. The local expertise of the locally recruited managers, because they are generally new to the corporation, will not always be given the necessary credibility. Their joint local learning, however, is critical and will be supported by organization systems that leave the necessary space for the learning to take place and establish clearly that local fitness matters.

This may seem obvious, but many companies seeking to expand internationally do not establish clearly *where* it matters to survive, locally or in the corporate offices. For example, short expatriate assignments encourage survival within the politics in the home office rather than on the local front. Similarly, locally recruited personnel who have no hope of career advancement globally, because those postings are reserved for home-country nationals, will not feel that local survival and fitness makes a difference for their future. Putting in place the organization systems that make it clear that local fitness matters is thus critical to generate the local learning that will sustain international growth.

CASE STUDY: HOW BOOTS EXPANDED IN SOUTH-EAST ASIA WITH
A LEARNING AGENDA

The Boots Company is one of the best-known retail brands in the UK; its chain of Boots the Chemist stores are market leaders. In the late 1990s it decided to investigate the potential for leveraging the brand into Japan because the company felt it should have a presence there as it is the second largest health and beauty market in the world. Also, it was getting difficult to find good locations for new stores in the UK and it was time to transport the successful formula into new territories.

The successful formula it employed in the UK relied mainly on one of the best-known brands in the country, covering a broad but focused range of products aimed at its target female audience. It also had developed leading-edge sourcing and logistics capabilities.

Research in Japan, however, found that while the brand was not really known there, what Boots could exploit was its "globalizable" sourcing and logistics capabilities to develop a retail concept based on women's personal care with European products – a concept with global potential. In July 1998 a joint venture agreement was signed with Mitsubishi Corporation to open stores in Japan. By 2000 there were several stores in Tokyo and other high-profile city centre locations, as well as one within a major department store in Yokohama. So the company rebuilt its business model using core elements, reconfiguring them for the local market and basing them on its logistical capabilities. In other words, the company listened and learned from a new environment.

The company followed a similar route in Thailand, where it used pilot stores to test the market in 1997 to learn more about the customers. By October 2000 there were almost 70 stores, primarily in Bangkok but also in tourist locations and other cities. It is also opening stores in Taiwan.

Managing the build-up of local–global tensions

Locally, embedding a robust learning agenda will generate adaptive behaviours that will, in turn, trigger more focused feedback. It will progressively shape into a more local version of the original entry learning agenda. As a result, the locally perceived reality will progressively drift away from the centrally perceived local reality – and from centrally perceived business-model priorities and imperatives. After all, the person on land cannot see in the sea what the sailor can. There is then the danger that, if not managed carefully, this local–global tension may cause the pendulum to swing back in favour of central fitness and block local learning.

Again, when local outposts are also seen as learning outposts in fast-changing markets rampaged by hyperactive competition, the tension can be uncomfortable. The local learning must not be blocked, however. If there is no local learning, there will indeed be no central–local tension of that nature. But there will also be no chance either to sustain local fitness.

In fact, when local curiosity and imagination are allowed to operate actively, what you get is local entrepreneurship. Previously untapped features in the local context and untested behaviours will be brought into the picture and new, unverified business models imagined. Tired with the known and tested causalities, the local entrepreneur will try some new ones that will ultimately stretch the learning further away from the relative comfort zone of the initial working business model. Many organizations will find that drifting away from the orthodox business model is threatening and, to the extent that some of the benefits of a global business model are jeopardized, it can be a threat. On the other hand, leaving enough room locally for this entrepreneurial experimenting is essential if learning "out of the box", learning beyond what is already half-known, even disruptive learning, is considered valuable. In businesses where contexts evolve very rapidly, where competition is hyperactive, this form of renewal is indeed critical.

CASE STUDY: BRL-HARDY: ALLOWING THE EUROPEAN SUBSIDIARY TO LEARN GLOBAL BRANDING

BRL-Hardy, the Australian wine company, was keen to expand its international exposure. It had made a few acquisitions of French and Italian vineyards and exported domestic wines through its European subsidiary based in the UK.

The newly recruited European manager, Christopher Carson, had in fact many years of experience in wine marketing in the UK, a lead market with respect to wine retail sophistication. Not only did he quickly earn his stirrups by growing the BRL-Hardy market share in Europe, but he also started diversifying his sourcing through alliances in Italy and Chile, to be marketed through European-wide brands.

At the same time, the (also) newly-appointed corporate marketing and export manager, Stephen Davies, was keen to develop corporate brands based on the company's Australian wines. The tension quickly mounted between the two men. Davies resented the European efforts to bypass his corporate projects. Carson was dead set against most of these projects because he did not believe that they would meet the needs of his markets; he found their positioning was too idiosyncratically Australian; the labels were uninspiring, the prices were not right.

Yet, the CEO, Steve Millar, seemed to believe that the learning undertaken by Carson in Europe could have global value. In spite of his unambiguous support for Davies's projects, he allowed Carson to go ahead with his Italian and Chilean ventures. He even compromised his "orthodox" organization design by having Carson report directly to him, instead of reporting to Davies as would have been the case in most organizations. His dilemma was to maintain the global vision, while at the same time allowing local learning.

Adapted from Bartlett (2000).

Organization systems to support local learning

Deploying a business model in a new geographical context is thus action learning. Local action learning must be supported by the organization systems. Tables 9.2–9.5 provide examples of how specific dimensions of local learning can be supported by the organization systems: the *organization culture*, the *leadership style*, the *organization processes* and the *organization infrastructure*. Within each of these dimensions, as suggested in Chapter 8, organization learning relies on four steps that activate and exploit the learning tension: *fostering information openness*, *shaping the business model*, *action–learning* and *debriefing*.

Fostering information openness locally

Fostering information openness into the learning process is meant to stretch the learning by keeping the local learning tensions in a state of unstable equilibrium. It can be promoted through the following capabilities:

- The local team should have the *willingness to admit ignorance* on some matters and open the door to new information. In a multicultural context, where regional pecking orders are frequent, this can be particularly threatening.
- The local team should have the *curiosity* to perform further the search for new information. Sometimes, just as the fish does not know that it is in water, the local team does not see the obvious.
- The local team should have the *open-mindedness* to look for diverse information sources. Local myopia can easily develop as a result of everyone thinking alike.
- The local team should have the *receptiveness* to allow even the most disruptive information not to be filtered out and, instead, to be given due attention. Locally, it may be tempting to push annoying information under the rug quietly.
- The local team should provide *transparency* to allow a free flow of information throughout the organization. Defensive local teams often prefer to keep the local situation somewhat opaque from the outside. More traditional hierarchical systems may also do the same internally.

Examples of how these local capabilities can be supported and enhanced by the organizational systems – culture, leadership style, processes and infrastructure – are provided in Table 9.2.

Shaping the local business models

The local ability to shape a business model at the same time encapsulates the learning and serves as the reference to derive feedback for future action. It sets the learning agenda. This critical phase in the learning process can be promoted locally through the following capabilities:

- The local team should be able to *grasp the different local dimensions* of business issues. This implies that it has these dimensions – business functions – locally.
- The local team should be able to *imagine possible interactions* between these dimensions, through working hypotheses and game plans. There can be a tendency not to imagine different interactions, "because it is the way it has always been done here; this is the way to work with local retail here".

Table 9.2: *Which organization systems will support local information openness*

Information openness	Organization culture	Leadership style	Organization processes	Organization infrastructure
Local willingness to admit ignorance	It is OK not to know	Senior management admits not to know about local environments	Recruitment of expatriates emphasizes learning capabilities	Local teams are supposed to know better
Local curiosity	It is OK to question beliefs and assumptions	Senior management asks many questions about local environments	Recruitment emphasizes international exposure and languages	Local intelligence is in place
Local open-mindedness	Familiarity with local environments is a must	Frequent local physical presence of senior management	Recruitment emphasizes the variety of experience in local teams	Corporate support for local intelligence
Local receptiveness	Listening to local feedback is part of the corporate culture	No sacred cows attitude; no axe to grind	Recruitment emphasizes open-mindedness	No location-related pecking order
Local transparency	No cultural or language preconceptions	Senior management goes straight to those who know locally	Performance assessment includes support to local teams	Seamless information channels

- The local team should be able to *assemble and formulate* a local business model. This requires conceptualization capabilities that may have been inhibited through previous experience. A local team that has evolved from a sales outpost will have difficulty coming up with a business model that is in fact *not* a sales plan.
- The local team should be able to *adapt* its working business model, taking disruptions into account. Local myopia can mean that the local team, seeing itself as immune from changes that have happened elsewhere, is taken by surprise.
- The local team should be able to *communicate* the local business model and the corresponding priorities. This is particularly critical in more traditional organizational cultures that separate the thinkers from the doers, which says that the doers do not really need to know.

Examples of how these local capabilities can be supported and enhanced by the organizational systems are provided in Table 9.3.

Supporting local action–learning

For the action–learning tension to be operational locally, the local team essentially needs to perceive itself as the master of its own destiny, with nobody else to blame or praise. Then the learning tension is compelling. Several capabilities will promote this local sense of accountability:

- The local team should *be in charge*, rather than merely execute. Without local empowerment, central guidelines will have the precedence over local feedback and there will be no local learning.
- The local team should be in a position to *take initiatives* and establish its local agenda. Without its own agenda, whatever feedback occurs, it will not be its problem.
- The local team should be expected to *pursue local fitness* by localizing the business model according to the circumstances. In some instances, the centre keeps such a close eye on the local team that fitness with the centre becomes more important than local fitness.
- The local team should have the readiness, ability and know-how to *experiment locally*. This should not be perceived locally as being particularly risky. On the contrary, doing nothing should be perceived as very risky.
- The local team should maintain a work-in-process, *ongoing learning agenda* to sustain the local fitness. The learning tensions must be kept in an unstable state of equilibrium. This can be done by injecting disruptive information from the outside, and even better by promoting local entrepreneurial attitudes.

Examples of how these local capabilities can be supported and enhanced by the organizational systems are provided in Table 9.4.

Table 9.3: *Which organization systems will support the shaping of the local business models*

Shaping local business models	Organization culture	Leadership style	Organization processes	Organization infrastructure
Grasping the different local dimensions	Local units are viewed as running a business	Hands-off approach, no micro-management	Local units have the local competencies covering different business dimensions	Local units master the key dimensions of their business
Developing hypotheses on how they interact locally	Discussions on "what would we do if" are frequent	Senior management routinely raise "what if" questions	Performance assessment looks at local anticipation capabilities	Methodologies are available locally to set up experiments
Putting them together in a local business model	Trade-offs are not escalated	Senior management refrains from being a referee	Local management has frontline experience	Information is available locally to make the key decisions
Adapting the business model to respond to local changes	It is OK to challenge, to question, to propose better alternatives	Senior management provide stretch and challenge	Plans are there to be revised	Local teams are expected to come up with alternative plans when needed
Communicating the local business model	Local vision, intent and business model are widely shared locally	Senior management insist on clear, crisp business models and priorities	Performance assessment looks at communication capabilities at the frontline	Intranet information on local units includes business model description

Table 9.4: *Which organization systems will support local action-learning*

Local action-learning	Organization culture	Leadership style	Organization processes	Organization infrastructure
Being in charge, locally	People on the spot are trusted	Senior managers expect people to take over locally	People on the spot are involved early on in entry projects	Infrastructure, like assets, human resources, etc., is available locally
Ability to take local initiative	Better to apologize than ask for permission	Senior managers refuse to be used as "global referees"	Recruitment and performance measurement focus on initiative	Local decision rights are clear
Ability to pursue local fitness	Local responsiveness rather than corporate conformism	Senior managers are curious about local learning points	Geographic expansion provides early front-line management exposure	Best practice from different countries is documented and published
Ability to experiment locally	Well-intended mistakes are learning opportunities	Senior managers expect local people to question business models	Methodologies using test countries and reference countries are available	Local investment authorizations are sufficient to experiment
Keeping an ongoing learning agenda	Debriefing locally is part of the culture	Senior managers provide stretch and challenges to local people	International career paths pursue a learning agenda	Competitive approaches are used to stimulate best practice

Encouraging local debriefing

Exploiting the feedback locally is the part of the learning process that ensures sustained local fitness. It builds up the experience that gets encapsulated in the work-in-progress, local business model. Several capabilities can help support effective local debriefing:

- The local team should have the *urge to improve*, across the board, as opposed to seeking a state of equilibrium in the action–feedback tension, such as, for example, by focusing on limited measures of performance that say that the results are good.
- The local team should pay attention to *the "how", in addition to the "what"*: debriefing processes that have led to the results, rather than discoursing on the results, are what allows learning and progress.
- The local team should adopt an attitude of *non-defensiveness and constructive criticism* in order to integrate the feedback from failures and successes alike.
- The local team should have the *capacity to change*, so as to transform the learning into action.
- The local team should carry out systematic *follow-ups*, establishing milestones and measurements. This critical part of the process is often forgotten: the meeting is over, everyone goes with a plane to catch, and local routines go on.

Examples of how these local capabilities can be supported and enhanced by the organizational systems are provided in Table 9.5.

Learning how to learn locally

The most important learning, from these early international entries, is probably not how to adapt the domestic business model locally, although this should definitely happen for the local fitness to be sustainable. The most important capability should be learning how to *learn locally to accelerate subsequent international initiatives*. This learning, however, will not leave the company the same. As it gets redeployed across the company, its original domestic business model will necessarily be stretched and evolve. For some companies, as we will discuss in Chapter 10, this is even the whole purpose of their international expansion.

Table 9.5: *Which organization systems will support local redeployment of feedback*

Encouraging local debriefing	Organization culture	Leadership style	Organization processes	Organization infrastructure
Local urge to improve	Debriefing activities and projects is normal practice	Senior management always insists on formulating key learning points	Processes for effective debriefing are available locally	Information infrastructure provides transparency of processes and results
Local attention to "how", in addition to "what"	No "sweeping under the rug"	Senior management expect feedback on corporate processes	Performance assessment looks at local ability to learn from experience	Local management is also responsible for the "how"
Local non-defensiveness and constructive criticism	Constructive criticism is well accepted	Senior management expect local feedback on corporate decisions	Processes exist to analyse reasons for performance	Information infrastructure publicizes lessons from local debriefing
Local capacity to change	Team development is part of the culture	Senior management is involved in local learning initiatives	Performance assessment takes into account local learning initiatives	Corporate support to local learning is available
Local ability to carry out systematic follow-up	Implementation and follow-up, not only ideas, are what matters	Senior management does not micromanage, but follows up	Local performance processes focus on follow-up to debriefing	Corporate support to local change projects is available

SUMMARY

Going international is often seen as extrapolating abroad what has already been done successfully at home. But this is misconceived. The key question firms should ask themselves is "How are we going to be better off after the move?" Addressing this question is critical in shaping the business model for the internationalization move as a learning agenda will be on everyone's mind.

Applying successful past experience is the first step in this learning process. For this to happen, however, the past experience must be sufficiently explicit, formalized and made available. For a number of reasons, however, this past experience is often not readily available: the company is not aware that it has it, those who had it have left, past experience is not a good memory, or the necessary infrastructure to document it and share it is not there.

Allowing the business model to remain a learning agenda, rather than just directives to be implemented, requires that local management is accountable for local fitness and has the means to pursue it: local initiative and even some degree of entrepreneurship are expected, even though they will generally create organizational tensions. Pursuing this learning agenda requires local learning capabilities: information openness, the ability to shape a local business model, the ability to experiment, and the ability to debrief and draw lessons to improve the local business model.

These local learning capabilities will, in turn, be supported by the organization systems: the culture, the leadership style, the organization processes and the organization infrastructure.

 **LEARNING POINTS**

- Before embarking on international expansion, first ask yourself: how are we going to be better off after the move? In other words, how, precisely, is the international move expected to improve our global competitiveness? What do we need to do for these advantages to accrue?
- Exploit past experiences vigorously. This will not always be straightforward, particularly if those experiences have been forgotten, are unavailable or are misunderstood. Be determined to find out what you can and learn from it.

- Make sure that the organization systems – culture, leadership style, process and infrastructure – support documenting, disseminating and accessing past international experience. To achieve this, they should emphasize the following five capabilities: willingness to admit ignorance, initiative in seeking information, developing broad networks for information gathering, avoiding the "not invented here" syndrome, and making information-sharing the norm. Also remember that informal information networks are the most effective.

- Base the international entry on a game plan, rather than on a road-map to be followed strictly; a game plan encompasses hypotheses to be verified, what-if questions, simulating possible feedback responses and alternative routes.

- Make your entry mindset a learning mindset: the learning agenda is to verify the premises on which our improved global competitive position is based, and to develop and test new approaches as needed.

- Manage the resulting local/global tensions as they emerge to the benefit of both global and local learning; avoid suppressing one of the two by voluntarily or inadvertently removing the tension.

- Develop a culture, a leadership style, processes and an infrastructure which foster local learning: local information openness, local ability to shape an appropriate local business model, local action learning, and local urge and ability to improve the business model.

Reference

Bartlett, C. A. (2000) BRL Hardy: Globalizing an Australian Wine Company, Harvard Business School case no. 9-300-018.

10

Stretching the Business Model Globally: The Outside-in Approach and the Learning Intent

Smart companies have a global learning agenda from the outset. These firms not only take the best lessons from wherever they expand, but they expand depending on where they think they can best learn. As **Xavier Gilbert** shows, they develop a culture, leadership style, organizational systems and infrastructure which not only encourage shared learning, but which successfully manage any strategic conflicts.

Overview

What is the difference between inside-out and outside-in international growth? In the former, you go out and happen to learn something new; in the latter, you go out with a learning agenda right from the start to improve your company's global fitness.

What is on this learning agenda? You start from the existing know-how that you believe you can apply; then you have a local learning agenda – what you want to learn in that particular classroom you are expanding into; then, you have a global learning agenda – how that local learning will be integrated into the global business model; finally, you have a hidden agenda – the mindset changes that you need to make to improve your overall global fitness.

How do we fulfill this learning agenda? The first step is to decide where and how we will learn what we believe we need to learn. The second step is to share globally this local learning through learning-oriented communication systems. The third step is to manage the tensions resulting from knowledge imbalances throughout the organization, in such a way that they are true learning tensions. To orchestrate this effort, the leadership style must be focused on learning, rather than on more traditional attributes such as telling the troops what to do.

So, a learning intent is driving the company? This is what it all boils down to; the purpose of this global learning pursuit is develop a global mindset or a global intellect throughout the company so that global fitness becomes natural.

How do we sustain this learning intent over time? It must be supported by the company's organization systems: its culture, its leadership style, its processes and its infrastructure must all be focused on global learning.

The business model strikes back

In Chapter 9, we addressed situations where the proposed business model was challenged by the realities of the local environment and had to be re-crafted to achieve local fitness. But for the smart companies, local fitness is not an end in itself. Instead, the business model is stretched in ways that have potential to affect it globally, ending up with a smarter, more global business model and providing new global competitive advantages, rather than a replication or adaptation of the domestic ones. The outcome of local action–learning is thus not only how to adapt locally. More importantly, it can lead to a different, more effective company, globally.

Instead of just recognizing after the fact that some of the local learning can be reapplied globally to constitute a more effective, global business model, some companies actually plan, as their rationale for expanding internationally, to learn locally specific building blocks for the future business model they want to deploy globally. The intent behind their international expansion is to address a corporate learning agenda. This realization may seem to be a small mental step. As we will see, however, it requires a substantial organization mindset change.

As the case study in Chapter 9 showed, for example, Boots, the UK retail drugstore chain, did not walk away unchanged from its Japanese venture. As a result of the learning that was allowed to take place in this instance, the company built a more globally robust business model. But this was an ex-post realization. A more ambitious corporate learning agenda than mere local fitness was only developed later on: to enter unknown territory so as to develop global capabilities there that could be re-applied globally from outside-in.

The proposed approach, instead of transferring inside-out the domestic wisdom to foreign territories, is learning, from the best classrooms, the wisdom that will make the company better off, globally. When the founder of Business Objects (see Chapter 8) decided that his company had to be US based right from the start, instead of being French based first and internationalized in a subsequent move, the intent was to learn from the US the building blocks of global competition in its business. Similarly, when Nokia Mobile Phones decided that a successful presence in the US was necessary to establish its global brand recognition, this learning was intended to be used globally.

In those cases, two components of the business model were critical:

- first, the past successful experience with some of its building blocks, which could be applied as a reliable vehicle to explore the new lands;
- second, an explicit learning agenda covering the pieces of the new, globally deployable business model, which needed feedback to be confirmed or modified.

An *explicit* learning agenda is obviously quite critical when the working business model is essentially untested. The expected competitive advantages are no longer an extrapolation of the domestic experience – inside out. They flow back from the global presence that is being built up – outside in. How the international presence is expected to help learn the building blocks of these global competitive advantages, must be made quite explicit. If you do not know what matters, it is unlikely that you will learn it. A list of specific points to be verified, a plan to verify them, the resources to verify them: these must constitute the agenda of the outpost team.

CASE STUDY: HOW MERCEDES DEVELOPED ITS SPORTS UTILITY VEHICLE IN THE US

In the early 90s, Mercedes was confronted with mounting global competition in its traditional segment of luxury passenger cars. The CEO himself, Helmut Werner, had recognized publicly that Toyota's Lexus offered better value for money to the US market. The high production costs of Mercedes, he felt, were not only due to high labour costs in Germany, but also a reflection of the company's conservative mindset, hierarchical structure and over-engineering approach. The decision was made to evolve from a German exporter strategy to a true global strategy, particularly through global manufacturing, and to enter other segments of the passenger car segment, such as the sports utility vehicle (SUV).

The lead market in the world for SUVs was undoubtedly the US market where one million such vehicles were sold annually, four times as many as in Europe. The market was dominated by the then US big three, GM, Ford and Chrysler, but the Japanese also had a 13% market share. There was no other place in the world to learn about the SUV concept, the market expectations, the car design and its manufacturing, as well as in the US.

The learning agenda was clear: learn how to compete globally, which meant learn your way in a global classroom, with a new market-product segment.And, more importantly, show that, to achieve this, a new "Mercedes mindset" works best. To fulfil this learning agenda, Mercedes followed an unproven path, but signposted with proven practices.

The first step on the unproven path was a greenfield investment in the US – in Alabama, a state with little industrial infrastructure, a low education level and certainly no car manufacturing resources (workforce, suppliers, etc.). The learning point was, as a late entrant into an already well-structured market, the quality advantage will be critical; then you need fresh new manufacturing practices, not those of your competitors. The wisdom of doing this in Alabama, however, was still untested.

The next important element was the person who was put in charge of the project. He was a 35-year-old German, Andreas Renschler, who had gained most of his car manufacturing experience with Mercedes in Latin America, not in Stuttgart. If you want to start with a new approach, indeed, you do not choose someone who has spent his life in corporate corridors. But Renschler had never run a project of that scope and complexity before.

In fact, Renschler had unorthodox managerial approaches, by Stuttgart standards. He established a non-hierarchical, informal style, promoting open communication. Again, if you wanted to show that a new mindset worked better, this was the way. But it still had to be proven.

On the other hand, many of the Mercedes production and quality practices constituted a valuable and proven baggage to take across the Atlantic. This was done without compromise, from the design stage when a virtual team was put in place, with half the team in the US and the other half in Germany. Newly recruited production operators and foremen were selected very carefully, on the basis of their drive for quality and improvement. Many were sent to Germany for several months to be trained on the production lines there.A whole team of 70 German operators was then sent to Alabama to continue the training on site. The proven methods were implemented fully.

Production started in 1997 at the rate of 65 000 units per year and was increased shortly after to the level of 80 000 units. Was the Alabama learning, however, effectively redeployed through the organization? Perhaps the jury is still out.

Adapted from Rosenzweig (1997).

The learning agenda: what's on it?

- The existing know-how that will be applied.
- The local learning agenda: what we want to learn locally.
- The global learning agenda: the business model we want to redeploy globally.
- The hidden learning agenda: how we need to change to improve our global fitness.

As exemplified by the Mercedes case, the learning agenda has several building blocks. The first is anchored in the usable experience that serves as a starting point, but must be stretched to new territories – in the case of Mercedes, top-quality manufacturing know-how. The robustness of this experience when transferred to the new territories needs to be tested and perhaps worked on; it was not certain from the outset that the Mercedes way of manufacturing could be transferred to Alabama and it certainly required some adjustments. The essentials of the know-how, however, were in-house.

The second building block focuses on learning to master the remaining elements of the business model, those that the company has never tested before, and are meant to be learned in this particular classroom. In the case of Mercedes, this was achieved by attending the best school on SUVs, under a new management style that would ultimately allow it to become a global business. This learning agenda really stretched the quality-manufacturing experience to untested limits. It applied it to a product Mercedes had no experience with, in a country where Mercedes had merely been an exporter of passenger cars, with a management style that was unknown in Stuttgart, under the leadership of someone who had never run anything in Germany. And a business model for competing globally in the SUV segment was the expected outcome. This was the *local learning agenda*, for the US team.

The third building block of this learning agenda was that the rest of the corporation would learn that the business model developed in the US was indeed a good business model for competing globally, that it could be done and, in fact, that it worked best. How will the rest of the corporation integrate this learning into a new global business model? In the case of Mercedes, it was probably expected that the new management style followed by Andreas Renschler in the US would be contagious because of its effectiveness and would then allow a more entrepreneurial, outside-in rather that inside-out, global expansion. Indeed, why could Helmut Werner observe publicly that the Lexus gave better value for money in the US market? Because the Stuttgart-centric mindset of Mercedes could not learn what perceived value meant to the US market. The SUV venture was meant to prove that, with the right management approach, this could be learned locally and redeployed globally. This was the *global learning agenda* for Helmut Werner, Andreas Renschler and potentially many others.

But the very reason for doing all this was in fact a fourth building block in the learning agenda. Why could Stuttgart not launch a SUV line in the first place? Essentially because of the corporate mindset reasons, corporate culture reasons, leadership style reasons, corporate processes reasons, corporate infrastructure reasons – the whole DNA of Mercedes. This was the opportunity for the whole corporation to learn that, if it wanted to be an effective global competitor in passenger cars – not only in the SUV segment – it had to adopt the mindset tested in the US, the ambitious vision of Helmut Werner: his *hidden learning agenda* that he wanted to share with the entire corporation.

This entire learning agenda, local, global and hidden, in addition to the existing know-how we want to apply, constitutes the working business model that a company needs to adopt to support and accelerate its international expansion. This learning agenda must be made explicit. It must be on the minds of all those involved in the international expansion. Some of the essential points that should be in the learning agenda of a global business model are given in Table 10.1.

Table 10.1: *The learning agenda of a global business model*

The hidden learning agenda: the corporate change agenda to achieve better global fitness?

⇨   The global business model

●   The overview, the building blocks, how they relate to each other

●   How to formulate it? The "tangible vision", the "elevator statement" that can be kept on the top of everyone's mind

●   How will it be communicated?

⇨   What is the corresponding corporate change agenda?

●   Corporate mindset

●   Corporate culture

●   Leadership style

⇨   The change project

●   Phases, timing, team, resources, etc.

The global learning agenda: how will we redeploy the local learning?

⇨   Which corporate processes are needed to deploy the learning?

●   The human resources processes: recruitment, career paths, performance assessment, human resources development, . . .

●   The decision processes: accountability, decision rights, . . .

●   The corporate resources

⇨   How will the organization infrastructure support it?

●   The organization structure

●   The information infrastructure

The local learning agenda: what needs to be learned to achieve all of the above? Where are the best schools? How do we enroll?

⇨   What do we expect to learn from this school?

⇨   Which learning points are unique to the "classroom" we are entering? Our reasons for attending?

●   Market sophistication

●   Competitors' approaches

●   Business system (local value-chains) architecture: how are the activities provided?

●   Specific business system activities that are particularly developed in this market: solution orientation, services, marketing, . . .

CASE STUDY: HOW NOKIA LEARNT ITS WAY INTO THE MOBILE INTERNET

Over the 90s, Nokia has developed a dominant position in mobile handsets, and a very strong position in mobile infrastructure. This was achieved with very strong roots in the GSM standard which is the dominant worldwide mobile standard. As a result of this ten-year learning, one could say that Nokia has developed a GSM mindset: its winning business model, on the network side, has been to work very effectively with telecommunications operators, providing them with strong technology and well-implemented infrastructures that allow numerous operator services.

On the handset side, Nokia is perhaps less GSM minded. In fact, it is rather what could be deemed "standard agnostic", since it is extremely consumer conscious, imposing the strongest global brand in the handset business, with a unique fashion-oriented approach.

But the information world is changing very fast. The internet global culture that has exploded over the last few years relies on the instant access to information anywhere in the world: business data, news, entertainment, shopping, whatever can be digitized. The consumer expectations have no limits. The need for mobile access to this information is obvious: not only information anywhere, but from anywhere. Since the number of handsets is growing faster than the number of PCs, as people get tired of carrying kilos of laptop hardware, the writing is on the wall.

But in this new world, the telecom operator is no longer the most obvious point of customer contact. In fact, everyone involved is fighting to be there, right in front of the customer: the application providers (Microsoft), the media (Bertelsmann), the portals (Yahoo), the portals media (AOL Time Warner), the operator media (Vivendi Universal), the operators (Vodafone, NTT-DoCoMo), . . . the list goes on. It is vital to be at the forefront in order to learn what "information experience" consumers may end up paying for. This is a challenge for any hardware player in this business system. Margins will obviously migrate to where a valued information experience is provided to the consumer.

For Nokia, the learning agenda is breathtaking; it must transform itself from a GSM company to a provider of consumer information experience. The vision is to help shape the "mobile information society", as the company puts it. It is attending any classroom in the world where this can be learned: not only in Silicon Valley, but also wherever in the world people are trying to develop new products and services. It is active in seeding ventures worldwide to support information applications. It is involved in numerous partnerships worldwide with media and information players. It has set up research centres in many parts of the world, close to technology or close to customers. It has deployed outside-in learning.

At the same time, the mindset transformation that must be achieved is also overwhelming. Over the last ten years its top team has built a hugely powerful position in mobile infrastructure and handsets. This does shape mindsets. Visioning a totally different business model is not a small challenge. It is the challenge of closing the gap between learning at the right schools and transforming all that learning in a compelling business model.

Implementing global learning: the global learning intent

Several steps are involved in implementing global learning:

- Identifying the new sources of learning – local learning. The location of foreign investments is one way, but there are many more; today you can be international without infrastructure, bricks and mortar all over the world.
- Sharing this local learning globally; this will challenge and stretch the existing business models.
- Managing the resulting learning tensions: the information imbalance that will result from this dispersed learning will result in organization tensions. These tensions must be managed in such a way that the learning gets integrated into new business models.
- Focusing the leadership style on learning: clearly, these steps need a conductor. The role of leadership in supporting global learning will also be discussed.

Identifying the new sources of learning

There are a number of avenues to explore such as:

- the location of foreign investments;
- the location of R&D outposts;
- the "windows" on the world provided by the organization structure;
- developing a venture-capital activity;
- using information technology resources generally, such as the internet.

The location of foreign investments to fulfil a global learning agenda is the most obvious approach to creating new learning sources. It takes the company physically close to the site of knowledge that matters: customers, consumers, technology, sophisticated competitors, unique resources. The examples of Business Objects and Nokia selecting their location for critical operations according to this logic have already been discussed.

Another example is the Swiss firm, Logitech, one of the key players worldwide in interactive devices between a human being and a computer, such as pointing devices (mice and trackballs chiefly), game controllers, keyboards, PC video cameras and multimedia speakers. Logitech started in Switzerland, the country of its founders, in an area that was close to the technology sources it tapped (the Lausanne campus of the Swiss Federal Polytechnic Institute), that provided precision manufacturing know-how (micro-mechanics, watches). It was also close to a company that had had a very early venture in word-processing hardware and software where the founders had worked and developed the idea for the need for interactive devices (at that time the only form of interaction with a computer was the keyboard and clicking desperately on the cursor key).

Early on, however, the company started an operation in California. Hewlett Packard (HP) had seen the potential of Logitech's very primitive mouse and had decided to help the company develop it. Logitech had to be physically close to this great school where it learned selling, making contracts, mass manufacturing and logistics: all, in fact, that was needed to build a business.

The location of R&D outposts is another obvious choice related to a learning agenda. Which electronics company does not have an operation in Silicon Valley today? But there are also less obvious locations from which to learn. Nokia has a development operation in Australia for entertainment applications because there are sophisticated partners there with which to do this work. General Electric (GE) has built an R&D centre in a research park near Bangalore in India in order to take advantage of the country's world-class software talent.

Selecting an organization structure can also be part of the learning agenda. This choice should optimize the learning that matters. Many companies have a geographical dimension in their global matrix. However, this is often for legal reasons rather than for learning reasons. But the country regional dimension may not be the best one to learn how to compete globally. Companies with global customers have often taken these accounts out of the country structure, to provide better focus. But they should make sure they do not miss the opportunity to use them as their global school.

Many companies have found that adding a product dimension to their organization structure has helped them capture product-related learning globally. The building materials company, Lafarge, which is mostly a set of local businesses, has found that its product divisions facilitated such learning much better than its previous country-based organization.

Similarly, ABB started with a balance between its country focus and its global focus that was meant to provide local and global learning. This approach, however, evolved towards more local fitness, at the expense of global fitness: the learning was more local than global. As a result, in the late 90s, the global focus was reinforced to secure global learning. It changed, in early 2001 to a structure focused on four customer segments – utilities, process industries, manufacturing and consumer industries, and oil, gas and petrochemicals. This will provide end users with faster and easier access to the full range of ABB's products, services and solutions and it will help ABB secure global learning on how to deliver *customer solutions* globally and seamlessly, a necessity due to the internet-triggered, corporate-information revolution. In addition, the newly created central unit, Corporate Processes, should ensure that the global learning generated in each customer segment is shared across these segments.

Developing a venture-capital activity is another approach to learning globally, but without local presence. This approach also responds to the general inability of large corporations to learn from small local experiments that either get forgotten or entangled into inappropriate corporate processes. Nokia Ventures Fund, based in Menlo Park and in Washington DC, attracts essentially US knowledge. However, by being involved in early funding, it has a broad reach of applications in the making. Some of the ventures are also moving internationally, especially in the UK and Japan. One of them, PayPal, which has developed a payment application through mobile phones, is active in more than 25 countries. Similarly, in early 2001, ABB created New Ventures Ltd, an incubator for new businesses, as a way to reach and nurture learning opportunities that would otherwise be missed.

Using the internet has also evolved, for many companies, as an access to global learning about stakeholder groups that matter in ways that were never feasible before without a local presence at the micro level. E-commerce enables them to learn about customers wherever they are located, with a global learning infrastructure that was never available to the local stores. Amazon.com can profile its customers wherever they are and personalize its portal display because it has learnt their buying patterns. Fnac.com, the French-style Amazon, uses its site as a cultural portal, which also helps it to learn about the tendencies of potential customers wherever they are. Shell uses its recruitment portal to survey interactively the opinions of younger generations worldwide on societal issues such as the environment or ethics.

Using information technology resources, a corporation can today develop an organization culture of information openness to the entire world by providing subscriptions to some of the many free e-mail news services. These services, such as TheStandard.com or RedHerring.com, for the internet economy, or GenomeWeb.com, for the life sciences sectors, provide worldwide insights on every desktop. *But it is not only the information that matters here; it is also the more globally oriented mindset that the company promotes in that manner.*

Sharing the local learning globally

Circulating the local learning across the corporation is the next step in the global learning process. This information is meant to be challenging, stretching and stimulating to the other local units, so that it becomes integrated and redeployed, and progressively evolves into global learning. Many approaches can be used to circulate globally the locally developed learning:

- celebrating the local achievements;
- making the local results totally transparent;
- the role of senior management in circulating the learning;
- exploiting the potential of their corporate intranets.

Celebrating the local achievements is an approach that is frequently used. It creates cross-unit competition and stimulates the other units to learn from the successful ones. For example, a newly appointed European product manager in a global chemical company was trying to convince the European sales force, who was of course not reporting to him but to the country managers, that they should sell their product as high-value, service-heavy solutions, rather than as commodities. In other words, he was trying to convince them not to compete on prices. The sales force responded very negatively, arguing that this was typically a headquarters view that ignored the realities of the local markets.

Nevertheless, the European product manager succeeded in building up two test cases, in two countries where new sales people had been appointed, by providing them with a lot of local support to use his new positioning. These two cases were then widely publicized and documented in the remaining countries, promoting the local sales people as the owners of the knowledge. It then became easier for the other sales people to learn from their sales colleagues, rather than from the central product manager, how to make the new approach work. They were also stimulated by the fact that two newer colleagues had built up their market share so fast.

Making the local results totally transparent can go a long way in circulating the local knowledge that is behind these results. ABB's ABACUS transparent information system, for instance, delivers the results of all local units to every local manager, thus creating a great incentive for these local managers to communicate and exchange their approaches and special programmes.

The role of senior management and of corporate offices can also be very effective in sharing the knowledge, experiments and approaches across local units. Senior managers who spend a substantial amount of time visiting the local units can hardly pretend to tell them what to do and to micro-manage them; with the few days they can spend every year on the spot, the best they can do is trust that the local management they have placed there is competent. On the other hand, they can tell the local managers what they have seen elsewhere, ask questions as to whether and why it is different or the same here, compare, stretch and challenge.

CASE STUDY: JAN CARENDI, THE TRAVELLING STORY-TELLER AT SKANDIA

Skandia Insurance Company is a Stockholm-based insurance and financial services company with sales in 1999 of $14 billion. It was founded in 1855. Although it had been active internationally for many years, by the 1960s its interest in overseas markets had waned. What really changed its pace of growth, however, was the arrival in 1986 of Jan Carendi as head of the company's international life assurance business. He oversaw a 45% growth per annum between 1986 and 1995.

When Carendi took charge of Skandia's Assurance and Financial Services (AFS), the business was anything but flourishing. In fact, it was in such a marginal situation that it was in danger of being closed down. Carendi, however, quickly saw the potential in the variable unit-linked life assurance products that had been developed by an entrepreneurial group at the company's UK subsidiary, in which Skandia had a 60% stake.

He arranged to buy the remaining stake and used it as a base to build - quickly and smartly - a new alliance-based business model. AFS became the link between distribution and investment, adding value by packaging long-term savings products for insurance brokers and their clients, and by bringing wholesale distribution to brand-name money managers. Backing this up was a PC-based, modular system which would enable the local companies to design and tailor products for new markets much more quickly and cost effectively by prototyping the products and adjusting a number of locally driven parameters. Market entry into Germany, for example, was done based on lessons from the entry into Switzerland, and adjusting the parameters in the model for Germany.

His international expansion strategy was thus based on three main planks: an innovative new life-insurance product, a partnership-based business model and a prototype-based learning processes. His belief was that the company had to be in a "permanent state of readiness", with people throughout the organization being encouraged to share information and knowledge across units, to encourage flexibility and speed. He also created temporary project teams, an integrative global area network infrastructure, and a small head office of only 40 people out of the total workforce of 1700. Product development was to take place close to the customer.

For Carendi, it was vital to treat employees as "volunteers". He saw himself as the coach of the team and an agent of change. He travelled constantly, conveying the experience and ideas from the other units, challenging the local assumptions and encouraging discussions. He established local centres of excellence which would compete with each other to retain their status. In his view, if you orchestrate the learning process, the rest takes care of itself.

His belief in the crucial role of intellectual capital was underlined when he appointed the world's first director of intellectual capital in order to translate what was such a broad concept into management specifics. In other words, the objective was to take human capital – what people know – and combine it with structural capital – databases, customer files, manuals and so on – in order to create value for customers, investors and other stakeholders. To further that vision, he developed a new measurement model called the Business Navigator which took a holistic view by also tracking the knowledge renewal and development investments and achievements.

Adapted from Bartlett and Mahmood (1998).

Due to the current information technology, companies also have the possibility to circulate knowledge through their intranet. During the 90s, because of the vogue for organization learning, companies have been building considerable repositories of knowledge, cases and experiences. Consulting firms have actually been assigning enormous resources to what they call "practice development", where they revisit the engagements they have performed by industry, technology and issues to formulate all the learning that had taken place in the minds of the experienced consultants.

Some industrial firms have been doing the same. Lafarge, the building materials company, has assigned senior-management resources to see what similar lessons can be drawn from the locations, throughout the world, where it is involved concomitantly in cement, aggregates and concrete activities. In some locations, this mode of integration has been very effective; in others, it has not. The purpose has been to draw lessons, based on the local characteristics of these three businesses, to help decide when integration would make sense.

The difficulty that all these companies have, however, is ensuring that these repositories are actually accessed and tapped. Accessing and digging into large, fragmented, often not user-friendly, databases is a forbidding and time-consuming task. The intranet portal technology that is now available enables users to present this information in a more friendly way, to integrate information from different databases seamlessly, and to customize the information according to individual user needs at a certain point in time. So there really are no more excuses. When a manager, anywhere in the world, opens his or her computer every morning, the links that are relevant to them are there. Just click and the latest learning from anywhere in the company, worldwide, is on display. If it is found to be irrelevant, it is as easy to click it away in no time.

Managing the resulting learning tensions

This large mass of learning will create imbalances in the company; it will not be symmetric locally and centrally or across local units. This will result in knowledge tensions that are not always comfortable: different perceptions of the same reality confront each other. It is tempting to try to avoid these tensions by shying away from them, by escalating them upward, or by giving precedence to one of the two perspectives. For example, in many matrix organizations, one of the dimensions ends up dominating, which will block and debilitate the learning along the other dimensions.

Keeping the tension alive is a better learning proposition. The confrontation, if appropriately steered, will create new, joint learning, or the ability to see "the two sides of the coin". Even more crucially, senior management should be ready for a "new coin" to emerge from this confrontation. The business model gets reshaped as the units under tension learn jointly. This is how "learning organizations" develop new business models that are shared across the organization, are implemented faster, and are improved all the time. "Then, we are all ready to go," observed Matti Alahuhta, the CEO of Nokia Mobile Phones, reflecting on how the Nokia strategy resulted from the confrontation of learning in all parts of the organization through a series of strategic workshops. In those companies, strategic thinking is an ongoing learning process.

It is by managing these tensions skilfully that BRL-Hardy, the Australian wine company, evolved from an exporter of Australian wines, to a vineyard-agnostic, global-brand company – which is a long way from selling wine internationally as proposed by the initial business model.

CASE STUDY: HOW **BRL-HARDY** DEVELOPED A GLOBAL-BRAND BUSINESS MODEL

As discussed previously in Chapter 9, the tension had been mounting between Stephen Davies, the corporate marketing manager, who was keen to develop global brands based on Australian wines, and Christopher Carson, head of the European operations, who was pursuing a strategy that he saw as more appropriate to the European market. Carson was pushing several projects, based on wines sourced from Italy and Chile, that seemed to go head-to-head against the strategy pursued by Davies. The tension was becoming quite uncomfortable. In many companies, the CEO would have stepped in and cut across the mess to impose the solution that seemed the most appropriate as seen from the headquarters.

Not Steve Millar, BRL-Hardy's CEO, who saw the value of the knowledge from both sides. On behalf of the corporation, Carson was actually learning how to source globally, which is necessary to protect against the agricultural cycles of vine growing and to produce the more predictable drinking experience that is necessary to sustain a global lifestyle brand. In addition, he had valuable knowledge about the European wine consumers that was critical for the global branding strategy of Davies to succeed.

Davies, on the other hand, had considerable experience with the US and Asian markets that was also critical to support his strategy.

Short of intervening in the conflict, Millar did everything he could to make sure that the tension would result in a positive outcome, a win–win instead of making one winner and one loser, perhaps two losers. He coached both sides to help them see the concessions that would be necessary to progress; he made both sides understand that they were ultimately pursuing the same goal; he helped both sides respect and value the views of each other. And eventually, the logic of both sides evolved in such a way that they could see by themselves which of their projects did not fit and which had potential. This allowed both sides to refine a joint business model for a global, lifestyle-brand, wine company.

Adapted from Bartlett (2000).

In managing these learning tensions, the role of leadership, as exemplified by the BRL-Hardy case, is clearly critical. So is a corporate culture that allows open confrontation and well-intended dissent, that fosters mutual respect, and that encourages entrepreneurship. The organization structure, however, is also an important factor. In many cultures, open confrontation is not adequate, even if undercover confrontation is sometimes pervasive. The organization structure is then given the task of avoiding confrontation or, when it happens, of pushing it under the rug. This will inevitably prevent learning in some parts of the organization, with the danger that it will become more widespread as others realize that it is preferable not to make waves. More importantly, it will prevent the joint learning that allows all to focus on the same, work-in-progress, global business model.

Again, the organization changes announced by ABB in early 2001 seem to have been inspired by the aim to keep a productive learning tension that will foster the emergence of a new business model focused on providing a seamless solution to customers, a solution imbedded in their fast-evolving value chains. This learning will result from the tension between the customer-focused business units, the product groups retained from the previous structure, the corporate processes unit and the customer challenges. This new corporate structure makes the learning tension almost unavoidable.

Focusing the leadership style on learning

As suggested by the BRL-Hardy case, the role of leadership is critical in steering the global learning process. There are two important dimensions in this role.

- The first one is to steer the formation of the work-in-process global business model that is shaped through the learning agenda.
- The second one is to orchestrate the global learning agenda itself.

In many learning processes, the learners are not aware of what they are shaping; it requires regular debriefing–reflecting pauses to address the questions "Where are we? What does all this add up to? What should be the next learning point on the agenda?" In a way, the role of the leader is first to hold the mirror up in front of the learners to help them make their learning explicit. It is a synthesis task, putting all the learning points together in a work-in-process business model, and feeding it back to the learners so that they can decide on the next steps in the learning agenda.

"Steering" is the word that best describes this process. It is a lot more than summing up the debate; at the same time as the leader helps formulate the working business model, he or she also questions, challenges, stretches, prioritizes, shows the implications, and can maintain the overall direction and the destination. BRL-Hardy's Steve Millar had set a clear destination: make the company internationally competitive. How to get there depended on what would be learned along the route which meant that, in a way, he was ready for surprises. The business model that emerged was really the result of the joint learning of Davies and Carson. Millar agreed that this was right.

Nokia's destination is "shaping the mobile information society". Even though it has tentative road maps that are indeed pursued until they need redirecting, Jorma Ollila, the chairman and CEO, Pekka Ala-Pietilä, the president, and their colleagues steer a global learning process that synthesize the learning from throughout the company, in all parts of the world where it has placed sensors. This is done through a series of strategic workshops, involving a large number of people who have done considerable amounts of homework on specific key issues, during which the leaders help shape them into working business models and more learning agendas. This steering is not only performed by challenging the learning teams to come up with working business models. The leaders also finalize decisive choices at critical crossroads.

The second important role of leadership is to orchestrate the global learning process, in order to ensure the integrity of the global learning process. Interestingly, this role is very much like the role of a good "case teacher".

Hands-off and committed. People learn when they have to provide the response themselves. They do not learn when they know that someone else will. Leaders who are effective orchestrators of the global learning process refuse to act as referees when the tensions are escalated; they push back. On the other hand, they provide all the necessary support for the tension to be productive and, indeed, generate joint learning. They coach both sides, help them establish common ground, show the progress, makes sure they talk and prevent them from withdrawing.

Providing stretching questions. Effective orchestrators of the global learning process also help people to raise their nose from the grindstone. They do so by asking the naïve questions about what is taken for granted and they genuinely expect an answer. This is very different from senior managers who can sometime ask questions that are readily perceived as *the* answer.

Injecting disruptive and questioning information. The learning tension is an unstable equilibrium; unexpected feedback raises questions that call for adaptive responses; the equilibrium stabilizes when the feedback becomes predictable: the learning stops. The effective orchestrator of the global learning process ensures that the equilibrium remains unstable through timely disruptive information on what has been done in other units, on the competition, on new trends. Again, senior managers have to be careful that this information is not perceived as an order.

Remaining strict on the destination. The effectiveness of the learning processes is reinforced by demanding results. The skilful orchestrators of the global learning process are very strict about the end results, even though they may not have to be delivered immediately. They also provide a very systematic follow-up of the learning agenda, asking questions on progress, learning points and implications drawn since the last discussion.

Protecting the learning tensions. The learning tensions, as we have seen in the BRL-Hardy case, can become uncomfortable and many organization cultures will attempt to suppress them in some way or other. In addition, many people believe that the good manager is one who makes decisions, cuts across dilemmas and steps in early so that subordinates don't waste time. But "hands off" is not "laissez-faire" either. The effective orchestrator of the global learning process will resist these interventionist temptations and actively prevent the pushing of the learning tensions under the rug.

Protecting the learning experiments. Organizations generally resent experimenting. Proven processes and beaten paths are preferred. As a result, learning experiments are often discouraged and repressed as unnecessary, disruptive or risky. Effective orchestrators of the global learning process protect the learning experiments from the rest of the organization. They allow them to be pursued, they protect the experimenters, they give them the necessary time. They also insist, however, on solid experimenting methodologies with clear dependent and independent variables.

Being present where the learning takes place. The regular presence of the orchestrator of the global learning process, where the learning is taking place, will go a long way in communicating the importance of learning. These leaders often have hectic travel schedules; they cut across the organization to learn directly from the people on the front line; they speak the languages or try to. At every juncture they are sowing the seeds of commitment to learning.

Helping draw the lessons. In a learning process, it is essential to regularly take stock of the progress: what did we learn? Effective orchestrators of the global learning process do this routinely all the time. They keep asking for key learning points, for syntheses, for key conclusions and for priority implications. Debriefing reflection is what clinches the learning by making it explicit and then deployable. Their point is that if the learning cannot be formulated in a crisp way, it has probably not been registered and it will probably not be usable by others.

The systematic pursuit of a learning intent

The conclusion is that international growth can be accelerated by orchestrating it and steering it as a global learning process. It is an effective way to craft evolving global business models in such a way that it is shared by most and rooted in local learning. By focusing on global learning, by pursuing a global learning intent, the corporate leaders will allow new, global business models to emerge and evolve.

Unless a corporation is capable of mobilizing learning globally it can clearly not come up with business models that truly take advantage of its international presence. This what Jack Welch refers to when he comments on the necessity to globalize the intellect at GE.

CASE STUDY: GLOBALIZING INTELLECT AT GE

Jack Welch, CEO of the US diversified industrial group General Electric (GE), has been a keen proponent of globalization since the 1980s. As well as expanding into markets around the world, he has pushed for deeper and faster penetration of them by trying to replace expatriate managers with local talent as soon as realistically possible, in order to put the businesses in the hands of managers who really understand local markets. This has been done in the context of a corporate culture which balances local activity with centralized financial targets, rigorous personnel review procedures and the occasional initiatives like globalization, the Six Sigma quality programme in the mid 1990s and e-business since 1999.

The focus on cross-border leveraging is another powerful global weapon, or how to make sure the best ideas in terms of people, processes and products from wherever they are in the world get transplanted to enhance effectiveness in other markets. That is why the company is beginning to locate R&D resources outside the US home market for the first time.

But he is adamant that the company, which in 1999 had $111 billion in revenues, still has some way to go. According to an interview he gave to Fortune magazine, he believes that the next step for the company has to be the globalization of intellect: The real challenge is to globalize the mind of the organization. And at least in America, that's the most difficult part of the equation. When you start talking about globalizing intellect and building massive laboratories in Bangalore and building foundries in the Czech Republic, you start really challenging the organization, because moving intellect out of the home base is a tremendously threatening thing.

"Until an organization truly sees itself as capturing the intellects of other areas, it really does have a problem. I think until you globalize intellect, you haven't really globalized the company."

Fortune, October 2, 2000

In the process of mobilizing learning globally, other capabilities that characterize a global mindset will develop. The learning tensions across the company, the imbalances that will result and the consequent joint learning will develop a global awareness, stemming from the realization of the fact that one cannot learn alone but that one needs other perspectives in order to progress towards a more comprehensive learning agenda, which can result in a more effective business model. Locally, the global awareness will increase as a way to generate more effective learning. Centrally, the local awareness will also increase as a way to generate more effective learning. A global mindset, omnipresent throughout the company, will thus accelerate the global learning.

In addition to the example provided by the corporate leadership, the responsibility of the central human resources function is critical in promoting a global mindset or a global intellect. Recruitment and the corresponding competence profiles obviously play an important role in this regard. Career management processes contribute

even more in the way they provide global exposure, in the way they deploy experience and knowledge, and in the way they stretch and challenge the local perspectives. The way that central human resources emphasizes global learning and the
development of a global mindset is a key ingredient of fast international growth.

Which organization systems will support global learning?

The previous examples highlighted several organization systems that can be helpful
or critical in supporting global learning. Some best-practice examples of how the
organization culture, the *leadership style*, the *organization processes* and the *organization infrastructure* can support global learning are summarized in Tables 9.2–9.5
for each building block of global learning: fostering *information openness globally*,
shaping *global business models,* leveraging *action-learning globally*, and *debriefing
and redeploying the feedback globally*. Many of the best practices suggested in
Chapter 9 to support local learning can, of course, be transposed to supporting global
learning. A few additional ones that are more specific to global learning are also
proposed here in Tables 10.2–10.5.

Table 10.2: *Fostering global information openness*

Organization culture	Leadership style	Organization processes	Organization infrastructure
Local-to-local and local-to-central communication at all levels is normal Local awareness is promoted centrally and global awareness locally No "not-invented-here" syndrome Side conversations in un-understood languages are not considered right	Naïve questions can help everyone Local assumptions and idiosyncrasies are routinely questioned Intensive travelling to meet local teams Language capabilities Acts as travelling story-teller, carrying experiences across units	Local managers, rather than expatriates, run the show locally Expatriates are there to learn Multi-cultural awareness training and development Language training; use of a neutral working language	Use of local intelligence to collect information An intranet portal allows the access of corporate information in an intuitive and seamless manner

Table 10.3: *Shaping global business models*

Organization culture	Leadership style	Organization processes	Organization infrastructure
Local-to-local and local-to-central testing of hypotheses is normal Tensions and confrontations are handled openly, preferably face to face The ultimate destination is shared by all	Provides continuously a very clear ultimate destination (vision) Stretches and challenges the thinking to stimulate learning Provides very clear expectations with respect to behaviours and results Provides support in the resolution of learning tensions	Local managers can be globally responsible for some issues Cross-organization taskforces are frequently used The impact of local results on global results is made transparent	The organization structure does not hide tensions The information infrastructure supports always-on communication

Table 10.4: *Global action–learning*

Organization culture	Leadership style	Organization processes	Organization infrastructure
Single-minded local focus is discouraged Cross-border projects are frequent and do not have to involve the centre It is common practice to give feedback across borders Experiments are given global visibility	Provides personal support to local projects and initiatives, and shows personal interest in their success; reassuring Happy to put local management in the limelight Willing to take the flack for not intervening as a referee in tensions and conflicts Willing to take the flack for allowing experiments to continue Follows up on discussions held locally	Decisions are made locally; central decisions are the exception Processes are designed to avoid complexity and redundancy at the local level Performance assessment also includes global performance measures Career paths include local start-up experience Local experiments are publicized globally	Flat global organization, as simple as possible Local "businesses" kept as small as possible The central, global infrastructure is kept at a minimum Global interest groups are supported by information technology

Table 10.5: *Redeploying the learning globally*

Organization culture	Leadership style	Organization processes	Organization infrastructure
Cross-business global initiatives are launched regularly Knowledge belongs to the company, not to the local units	Follows up on best practice projects Plays a personal role in circulating best practice Personally behind global initiatives	Best practices are documented centrally Massive push of information on best practices through corporate-wide meetings and information technology Performance assessment looks at local implementation of global best practice Career planning is designed to accumulate local exposures	Global competitions and prizes are organized on the implementation of best practice Successful local implementation of best practice is publicized globally The corporate intranet works as a best-practice portal

 # SUMMARY

Outside-in international growth relies on learning; rather than extrapolating what is known to new geographies, it seeks to learn from the best classrooms worldwide and bring the learning back in to craft a global business model.

So, a global learning agenda is the starting point. This learning agenda, of course, has its foundations in the company's existing know-how, but it also covers what needs to be learned and where, how this learning will be shared across the company, and how the company's overall mode of operation needs to change to pursue a global business model.

Deciding where to expand next, internationally, will thus be based on where we can best learn what is on the agenda, rather than on where we can best apply what we already know. This concomitant learning, taking place in different parts of the world, must then be shared and integrated into global learning. The organization systems must support the urge to learn from each other. But, at the same time, different pockets of learning, across the organization, could draw conflicting conclusions on how the global business model should be crafted. These potential conflicts must be managed in such a way that they remain true learning tensions. Focusing the leadership style on orchestrating the learning, rather than on providing the answers, is essential to sustain this global learning.

In addition to building an effective global business model, also on the learning agenda is the promotion throughout the company of the global mindset or global intellect, which constantly updates the business model to pursue global fitness in the longer term.

Pursuing a global learning intent allows new, global business models to emerge and evolve in real time; it accelerates international growth.

 LEARNING POINTS

- Establish a global learning agenda: what do we need to learn to compete globally more effectively? How do we need to change? How do we see our global business model?
- Build your international expansion on where you believe you can get the know-how that is on your learning agenda.
- Focus your leadership style and communication systems on disseminating the learning: global business models are crafted through the resulting learning tensions. As a leader, orchestrate these learning tensions; give them space and time; refrain from stepping in immediately when questions are still looking for answers.
- Keep in mind that you want to build your company's learning mindset or learning intellect: a reflex to think globally, throughout the company; a reflex to pursue global fitness.
- Align the organization systems to support global learning: a culture of sharing best practice; a leadership style of orchestrating learning; organization processes that move the know-how around; an infrastructure that immerses everyone in the corporate global know-how.
- Do not be impatient with learning; ultimately it will accelerate global fitness.

References

Bartlett, C.A. (2000) BRL Hardy: Globalizing an Australian Wine Company, Harvard Business School case no. 9-300-018.

Bartlett, C.A. and Mahmood, T. (1998) Skandia AFS: Developing Intellectual Capital Globally, Harvard Business School case no. 9-396-412.

Rosenzweig, P.M. (1997) Mercedes-Benz: Setting up in Alabama, IMD case.

Part Five

Adapting the Global Organization

11

Changing Perspectives on Global Strategy and Organization

Traditionally, companies have evolved their international strategies based on leveraging their existing strengths globally through either centralized or decentralized structures. In today's competitive environment, however, this is no longer enough. As **Thomas Malnight** explains, firms need to develop fundamentally new approaches to structuring and managing worldwide operations, creating flexible, global networks where the emphasis is on value creation.

Overview

As earlier chapters discussed, there are various motivations for international growth. For example, in some industries competitive pressures *require* companies to grasp global opportunities at some or all stages of the value chain. In other industries, while global strategies are not such an essential requirement, they can nevertheless offer *rewards* to the expanding firm.

There are also distinctions to be made in terms of how companies approach new markets. One of the oldest motivations for foreign investment was to *seek natural resources*. Over time this has evolved into categories such as *market seekers*, where emphasis is put on factors such as market size and disposable income, *cost seekers*, who move abroad more for the ability to produce high-quality goods at low prices, and, most recently, *knowledge seekers*, where tapping into know-how becomes the prime motivation.

What this chapter sets out to do is to take this perspective to the level of the firm and its organization, addressing how individual firms build strategies to enhance their competitive advantage, and the organizational challenges of effectively building and leveraging global networks of operations. It will discuss how being global offers an expanding array of opportunities for enhancing firm competitive advantage based on leveraging these global networks of operations.

Background

In a study of the evolution of modern global competition, Alfred Chandler, the renowned business historian, highlighted the emergence of firms operating across national borders resulting from the development of mass transportation, communication and production technologies beginning in the 1850s and 1860s. As a result, the early development of firms with international operations concentrated in industries with high volume production or distribution processes, a situation that remained even through the early 1970s. As late as 1973, 65% of the largest industrial corporations in the world were concentrated in a few industrial sectors – food, chemicals, oil, machinery and primary metals.

However, there have been dramatic changes in the form and focus of international trade and competition since the 1970s, driven by the new technologies – including communication and information, and product-specific production technologies – as well as the transfer of managerial methods across borders as sources of firm advantage. The number of industries affected today by the potential for global strategies has expanded dramatically, as has the mix of strategic opportunities for firms operating globally. As a result, the need for companies to have global strategies has become an accepted wisdom in most industries, with management at more and more firms having to address the impact on their company's competitive advantage of how and where they operate globally.

This acceptance has brought recognition of both the opportunities and the challenges of operating globally, not only for firms with established networks of worldwide operations but also for small-to-medium-sized companies. The complexity of these opportunities reflects the fact that there is no single ideal approach for operating globally. Companies like ABB, Intel, McDonald's, Yahoo! or Gillette are global in different ways, and the opportunities and challenges for each firm to benefit from being global clearly need to be analysed within the context of their environment. Intel has an integrated worldwide organization to develop, produce and sell highly innovative components around the world. What would not work for Intel is the McDonald's model of providing a worldwide formula for franchising locally.

On its part, the ABB approach of occupying over 5000 "local" markets is the antithesis of a company like Gillette, which is based on selling almost identical products globally. Yahoo! typifies how the Web has enabled even very young companies to exploit global expansion from a very early stage by developing a global brand with local content, by leveraging the company's common technology platform. In all of these companies, the issue is not a question of *if* they need to be global or not, but rather how operating globally can enhance their competitive advantage and how they can structure and manage their operations to capture these potential advantages.

CASE STUDY: YAHOO!: GOING GLOBAL AND ACTING LOCAL

Yahoo! is a global internet communications, commerce and media company offering a branded network of services to more than 166 million individuals each month all over the world. Having begun as an free online navigational guide in 1995, when two Stanford University doctoral students decided to turn what was a hobby into a business, Yahoo! has served as a prominent example of how a young brand can exploit the global reach offered by the internet and rapidly emerge into a multinational player by bypassing the slower, step-by-step approach to internationalization which has characterized global expansion in the past. Whatever happens to the brand, its growth is still instructive.

According to a research report on Yahoo! by Lehman Brothers (29 June, 2000) the portal is one of the few companies that has lived up to what it calls the mythical "internet business model" or a virtual business with highly scaleable revenue streams, a large amount of operating revenue, strong profits and a cash flow. Revenues in 2000 were $1.1 billion, up 88% from 1999. Its growth is mainly the result of online advertising from both online and offline companies; it continues an aggressive programme of investing in new services and initiatives, including the business-to-business area, focused brand-building and accelerated entry into new markets.

It is its global capabilities which have been one of its greatest strengths. Yahoo!'s strategy has been international in outlook from the early days of its founding. That strategy has combined exploiting a consistent brand identity with a common design and services, and establishing local offices to create local content. It had already set up satellites in Canada and Japan within a year of its emergence, and by September 1996 it made its first foray into Europe with the launch of a localized version in the UK, quickly followed by sites for France and Germany. Yahoo! has an audience of more than 30 million in Europe, including 9–10 million in the UK.

Although it is such a stalwart member of the new dot.com fraternity, Yahoo!'s approach to global expansion is in some ways not that different from its bricks and mortar counterparts. For example, its entry into markets has often been done in alliances with partners: it launched in Europe with Ziff-Davis, a leading publisher of computer magazines and online computing content. It also faces local regulations and restrictions: in France its ability to conduct online auctions was delayed because of complex legal issues, while the slowness of many countries to come to terms with online shopping puts a brake on revenues.

Nevertheless, exploiting its first-mover advantage, it is now in first or second place in all the main markets around the world, including Europe, Canada, Korea and Japan. Having built up strong audience figures by acting as a free-to-users content aggregator and thus generating substantial online advertising, Yahoo!, like other portals, has embarked on a number of strategic initiatives to find more sustainable revenue streams from more value-added activities such as e-commerce, and differentiate itself from its competitors both in the old and new economy. The challenge will be to maintain its momentum as the market matures and big companies in sectors like telecommunications get to grips with their internet strategies.

Yahoo!'s management have outlined five key initiatives in order to capitalize on the next wave of internet growth:

- *Leverage further the e-commerce opportunities throughout its network.*
- *Extend the depth and breadth of services on its international properties and monetize its global reach.*
- *Integrate more broadband content into its sites.*
- *Make Yahoo! services ubiquitous across platforms and devices.*
- *Develop additional services for small and mid-sized businesses.*

Yahoo!'s vision is to be the world's portal, so it aims at providing a similar home page to internet users across the world. This determination to build a global brand is tailored to the local language, culture and legislative framework, however. In France, for example, the management style is modelled as much as possible on that of its Silicon Valley parent, but adapted to the French work culture as well as legislation. And while what the French users see almost exactly what their American counterparts see, the content is very much geared to a French audience.

Table 11.1: *Yahoo! – global expansion at blistering pace*

Country	Launched	Country	Launched
Yahoo! UK and Ireland	4Q96	Yahoo! Asia	4Q97
Yahoo! France	4Q96	Yahoo! EN	4Q97
Yahoo! Germany	4Q96	Yahoo! Italy	2Q98
Yahoo! Japan	4Q96	Yahoo! Spain	4Q98
Yahoo! Canada	4Q96	Yahoo! Taiwan	1Q99
Yahoo! Australia (incl. NZ)	2Q97	Yahoo! Singapore	1Q99
Yahoo! Korea	3Q97	Yahoo! Hong Kong	1Q99
Yahoo! Sweden	4Q97	Yahoo! Brazil	3Q99
Yahoo! Norway	4Q97	Yahoo! China	3Q99
Yahoo! Denmark	4Q97	Yahoo! Mexico	4Q99
		Yahoo! Argentina	1Q00
		Yahoo! India	2Q00

Source: Lehman Brothers (2000).

Traditional approaches to global strategy: value-leveraging strategies and organizations

Initially many companies expand around the world for two major reasons, both of which focus on primarily *leveraging* existing company strengths. These two inter-related reasons are:

- reducing costs through increasing volume or accessing low-cost labour or other resources; and/or
- expanding sales of existing products or know-how.

Underpinning these motivations is a belief that the centre, the headquarters and home market operations are the primary source of a company's "value" creation. Company advantage focuses on the strength of the domestic operations and the ability to manage the transfer of products and know-how across national markets (Figure 11.1). Managing the transfer of products involves developing the capacity to sell and distribute products, with these products often produced by home market operations. Managing the transfer of know-how involves developing the capacity to set up local operations that can mimic or duplicate domestic operations, thus leveraging such know-how within multiple local markets.

At this stage of expansion, the definition of a company being "global" is often meas-ured based on the percentage of its sales outside its home market and the number of countries in which it operates. In both cases, the higher these numbers the more "global" a firm is considered. Thus a firm having 60% of its sales outside its home

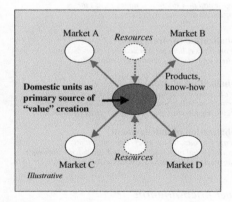

Strategic motivation
Companies operate globally to reduce costs or expand sales of existing products or services

Company advantage
Based on strength of domestic operations and ability to manage the transfer of products and know-how

Definition of "global"
Typically based on:
- the percentage of sales outside a company's home market, and
- the number of countries in which a company operates

Outcome
The need to be "global" leads companies to built extensive worldwide networks of operations

Figure 11.1: *Value-leveraging strategies*
Source: Adapted from Bartlett and Ghoshal (1989).

market and with operations in 80 countries is more "global" than one having only 30% of its sales outside its home market and operations in only 20 countries. An important result of these "global" expansion strategies is the building of extensive worldwide networks of operations.

WHAT IS GLOBALIZATION?

One of the most frequently used, and often abused, terms describing business challenges today is globalization. The world is globalizing!! Firms are globalizing!! Managers need to globalize!! The challenges associated with globalization are very real, but it is important for managers to understand and consider more carefully what is meant by the term globalization and how it affects the way they operate. Although much has been written about globalization, no clear definition has emerged, and, as a result, significant confusion exists about the topic.

Globalization is not a single, monolithic trend but occurs at multiple levels (Figure 11.2). At the macro level, globalization of industries involves how the external and competitive environment facing firms is changing and how these changes impact the competitive requirements, opportunities and challenges facing firms. As a result of industry trends, emerging competitive requirements are changing to include a growing emphasis on speed and flexibility, an expanded focus on learning and innovation, and the ability to draw and integrate information from multiple sources to create organizational knowledge. In many cases the requirements are a direct result of changes in the competitive environment.

Figure 11.2: *Globalization: A multi-level phenomenon*

Globalization of strategies concerns how firms are enhancing their competitive advantage based on where and how they operate globally, and the specific strategic objectives and positioning firms can develop to meet the requirements arising from changes in their industry.

Globalization of firms is about the organizational model itself. What operational models will allow firms to structure and manage their worldwide operations in line with their changing strategies? There has been much discussion on the need to move toward global models shifting from a traditional vertical, hierarchical structure to a growing horizontal orientation across dispersed and interdependent worldwide operations. Frequently these new models fundamentally alter how managers structure, control and integrate their worldwide operations.

Globalization of management centres on how the roles of executives are changing within integrated global organizations. What are the major management challenges facing senior executives?

Why is this integrated perspective important? Because it helps move beyond broad generalizations to address the specific challenges facing an individual firm. For example, when asking what types of managers a firm needs to run its overseas operations, there is not a single correct answer. It depends on the type of organization it is trying to create, which subsequently depends on its strategy. When asking what type of organizational model is appropriate, it depends on a firm's strategy and its specific competitive environment. When asking what is an appropriate global strategy for a firm, it depends on a combination of the specific competitive requirements in its environment, as well as an assessment of its own resources and know-how.

Factors influencing structural decisions

There are three factors influencing how firms in this value-leveraging stage of global expansion structure and manage their worldwide operations.

- First, the selection of a structure is influenced by firm-specific *evolution*, or the extent and nature of a firm's worldwide operations.
- Structures are also influenced by the characteristics of the worldwide competitive *environment*, including the extent of similarities and barriers across markets.
- Finally structures are influenced by *administrative* factors, including a firm's national origin or the mindset of its senior management.

In terms of the firm-specific evolution, a 1970s study by John Stopford and Lew Wells (Stopford and Wells, 1972), on structures as firms expanded internationally, observed an initial introduction of an international division, then a move to either a global product or geographic based (e.g., Europe, Asia, etc.) structure, then a move to a matrix or grid-type structure (Figure 11.3). In the initial stages of expansion, international divisions are often used to manage and control small and relatively simple "foreign" operations, minimizing the disruption to other busy units. These international divisions have the dual advantages of concentrating expertise on operating within "foreign" markets within one unit, as well as freeing other management to concentrate on their primary domestic market operations.

As international business grows in either importance (percentage of a company's sales) or complexity (e.g., number of businesses or markets), firms introduce new

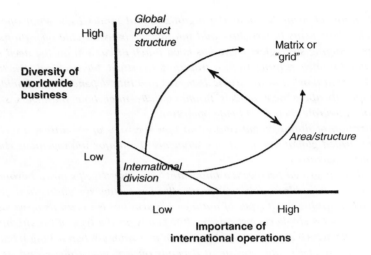

Figure 11.3: *Patterns of organizational evolution*

Adapted from Stopford and Wells (1972) with the permission of Perseus Books, from *Managing the Multinational Enterprise* by Stopford, John M. & Wells, L.T., Basic Books, New York.

structures. If business grows in importance, but remains largely concentrated within a few products or businesses, companies tend to introduce geographic or area-based structures. Area-based structures reflect a high degree of decentralization within regions and provide the management of each territory autonomy over its value-creation activities to adapt to local or regional conditions. If international business grows in importance and complexity, firms tend to introduce global product or functional structures, reflecting a high degree of centralized controls within globally focused units. These structures are based on the notion that each product division should have full authority to rationalize and coordinate its value creation activities, improve communication and resource transfers, and strategically respond to the competitors globally. If international operations grew in both importance and diversity, Stopford and Wells found that firms employed some type of matrix or grid structure.

A second factor influencing structural choices within value-leveraging strategies is the nature of the industry competitive environment. Prahalad and Doz (1987) characterized these environments based on two conflicting pressures, for both "global integration" and "local responsiveness". Some environments reflect relatively independent national markets, with primary pressures for local responsiveness. These environments typically have high barriers between and significant differences across markets, and competition occurs largely within each national market. Other environments reflect integrated world markets, with few and falling barriers between and growing similarity across national markets, with competition occurring across large continuous world markets. Strategies and organizations will vary dramatically across these environments. With high pressures for responsiveness and few for integration, firms tend to introduce decentralized, geographic-focused structures. When pressures for integration are high and there are perceived to be few benefits from local responsiveness, firm structures tend to reflect globally centralized product or functional structures (Figure 11.4).

"Global" environments	"Multidomestic" environments
◆ **Pressures for cost reduction** • scale, experience, low factor costs, etc.	◆ **Differences in customer needs**
◆ **Technology intensity** • increasing fixed asset investments, proprietary assets	◆ **Differences in product positioning, promotions, pricing, distribution, etc.**
◆ **Similarity in demand, multinational customers** • demand consistency in products, processes, support	◆ **Local availability of substitutes**
◆ **Multinational competitors** • gather intelligence, identify and respond to moves	◆ **Different market structures**
	◆ **Host government demands** • e.g., non-tariff barriers

CENTRALIZE: DECENTRALIZE:
INTEGRATE GLOBALLY!!!   BE LOCAL!!!

Figure 11.4: *Conflicting environmental pressures*

Adapted from Prahalad and Doz (1987) with the permission of The Free Press, a Division of Simon Schuster, Inc., from *The Multinational Mission: Balancing Local Demands and Global Vision* by C.K. Prahalad and Yves Doz. Copyright © 1987 by The Free Press.

The third set of factors involves firm choices, often influenced by management or cultural styles or preferences. For instance, US or Japanese multinationals have traditionally been more likely to employ structures with stronger centralized controls. On the other hand, European multinationals have been more likely to employ decentralized structures, with higher autonomy given to national affiliates. In terms of the mindset of senior management, Perlmutter (1969) distinguished between ethnocentric (i.e., home-country), polycentric (i.e., host-country), and geocentric (world) orientations, with a significant influence on resulting strategies and organizations.

Traditional value-leveraging structures

Overall these factors result in two primary approaches to structuring and managing worldwide operations within a value-leveraging global strategy. The first approach reflects a *centralized* globally focused organization, while the second reflects a *decentralized* (Figure 11.5) or geographic-focused organization. The strategic objectives and associated organizations of centralized and decentralized approaches vary dramatically. Centralized approaches focus on the benefits of global structures and are associated with environments emphasizing the benefits of global integration. Organizational characteristics of centralized structures include having strategic, value-creating resources and operations that reside in the home market with tight centralized formal controls over foreign operations. There are frequently separate domestic and international units, with a one-way flow of products, resources and ideas, and with the international units at both a strategic and geographic distance.

Competitive environment

- Primary pressures for global integration

Global strategy

- Primary focus on domestic operations with incremental, but opportunistic approach to expansion
- Foreign strategy to leverage domestic resources

Organization

- Separate domestic and international units
- Primary value-creating, strategic operations centralized in domestic market with dispersed supporting operations
- Strong centralized formal controls over international operations
- Key decision-making positions held by home-country executives, often with we/they (home country–foreigner) mindset
- One-way flow of products, technologies, staff, ideas from domestic to foreign operations

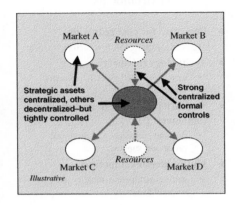

Figure 11.5: *Centralized strategy and organization*

Adapted from *Managing Across Borders: The Transnational Solution* by C. Bartlett & S. Ghoshal, 1989.

Competitive environment

- Country markets perceived as different and unique, with each market requiring local customization and expertise

Global strategy

- Foreign strategy to transfer know-how within national markets and value-creating activities to adapt and exploit this expertise within national markets
- Strategy to operate as portfolio of largely national focused affiliates

Organization

- Autonomous affiliates in each market
- Primary value-creating operations duplicated within major national markets
- Control systems focused on profitability, with measurement and rewards based on local results
- Key decision-making positions held by local executives
- Limited flows of products, technologies, staff, ideas from domestic to foreign operations

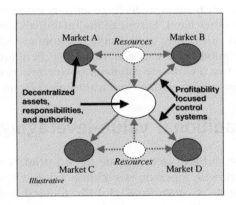

Figure 11.6: *Decentralized strategy and organization*

Adapted from *Managing Across Borders: The Transnational Solution* by C. Bartlett & S. Ghoshal, 1989.

The decentralized structure reflects the benefits of geographic-oriented structures and environments emphasizing the need for local responsiveness. Foreign markets are seen as different and unique, with a strategic focus on transferring know-how within national markets, and locally adapted to reflect differences across markets.

Organizational characteristics include operating as a portfolio of autonomous affiliates in major markets. Most value-creating operations are duplicated within national markets, which are monitored through financial controls focusing on affiliate profitability. There is a tendency to emphasize the use of local executives in decision-making positions within each market.

Advantages and disadvantages of traditional structures

Centralized and decentralized structures offer the management of firms operating within value-leveraging strategies numerous benefits, but also have important limitations as well. While centralization can be an effective structure to manage worldwide flows of standardized products, decentralization can be effective for managing flows of know-how to each national market, allocating largely autonomous operational management to local executives. Within both approaches, structuring decisions are typically made at the level of the firm and this consistency of structure across operations simplifies the management of worldwide operations, with clear roles and responsibilities across the organization. Global controls in centralized firms are managed through direct reporting relationships, while in decentralized organizations national affiliates are measured and controlled based on local profitability. Both structures also are associated with an alignment of responsibility and accountability. Finally each approach has a clear set of strategic benefits, with centralized structures focused on developing the advantages of global integration, and decentralized structures the benefits of local responsiveness. Both structures enable firms to build significant international sales and operations across world markets.

However, there are also important limitations for these structures. Both centralized and decentralized structures focus on making decisions on strategy and organization *at the level of the firm*, with this selection involving a balancing or trade-off among various opportunities. Both structures emphasize some motivations from operating globally, trading off against other potential benefits. As will be discussed later in this chapter, in many industries firms are now focused on simultaneously pursuing multiple strategic opportunities from operating globally, as opposed to selecting among potential benefits.

There are additional important limitations for both type of structures. Centralized structures emphasize home-country resources, personnel and market requirements, limiting a firm's willingness and capacity to access local personnel, resources, or know-how or respond to local market requirements. Innovations – or market requirements – outside the home market are frequently not given adequate weight in the company strategic decision-making process. Additionally, there is a clear limitation on the ability of a firm to develop and utilize operations outside the home market, with executives and operations frequently delegated to a supporting position.

On the other hand, decentralized structures have similar limitations. While offering important opportunities to strengthen positions within national markets, the organization results in duplication and fragmentation across markets. Duplicating operations across countries results in a high cost structure, limiting a firm's capacity to develop economies of scale in critical cost-focused operations. This fragmentation also limits a firm's ability to leverage expertise, innovations or resources across markets, with exchanges primarily being financial in nature. Finally the structure limits a firm's opportunity to develop advantages associated with flexibility from coordinating operations across markets.

Current debate on global operating structures

Thus, overall traditional structures for operating globally offer numerous benefits, but with severe constraints as well. The current debate on structuring decisions reflects this situation (Figure 11.7). Many firms, especially during the initial stage of building international operations, elect either the centralized or decentralized structures. While often effective during the value-leveraging stage of development, these single-minded approaches to structure often result in frequent reorganizations. Both structures focus on some strategic advantages at the cost of others, essentially focusing the organization on the primary challenges or opportunities a firm faces at any time. As the mix of these challenges and opportunities changes, many firms have been found to respond by undergoing frequent reorganizations, moving between product and geographic structures. Other firms respond to growing strategic complexity by

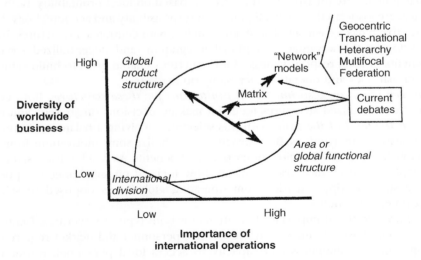

Figure 11.7: *Debate on patterns of organizational evolution, including the emergence of potential new organizational models*

Adapted from Stopford and Wells (1972) with the permission of Perseus Books, from *Managing the Multinational Enterprise* by Stopford, John M. & Wells, L.T., Basic Books, New York.

introducing a matrix structure. However, for many firms, matrices have been associated with bureaucratic conflict and power struggles.

A further option under development at many firms involves the introduction of fundamental new approaches to structuring and managing worldwide operations. These emerging structures are associated with leveraging the advantages of a firm's network of operations, and are often associated with new strategic challenges and opportunities from operating globally that will be described in the section on value-creating global strategies.

Emerging challenges and opportunities in operating globally: value-creating strategies and organizations

Today many firms – large and small – compete globally with established networks of worldwide operations. These networks include both operations owned and operated by the firm, as well as strategic alliances and other partner firms. The opportunities associated with operating an established network of operations extend beyond those reflected in value-leveraging strategies. But also so do the challenges (Figure 11.8). Today many firms globally perform a series of *functions* to produce multiple *products* with operations spanning multiple *geographic markets* and serving the needs of different *customer* types. There are strategic and organizational pressures and opportunities across each of these dimensions of a firm's operations: today, firms simultaneously face pressures to develop leading edge functional skills, to develop and manage expertise and operating scale within and across major product areas, to develop and leverage expertise within major geographic markets, and to develop the capacity to serve a wide range of customers. For many firms, the need to *simultaneously* pursue each of these objectives has become critical, directly impacting their strategies and structures for operating globally.

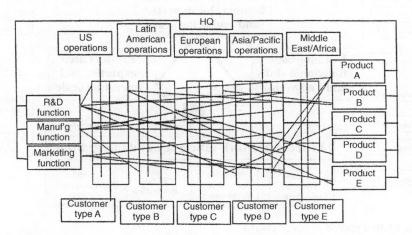

Figure 11.8: *Emerging strategic and organizational challenges*

In this increasingly complex global competitive environment, there is a fundamental transition taking place in the way companies of all sizes need to think about their strategies and organizations for operating globally. Moving beyond value-leveraging strategies and centralized or decentralized structures, firms are compelled to take new approaches to operating globally. This new approach involves shifting focus from not just *where* a firm operates and sell its products, but also *how* it structures and manages all of its worldwide operations to capture and create value across all activities. *The strategic pressures and opportunities for firms operating globally, both through their internal operations and through external partners, are accelerating over time.*

Building and managing process networks

In addressing strategies and structures for effectively competing globally today, companies have moved beyond looking for a single global strategy and structure for all their operations, and are rather focusing on discrete *processes* that cumulatively result in a firm developing, producing and supplying products to markets. Processes involve multiple operations that combine to perform a series of tasks or activities that create something of value (an "output"). Processes are distinguished to divide the overall industry value chain based on variations in the nature of work performed and objectives pursued.

A typical process flow (Figure 11.9) within many industries involves *creating, developing, making* and *selling* products or services. Each process can involve

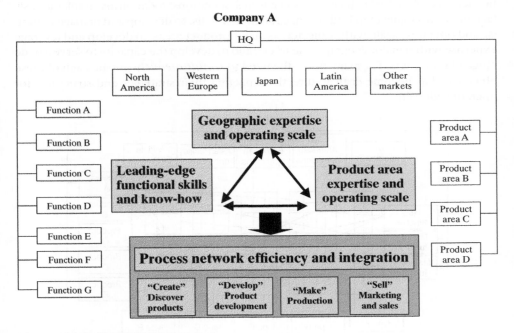

Figure 11.9: *Typical process chain*

either individual or multiple functions, can impact individual or multiple products, can impact multiple types of customers, and can involve individual or multiple geographic markets. Both vertically integrated and specialized firms typically perform processes. In the pharmaceutical industry, for example, the drug discovery process (creating new compounds) is performed not only by integrated pharmaceutical firms, but also by specialized (e.g., biotechnology) firms, research institutes, and universities. Overall, focusing on processes involves taking a managerial approach to global strategies and structures, by focusing on patterns of variations in objectives and tasks within and across firms in an industry. *Firm competitive advantage is based on building and integrating effective process strategies and structures.*

For building and managing effective process networks, firm management should ask three questions:

- *What* are our overall strategic objectives and how can we enhance these objectives based on operating globally?
- How can we enhance our overall competitive advantage based on *where* we should perform each operation, including how each process enhances our performance?
- How can we enhance our overall competitive advantage based on *how* we coordinate, integrate and manage both within and across processes to capture value?

Value-creating strategies: from strategic trade-offs to managing strategic tensions

As we have seen, one important limitation of traditional global strategies is that they involve trading off one set of strategic objectives for another. In the most basic sense, centralized strategies optimized value and efficiency in standardized products at the expense of local responsiveness and flexibility. Decentralized strategies focused primarily on local responsiveness and flexibility. As described earlier, there is an expanding array of potential strategic advantages associated with operating globally. The challenge facing management today is to focus simultaneously on multiple and often conflicting strategic objectives. For example, increasingly firms need to be efficient, flexible, responsive and innovative all at the same time.

Operating a global network of operations opens up a host of additional strategic opportunities for established multinationals. Some additional potential advantages include:

- serving the worldwide needs of customers;
- anticipating and responding to the movements of global competitors within and across national markets;
- locating facilities or sourcing materials from multiple locations, not only to lower costs but also to enhance their flexibility to respond to changes in foreign exchange rates or other market changes outside a firm's control;

- innovating new products or know-how based on their exposure to multiple national markets;
- gaining access to and exploiting specialized resources and skills from around the world;
- balancing revenue streams across markets that differ in their growth rates or risk profiles.

Reflecting these emerging opportunities, the strategic motivations for operating globally extend beyond leveraging existing products or know-how across national markets, to *value-creating* strategies building on the existence and management of a worldwide network of operations. *Value-creating strategies focus not only on enhancing the strength of each operations, which are increasingly dispersed globally, but also the ability to create and manage expanding flows and exchanges across these operations* (Figure 11.10). In other words, being global offers an expanding array of opportunities for enhancing firm's competitive advantage based on leveraging the global network of operations.

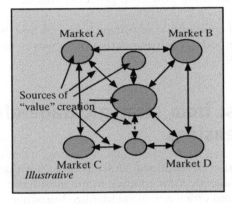

Strategic motivation
Companies operate to "systematically" develop and exploit global opportunities to enhance competitive advantage in each operation.

Company advantage
Based on strength of dispersed operations, as well as linkages between operations.

Definition of "global"
"Global" is defined in terms of enhancing firm competitive advantage based on:
- developing and accessing world-class resources and know-how for each operation
- integrating and leveraging the strengths of geographically dispersed operations

Outcome
The management of a global network provides the opportunity to simultaneously pursue multiple and conflicting strategies within and across a firm's operations.

Figure 11.10: *Value-creating global strategies*

In terms of moving beyond strategic trade-offs to pursuing multiple objectives simultaneously, the company needs to ask what its overall strategic challenges are both as a firm and for each process. What is happening in the environment? What are my objectives? What are the processes and challenges that I am facing across different parts of the business and what are the tensions that I am going to focus on? Then, once those tensions have been identified, the company can look at what kind of organizational structure is needed in terms of products, functions and geographies to make the most of each particular business stream, including the roles and responsibilities each part should play in pursuing these objectives.

Process networks focus on creating and capturing value based on advantages derived not just from the centre but from the strength of each dispersed operation and, importantly, the *linkages* between the process networks. As a result, these networks offer an effective potential mechanism for moving beyond single strategic objectives and the traditional approach of trading off some advantages against others. Within network approaches, different nodes or operations can focus on different and distinct potential strategic advantages offering the firm the potential to pursue multiple and often conflicting objectives simultaneously.

The emergence of a value-creating approach to operating means that traditional measures of the "globality" of firms may no longer be appropriate. Can we consider a company to be global if, although a large percentage of its sales are "international", the primary source of its value creation resides in a single home-market driven brand, with an assumption that as long as the world wants to consume this existing brand growth opportunities continue? Or are there fundamental opportunities for value creation that this firm is missing? Likewise, can we consider a firm to be "global" if, although it has operations only in one market and its sales are largely within this market, through linkages to other firms, with existing networks of worldwide operations, the firm captures the value associated with its focus of operations?

Within this perspective, an effective definition of "globality" has shifted away from the percentage of sales outside a home market or the number of countries in which a firm operates. *Increasingly an effective definition of "globality" involves how a firm enhances its overall competitive position, in all its value-creating activities, based on how it develops and accesses world-class resources and know-how for all its operations, as well as how it integrates and leverages the strengths of each of these operations within and across world markets.*

The limitations of traditional definitions of "globality" can be demonstrated by the recent comments of a senior executive of a leading US pharmaceutical company. This executive commented that the company was witnessing "reverse globalization" as sales and profit growth were increasingly driven by the company's home market. But what this executive had not considered was that the new products behind the company's success had been discovered using *worldwide* information and laboratories, had been rapidly developed and launched by using *worldwide* markets for rapid approval, and were produced in multiple worldwide locations to enhance tax and other cost considerations. So even though sales were accruing in the US, the company had enhanced its overall competitive advantage by operating around the world.

Strategic and organizational challenges in the pharmaceutical industry

The world market for pharmaceuticals, which totalled $303 billion in 1997, has long been considered attractive and highly profitable, with the average profit margin of the ten largest pharmaceutical companies being 30 per cent in 1997. Competing in this industry, integrated pharmaceutical companies discover, develop, manufacture and sell products. Discovery involves chemical, biological and pharmacological activities to identify and synthesize new compounds for the potential treatment of various diseases or medical conditions. The resulting "lead compounds" are tested to investigate efficacy, toxicity and potential side effects, and subsequently studied through a series of clinical trials as part of receiving regulatory approval. Data from all trials are included in a New Drug Application (NDA) that is submitted to regulatory officials. It has been estimated that for every 5000 to 10 000 compounds initially evaluated in laboratories one product is approved.

A series of new technologies have been fundamentally altering the drug discovery and development process, suggesting the potential for continued growth of the industry. These technologies include genomics (study of the way that genes interact to impact human development, health and sickness), combinatorial chemistry (combining known molecular building blocks to quickly create gigantic libraries of compounds for screening), high-throughput screening (robotic techniques for testing drug candidates against biological targets) and bio-informatics (using computers to collect and store huge volumes of data generated by biomedical research). These advances are expected to lead to an increasing flow of new product candidates, with one industry expert in the late 1990s commenting, "More drugs will be discovered in the next 10 years than have been discovered in the last 100 years."

Industry challenges

At the same time, a number of trends are challenging the traditional structure and profitability of the industry. These pressures are associated with rising R&D costs, lengthening development and approval times for new products, growing competition from generics and follow-on products, and rising cost containment pressures. Pharmaceutical companies spend about 20% of sales on R&D, and the cost of developing new products has skyrocketed. A 1992 study by the US Office of Technology Assessment estimated the pretax cost of a single new drug at $359 million, compared with $231 million in the late 1980s and $125 million in the early 1980s. Subsequent studies have estimated these development costs for a new drug at between $350 and $500 million.

Simultaneous with escalating costs has been a lengthening of the time required for development and regulatory approval. New regulations have increased the average time for obtaining regulatory approval in the United States to 8 to 10 years. Given the fixed patent life for products[1], these increases have had a direct impact on a product's effective patent life, the period in which the patent holder has enjoyed market exclusivity.

Once new products are launched, further pressures result from the growth of so-called "follow-on" products and generics. Follow-on products result from the incredibly rapid exchanges of information and the increasing focus of pharmaceutical

---

1. US manufacturers typically file a patent application when submitting an Investigational New Drug (IND) application, protecting themselves for 17 years from the date the patent was actually issued.

research on common therapeutic indications and disease pathways. Following the expiration of a product patent, pressures result from the rapid entry of generic products. According to industry sources, it is not unusual for sales of a drug to drop by more than 50 per cent in the first year after patent expiration as a result of generic competition, and they continue to decline rapidly thereafter.

Finally, health-care expenditures represent a large and growing portion of the gross domestic product (GDP) of most major markets, resulting in growing cost containment efforts in most world markets. Examples of cost-control mechanisms have included reference pricing (establishing a fixed reimbursement based on therapeutic equivalence) and establishing budgets for individual physicians. In the United States, managed-care organizations and government national insurance programs (e.g., Medicare) increasingly emphasize total cost management.

Cumulatively these trends pressure pharmaceutical firms to innovate in developing a continual flow of new products, to speed the development and launch of new products, to improve the cost efficiency of all operations, and to be aggressive in selling products to major world markets. These challenges and opportunities directly affected how pharmaceutical firms operate globally.

Process-level global strategies and organizations

This section examines the global strategic and organizational challenges facing pharmaceutical companies, focusing on the processes of discovering new compounds, developing and launching these products, and marketing and selling these products within world markets. (The processes associated with producing and supplying the products are not addressed.) Each of these processes involves multiple functional-, geographic-, and product-focused units.

The challenges facing pharmaceutical companies in *discovering new products* have reflected the need to ensure a continual flow of innovative new potential products (Figure 11.11). Operating globally has offered a number of potential opportunities to enhance these processes. Generally there are three different types of units involved in the discovery process: therapeutic area units responsible for overall innovation within a product area, functional units that provide common technologies and supporting tools to all research efforts, and research laboratories that may perform research activities for multiple therapeutic areas. Companies enhance their potential for innovation by accessing the best scientists, irrespective of national origin or geographic location, to oversee research efforts in each therapeutic area in which it operates. At the same time, research is conducted in pharmaceutical and biotechnology companies, universities and research laboratories around the world. In order to enhance innovation, companies need to access leading-edge knowledge and expertise, not just that located in their home country. Finally given the rising investment costs in supporting technologies and research tools, companies need to develop and leverage growing investments in these tools.

The overall challenges facing pharmaceutical companies in the *development process*, associated with obtaining regulatory approval for new products, involve increasing the speed of securing regulatory approval and launching new products in

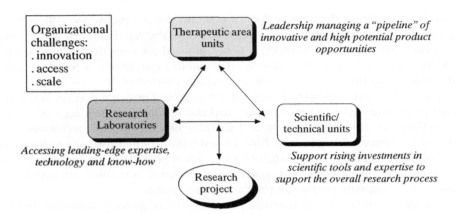

Figure 11.11: *Discovery process strategic challenges: Ensuring a continual flow of innovative new potential compounds*

the world market (Figure 11.12). According to one industry estimate, each year that the development time of an average product can be shortened results in an additional cash flow of $150 million. For "blockbuster" products, these gains in incremental cash flow could be substantially higher, reflecting both incremental patent-protected sales revenue and opportunities associated with beating competitive products to market.

Global opportunities for speeding the development and launch include accessing a larger number of clinical trial patients and leveraging regulatory variations across markets. For example, in some markets there are regulatory waiting periods for conducting some tests that can delay the development process by one or more months. Operating globally can allow a company to continue working on development testing, without compromising quality standards or procedures, by globally allocating these testing requirements. Similarly it is possible to more quickly access a large number of patients working across world markets, as opposed to duplicating the trials within each market or within a single market. Securing these benefits requires the standardization of testing procedures and standards, at the most stringent levels, to share the resulting data across markets.

Organizationally there are four types of units active in the development process. Functional and testing units (toxicology, etc.) establish and manage global development standards and procedures for all trials, as well as providing technical expertise to product teams, and performing testing and supporting services as required for the development of individual compounds. Therapeutic area units manage the overall development portfolio of the products under development in any area. Product-focused (cross-functional) teams are responsible for planning and executing the rapid global development and launch of new products across world markets. National affiliates are responsible for securing, as requested by the product teams, clinical trial patients for different products under development, as well as working with local regulatory officials to secure national approvals.

The process of *marketing and selling* pharmaceutical products globally also faces conflicting global strategic pressures and opportunities (Figure 11.13). On the

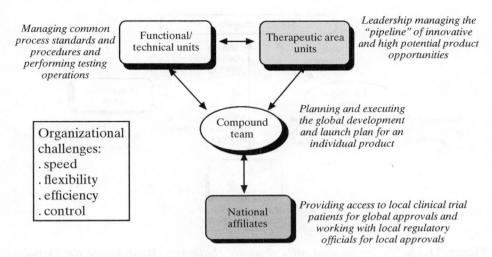

Figure 11.12: *Development process challenges: Speeding the testing, regulatory approval and global launch of new products*

one hand, pharmaceutical companies face pressures to maximize the returns on new products within a fixed, but shortened product patent-protected marketing periods. On the other hand, companies face pressure to maximize the returns on their portfolio of products within national markets that can vary significantly in local market characteristics (e.g., medical care systems, etc.). Maximizing global product returns and national product portfolio returns is a classic challenge facing companies in many industries.

Organizationally there are several types of units involved in responding to these challenges. Senior management is responsible for ensuring the overall returns across products that vary in their life cycle and the potential across markets that vary in their characteristics. Product units focus on maximizing the returns on individual products (even though they do not "own" the ultimate sales forces within the national affiliates), while national affiliates focus on maximizing the national returns on the company's total portfolio of products (even though they do not have critical expertise on individual products). Functional units play a critical role in developing the supporting interface systems for managing these interfaces. These include, for example, product strategy systems that support management in the evaluation of potential across products, as well as national market strategy systems that support the evaluation of differences in market opportunities in markets that vary in their characteristics.

These strategic challenges facing pharmaceutical companies vary dramatically across processes, and operating globally has a major impact on a company's ability to develop advantage in each process. Organizationally, however, the challenges involve developing multiple types of process networks within the firm, with each integrating the roles and contributions of multiple types of units and pursuing a mix of strategic objectives. Although the strategic and organizational challenges are severe, a

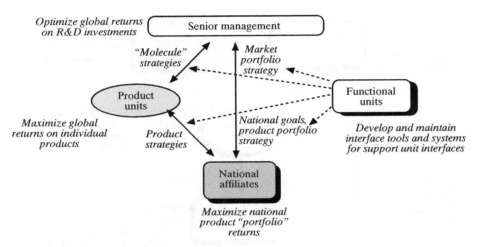

Figure 11.13: *Marketing and sales strategic challenges: Maximizing the global returns on new products and the local returns on the product portfolio*

company's ability to understand and respond to them will directly impact a firm's competitiveness. There is often a well known and common understanding across firms in terms of the challenges – often the issue is being able to effectively build, and establish and manage the organization.

Network structures: building efficient and effective process networks

Since the 1980s, many consultants and academics have developed a number of organizational models, accompanied by futuristic sounding names: heterarchy, transnational, multifocal, horizontal and federation, to name but a few. Most of these models have a few characteristics in common, suggesting approaches for managers to disperse their operations globally and manage expanding horizontal flows and exchanges of products, people, information and other resources. These models all build on the notion of the firm becoming a global network.

Overall the network approach calls on managers to look beyond transferring their traditional home-based products and know-how to worldwide markets. Instead, companies need to look to how they can enhance their ability to respond to growing competitive pressures by tapping into opportunities associated with value-creating global strategies, and then install organizations that optimize both their dispersed operations *and* the linkages between them. Structurally network challenges encompass two primary issues: *optimizing each operation for each task or activity and then managing and optimizing linkages between these operations.*

In terms of optimizing the performance of each unit within a firm's network of operations, process network structures dramatically increase the ability of managers to allocate flexibly roles and responsibilities globally. Some operations can be centralized at a single location, potentially at locations designed to enhance the performance of such operation. Other operations can be distributed across multiple locations, allowing managers to source flexibly from across these operations to respond to market changes outside its control (e.g., changes in foreign exchange rates). Other operations can be decentralized to serve the needs of local national markets.

These network configuration decisions involve a series of decisions by managers on how to structure the nodes of the network. These network configuration decisions include the following:

- location of worldwide facilities;
- roles of worldwide facilities;
- nature and extent of exchanges among worldwide facilities.

Subsequently the management of process networks often appears to be moving toward a loosely coupled organization that can be likened to a form of controlled anarchy. It can appear that each part of an organization in and of itself is strong but the linkages between them are also stronger across markets than they would be in more traditional models. An important shift has occurred in the notion of linkages between worldwide operations, moving from management and control toward alignment and integration, where the focus is on enhancing potential advantages of the entire network, as opposed to those of individual operations.

At the same time, increasingly, managers are recognizing a wide range of organizational variables that can be used to *align and integrate* worldwide operations, including the following:

- human resources, staff;
- reporting channels;
- decision authority allocation;
- management control systems;
- operating standards and procedures;
- planning and information systems;
- measurement and evaluation systems;
- corporate culture;
- informal communications and linkages.

Combinations of these organizational variables offer managers a wide range of structural alternatives. For example, for many processes, companies are centralizing operating standards and procedures (around best practices) and planning systems (to align and allocate activities globally), but employing dispersed operations with extensive decentralization of decision authority without defined boundaries. Is this centralized or decentralized? Other processes can be managed globally through decentralized operations, planning and decision making, but with a strong centralized culture and tight communication. Again, is this centralized or decentralized? Managers today have a wide array of structural alternatives – between traditional centralized and decentralized structural approaches – to integrate and align worldwide operations.

DETERMINING YOUR MIX OF STRATEGIC MOTIVATIONS FOR OPERATING GLOBALLY

As has been highlighted throughout this chapter, there is a wide and growing range of strategic opportunities for firms operating globally. Given the relationship between the strategic motivations for operating globally and the organizational challenges of doing so, it is important for executives to develop a clear understanding of their motivations and opportunities for operating globally across the different parts of their operations. To help determine the nature of opportunities facing your firm, the following list of opportunities can be used to understand the nature of the current potential global strategy, and thus the nature of your subsequent organizational challenges. In considering these opportunities, it is useful to consider these motivations at multiple levels, first at the level of the firm as a whole and then across your different functions, markets, and products or services.

Rank each motivation on a scale of 1 (low) to 5 (high)

Motivations for operating globally	Rank
Reducing costs	
• Reduce costs through increasing volume	___
• Reduce costs through accessing low-cost labour	___
• Access commodities or other standard inputs	___
• Minimize logistics costs	___
Expanding sales	
• Access new markets for existing products	___
• Meet unique local market requirements and build strong local relations	___
• Build presence in established and emerging markets	___
Average value-leveraging objectives	___
Enhancing operations, accessing specialized resources	
• Access skilled labour resources or professional staff	___
• Access unique or specialized technologies	___
• Access other unique specialized resources or inputs	___
Leveraging a global network	
• Enabling flexibility to shift operations (e.g., production) among dispersed facilities	___
• Innovate products or processes by operating across multiple markets	___
• Speed development and launch of new products	___

- *Serving the worldwide needs of customers* _____
- *Optimizing regulatory variations across markets* _____
- *Enhancing the ability to anticipate and respond to global competitors* _____

Average value-creating objectives _____

The more your motivations for operating globally across your operations (at the level of the firm, functions, markets and product) are associated with value-leveraging objectives, the more your organizational choices should likely be between the traditional centralized or decentralized structures. However, if your motivations are increasingly associated with value-creating objectives, the more the nature of your organizational challenges should involve introducing and managing global network-type structures.

Emerging management challenges: building and integrating process networks

Within individual firms today, there are multiple types of networks emerging that can directly enhance firm's competitive advantage. Some of these networks focus on accessing and leveraging knowledge and information, others on building and leveraging common data and information, and others on leveraging common facilities globally. Table 11.1 provides examples of the overall characteristics of these various types of networks.

Overall, management challenges today involve building and managing effective process networks, as well as sharing resources and integrating across process networks. In the pharmaceutical industry, firm competitive advantage is based on firms developing effective process networks to discover new compounds, develop and launch new products and produce, market and sell these products in worldwide markets. There is extensive sharing of resources across each of these processes, and management of each process is dependent on the inputs (requirements) and outputs of other processes.

Table 11.1: *Structural characteristics of a sample network-based multinational*

	Knowledge-sharing networks	Data-sharing networks	Facility-sharing networks
Global dispersion of operations: responsibility and location	Global product structure Dispersed global product-area responsibility for process output Dispersed and specialized operational facilities	Global process structure Dispersed global product-specific responsibility for process output Dispersed and duplicated operations for undertaking common activities within markets	Global functional structure Single unit with global process responsibility for all operations Dispersed and specialized facilities with global-product type responsibility
Cross-unit interdependence: exchanges and flows	Exchanges of know-how and expertise Global sharing of technology "tools" across units Operations coordinated within overall corporate strategy	Exchanges of data and know-how for individual products Operations aligned through common operating standards and procedures to ensure global process consistency	Primary flows of intermediate products to global markets Operational planning integrated through technical and operating standards focused on worldwide requirements
Structural flexibility: structures and linkages	Primary operational and budget flexibility within global product-area units Focus on identifying and sharing innovations arising globally and across centres Internal "contracting" system for cost transfers	Primary operational and budget flexibility within product-specific teams Focus on identifying and sharing of information and expertise for individual compounds Internal "contracting" system for cost transfers	Primary flexibility within global functional unit Sharing of best practices for common tasks across facilities Internal "contracting" through transfer price systems

SUMMARY

This chapter has addressed the movement from value-leveraging toward value-creating global strategies, and the associated movement from traditional centralized or decentralized structures toward network-type structures. More and more firms have to build an effective global network that will be able to deal with and manage the multiple and conflicting objectives of being efficient, flexible, innovative and responsive – *at the same time* – and be global, regional and local – *at the same time*. It will be based on answering questions such as:

- What is the objective of each process network across our overall value-creating activities?
- What tensions is it trying to manage?
- What different units need to be involved, both internally and externally?
- What kind of organization are we trying to create?
- What are the roles and responsibilities across the different units?
- What kind of mechanisms can we develop for both formal and informal linkages?
- How can I do this quickly?

Building and optimizing these process networks obviously require moving beyond incremental change to fundamental strategic and organizational design. Firms do not have the luxury of evolving this structure over a period of years; they need to move toward an optimum position for value creation as quickly as possible.

Networks are not for every company and they can also be organizationally costly to set up and run. So if you are simple, stay simple. But if your firm faces increasing external pressures along functional, product and geographic positions, has growing needs to share resources across businesses, and has pressures to improve flexibility and response time to market opportunities, then installing and managing a network-type approach are critical to a firm's overall competitive strategy, not just its global one.

 LEARNING POINTS

- Traditional strategies for international expansion are no longer effective in an environment of increasing complexity and speed.
- Firms now have to look beyond a single global strategy and structure, whether centralized or decentralized, to create new sources of value.

- In this process-based approach, firms should determine how to enhance their strategic objectives in terms of *where* they perform each operation and *how* they coordinate, integrate and manage both within and across processes to capture value.
- Network structures offer value-creating opportunities based not just on the centre and the strength of the dispersed operations, but on the linkages between them.
- This begins to shift the way firms oversee dispersed operations, from management and control towards alignment and integration, to enhance the potential advantages of the entire network.
- The challenge is to focus on multiple and often conflicting strategic objectives in the search for efficiency, flexibility, responsiveness and innovation – at the same time.

References

Bartlett, C.A. and Ghoshal, S. (1989) *Managing Across Borders: The Transnational Solution*, Harvard Business School Press, Boston.

Perlmutter, H.V. (1969) The Tortuous Evolution of the Multinational Corporation. *Columbia Journal of World Business*, January–February, pp. 9–18.

Prahalad, C.K. and Doz, Y. (1987) *The Multinational Mission: Balancing Local Demands and Global Vision*, The Free Press, New York.

Stopford, J.M. and Wells, L.T. (1972) *Managing the Multinational Enterprise*, Basic Books, New York.

12

Managing Subsidiary Evolution

The role of national affiliates in international firms is changing substantially. Rather than being outposts for the centre or independent fiefdoms, they now have to be actively involved in creating value for the whole firm. **Thomas Malnight** describes the challenges facing firms in developing effective national market strategies that reflect local potential globally and global potential locally.

Overview

As firms develop international growth strategies, a key question to address is the changing role of the national affiliates and country managers. National affiliates represent the nodes of a firm's global network of operations and their roles in and contributions to this network are instrumental to the capability of the entire network. As a result, an important challenge in accelerating the process of building an effective global strategy and organization – for both established and emerging multinationals – is understanding the changing roles and contributions of national affiliates.

As Chapter 11 emphasized, the role of national affiliates within *value-leveraging* global strategies is relatively clear and focuses on leveraging a company's home-country products or know-how within their local market. For the centralized multinationals this role focuses on selling and delivering products to the local market, while for the decentralized firms this role focuses on importing know-how within a market and building a relatively autonomous operation to exploit this know-how within their local market.

As companies introduce value-creating strategies, their management is increasingly charged with identifying where important resources and activities across all their processes and operations should be located, and how best to incorporate these dispersed resources into the global framework. Value-creating global strategies are dependent on a firm's ability to build, align and integrate globally dispersed operations.

The issue of the roles and contributions of national affiliates is directly related to the question of how "global strategies" affect "local autonomy", or in other words, whether national affiliates exist within truly global operations. What is the role of national affiliates in global strategies and how is this role changing? In addition, how can both established and emerging multinationals reorganize the way national affiliates operate to speed up the process of becoming global?

This chapter addresses these issues. First the chapter explores how firms are developing national market strategies within global firms, responding to the challenges of competing across diverse world markets. Then the chapter discusses the strategic and organizational challenges of building an effective global network of national affiliates.

National affiliate strategies in global firms

Despite the importance of national affiliates to a firm's global operations, there are conflicting perspectives on understanding how to manage local strategies in global firms. National affiliates provide a critical access to local customers, competing in markets that vary dramatically in characteristics. National affiliates provide access to critical local resources, which impact not only a firm's local but also its global operations.

Within this context, an important issue for managers is to understand the wide variety of strategies for national affiliates within a firm's global operations. There is not one common single strategy for all national affiliates, nor do all markets require unique strategies and approaches. An important challenge facing managers of global firms today is to develop effective national market strategies that reflect both *local potential globally* and *global potential locally*.

Citibank, as part of its Customer Focused Management Process (CFMP), developed a model of national markets strategies (Table 12.1). This was based on important financial services market characteristics that varied, according to the stage of economic development. As national markets evolved from "minimum potential" through "emerging growth" to "rapidly developing" to "newly industrialized" to "Organization for Economic Cooperation and Development" markets, the financial market environment, local market needs, local customer base and competitors, and products and their prices systematically varied. As opposed to developing national market strategies based on geographic proximity, this model allowed Citibank to segment its national market strategies based on market characteristics that drove its national potential.

A different market segmentation approach was taken by Coors Brewery, a traditionally family-owned US beer company. In its segmentation model, presented in Figure 12.1, the company's national market strategies – and thus its investment positions – were influenced by two factors. The first factor was the stage of beer market development, while the second was the market growth potential. The model resulted in markets being categorized into one of four strategies:

Figure 12.1: *Coors segmentation of world beer markets*

- Develop and maintain a stronghold position
- Great opportunity to invest, but carefully
- Long-term focus
- Leave for grandkids

In the pharmaceutical industry, Eli Lilly and Company developed another approach for establishing strategies across national markets. This model, presented in

Table 12.1: *Citibank national market segmentation model*

	Stage 1 Minimum Potential	Stage 2 Emerging Growth	Stage 3 Rapidly Developing	Stage 4 Newly Industrialized	Stage 5 OECD
Financial market environment	Limited capital and trade flows / Unconvertible currency / Unpredictable regulations	Limited access to world capital markets / Restricted currency convertibility / Unpredictable regulations	Growing access to world capital markets / Few currency restrictions / Established, growing financial markets	Full access to world capital markets / Generally stable regulations / Well developed capital markets	Complete access to world capital markets / Globally competitive regulatory environment / Fully developed local financial markets
Citibank customer base	Public sector / Financial institutions / World corporate group	Public sector / Financial institutions / World corporate group / Large local corporations	Public sector / Financial institutions / World corporate group / Local corporate / Investors	Financial institutions / World corporate group / Local corporate / Investors	Financial institutions / World corporate group / Local corporate / Investors
Local customer needs	Transaction banking / Local lending	Full-range commercial banking products	Significant investment banking products / Some disintermediation / Funds management	Commercial banking commoditizes / Full-range investment bank / Widespread disintermediation	Full disintermediation / Tax / Advisory
Local competition	Weak, unsophisticated	Emerging, Strong local lending and transaction services	Very strong / High volumes / Local funding strengths	Global, regional competitors emerge	World class
International competition	Generally not interested	Growing targeted interest	Strong focused niche in market	Established cross-border business	Cross-border businesses
Prices and fees	Very favourable	Favourable, but tightening	Competitive / Customer unbundling begins	Fully competitive / Full unbundling	Fully competitive

Source: Citibank Customer Focused Management Process (CFMP).

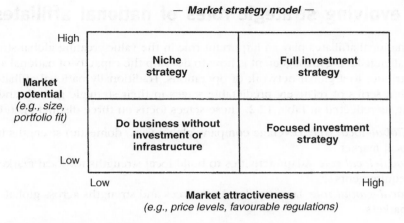

Figure 12.2: *Eli Lilly's national market strategy model*

Figure 12.2, again balanced two factors that directly impacted its profitability and potential across a wide variety of national markets. These factors include market potential (e.g., size, portfolio fit) and market attractiveness (e.g., price levels, favourable regulations). In large attractive markets, the model calls for full investment locally, as well as leveraging global investments across markets, to develop fully national market potential. In smaller but attractive markets, the model calls for focusing investments on developing the attractive opportunities. In the niche strategy, the focus of investments is on building a position for the future. Interestingly the no-investment strategy significantly increases the potential profitability (i.e., return on sales) of traditionally unattractive markets, by systematically eliminating direct investments and rather relying on partners or other parties to promote and sell its products.

These models enhance the management's ability to establish and manage national market strategies across a wide variety of markets. Each model reflects a common objective, that of systematically determining a firm's strategy for each national market by the industry and firm-specific factors that impact national profitability. This perspective is important in operating in complex world markets. Many companies tend to establish common strategies or objectives across all national markets, essentially treating each market equally, despite their differences. On the other hand, there is a tendency for country managers to focus on the differences in their markets. A common response by many country managers to headquarters initiatives is "You don't understand, my market is different." In many cases they are correct and their market is different, but it is also not likely to be unique. These models are important management tools. They focus management attention on identifying patterns across market characteristics that have a direct impact on national market potential and profitability. Beyond focusing on market differences, these models focus on patterns of similarity, giving management the ability to manage local operations across a wide variety of geographies.

The evolving strategic roles of national affiliates

While national affiliates play an important role in the value-creating global strategies, one challenge facing management is how to develop the capacity of national affiliates to contribute to a global network of operations. Traditionally national affiliates pass through a series of relatively predictable stages in their strategic growth and development, as reflected in Table 12.2. These stages focus on three distinct agendas.

- *Global–local role:* Leverage company global (e.g., domestic) strengths in a local market
- *Local–local role:* Adapt activities to build local strengths for local market requirements
- *Local–global role:* Leverage local resources and strengths across global markets

Table 12.2: *Stages in local affiliate strategic growth and development*

	Global–local role	**Local–local role**	**Local–global role**
Strategic focus	Expand sales of existing products or know-how in new markets	Adapt operations to expand sales beyond export levels	Exploit specialized local capabilities in world markets
Resource challenges	Primarily outside local market, with local resources focused on downstream operations	Build local resources to adapt operations to local requirements	Expand and focus on specialized local resources to meet global requirements
Organizational challenges	How to support and control local organizations linkages mainly from headquarter to affiliate	How to build and manage local operations: linkages mainly within local market	How to transfer local skills globally; linkages from local market to global
Country manager role	Entrepreneur; implementer	Local general manager	Global manager

Generally the first stage focuses on developing the local market potential for existing global capabilities (i.e., products or know-how). This stage emphasizes enabling entry into new markets and encourages transfer of expertise to local markets. However, without adapting products or know-how to local market conditions, there is a limitation on the potential for such products or know-how. The second stage addresses these limitations by concentrating on developing or adapting products, or know-how focused on the local market requirements. This second stage emphasizes distinguishing local requirements, opportunities and success factors, and builds the resources and organization to reflect these different market needs. The third stage emphasizes how a local national affiliate can contribute to a company's global operations, developing and leveraging local strengths as part of an integrated global network. This stage emphasizes leveraging local specialized resources and activities globally, and building the organizational linkages to enhance and support these other global operations.

The global–local role

The strategic role of the national affiliate in the *global-local* stage of development is to build national sales largely drawing on resources, products, ideas and know-how from the centre outwards to each affiliate. Organizationally, the most important value-creating activities are located outside the market, with local resources focused on downstream sales and delivery activities. As a result, a national affiliate is dependent on one-way flows and exchanges from the home country, or some other established national affiliate, to a local market. Headquarters' organizational challenges emphasize supporting and controlling local build-up and early growth.

In this initial stage of development, country managers, often expatriates, play an entrepreneurial role focusing on building a local business, often from scratch. As such, issues of concern involve market entry issues such as understanding what resources and activities are the basis of local advantage, what market factors will impact the ability to exploit this advantage and the competitive implications of their market entry. Early measures of the performance of country managers tend to emphasize sales and profitability, although transfer prices and other factors outside the control of the country manager can heavily influence profitability. An important challenge facing country managers is to begin to balance between the requirements for meeting short-term objectives while also building toward long-term market opportunities.

The local–local role

As an affiliate becomes more established in the market, the development stage shifts toward a *local-local* role, focusing on expanding the local position, and adapting products and operations to meet local requirements. At this stage of development, strategic challenges reflect market expansion issues, such as overcoming local opportunity limitations based on standardized products, know-how and resources. This development stage is critical in terms of building and maintaining local expertise with regard to:

- Local customers and suppliers. Frequently the majority of business in many affiliates comes from local, not global customers and country organizations have to be able to adapt standard products and services to local conditions to capture local value. They also have to deal with local suppliers.
- Local competitors. Multinationals compete against strong global and local competitors. Country organizations have to be flexible enough as well to respond to nimble and innovative local competitors.

- Government relations. Multinationals need access and contacts with governments around the world. Country organizations have to be mindful of national interests, as well as regional and global concerns.

Often this stage is associated with a build-up in the scope of local operations, with an affiliate performing an increasing array of activities locally, transferring resources that are necessary to meet local requirements. As such, the affiliate becomes increasingly autonomous in their operations, with an increasing emphasis on local resources and local value-creating operations. The headquarters' organizational challenges at this stage involve supporting this local build-up, often including the transferring of expertise and resources into the national market to support local market needs. Country measurement and reward systems tend to emphasize local profitability.

Country managers at this development stage tend to play more of a general manager role, overseeing an increasingly autonomous operation. The affiliate manager, increasing a local executive, focuses more on local market needs and requirements and local customers, channels, competitors and governments. As affiliates focus on local requirements and build local resources, new sources of opportunity also emerge – that associated with using the local resources outside the national market to pursue global opportunities.

The local–global role

As firms struggle with the conflicting objectives demanded by the globalization of markets and competition, national affiliates increasingly move from playing a purely local role to assuming a regional or global role. As this transformation occurs, firms seek to exploit locally based specialized resources and capabilities across global markets. In this stage of development, national affiliates move rapidly into a *local-global* role, seeking to develop and exploit each affiliate's role as part of a total global network of operations.

The role of the national affiliate changes substantially at this stage of development. As firms move to an integrated network, local affiliates shift their focus from local concerns alone to play more of a global role as well. National affiliates now have to widen their strategic view to reflect three areas:

- expanding local operations by accessing and leveraging the firm's globally dispersed resources;
- building managing operations where there is a local advantage that can be exploited locally *and* globally; and
- integrating local operations within a worldwide network in structure and systems.

For the local affiliate, this involves a selective resource build-up, emphasizing operations where there are local advantages that can be exploited within and outside the market, as well as eliminating operations where the affiliate can access similar or more efficient resources from other markets. Organizationally the firm's global challenges shift toward facilitating multidirectional exchanges of products, know-how, people and other resources.

The role of a country manager in an integrated network is complex, involving both local and global roles. The country manager is responsible for national performance, leveraging both local and dispersed global resources. Their role also includes managing locally based resources that serve global requirements. These challenges are particularly complex requiring local expertise and the ability to represent local operations globally, as well as global influence within the firm to represent local operations, and, globally, the ability to access and influence operations outside the local market effectively. Overall this role involves moving from a relatively autonomous general manager to a role demanding managing local interests globally, and global interests locally.

Although the role of the country manager becomes increasingly complex in global organization, it is also critical to a firm's ultimate success. One senior executive described the challenge this way. "*Country managers are like the 'hands' of the multinational.As you build 'muscle' (i.e., capabilities) across your worldwide organization, you still need your hands to touch the local markets and customers.*"

Organizational challenges of building and leveraging national affiliates

To better understand the process of building and leveraging national affiliates as part of a firm's global strategy, this section develops two distinct organizational challenges in the firm's globalization process that directly impact national affiliates. *The first challenge involves building up a network of globally distributed leading-edge resources to take advantage of specialized resources and expertise distributed globally. The second challenge involves building up organizational linkages between globally dispersed operations* (Figure 12.3).

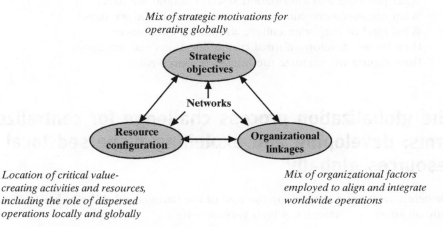

Figure 12.3: *Networks involve variations in strategy, resource configuration and organizational linkages*

Earlier it was described how the affiliate strategies systematically vary based on patterns of characteristics across national markets, as well as how the strategies of national affiliates develop and expand over time. The premise of the following discussion is that only by understanding and reflecting these dual organizational challenges can management speed up the process of building an effective global network of operations.

Network organizational decisions

As the traditional organizational structures have proven to be increasingly less effective as a result of the globalization of industries and strategies, managers are called on to move beyond traditional centralized and decentralized models. Instead, managers are employing a broader range of organizational decisions in building global networks. Some of these critical decisions include a firm's strategy toward its resources configuration and organizational linkages. Some of the important decisions include the following:

Network configuration decisions

● Where should we locate our worldwide facilities?
● What will the roles of these facilities be?
● What will be the nature and extent of exchanges among worldwide facilities?

Network organizational decisions

● What should the reporting channels look like?
● How do we allocate the authority for decision-making?
● What management control systems should we have?
● What planning and information systems should we have?
● What measurement and evaluation systems should we have?
● What kind of corporate culture should we encourage?
● How do we develop informal communications and linkages?
● How should we organize the human resource role?

The globalization process challenge for centralized firms: developing and exploiting dispersed local resources globally

For centralized firms, rethinking the role of the national subsidiaries has to focus initially on some key activities, which vary over time:

● building up specialized resources in the appropriate national affiliates, while formalizing linkages to enable sharing of resources;

- substantially integrating worldwide resources, reallocating roles and responsibilities, with supporting adjustments in systems and cultures, leading to a fundamental altering of the organization.

The following description focuses on the globalization process at one traditionally centralized firm, Eli Lilly and Company. The purpose of this description is to examine the process of change in terms of how the company moved from a centralized to an integrated global network structure.

Globalization of Eli Lilly and Company (1980–1995)

One company that moved from a traditionally centralized structure to a global network structure was Eli Lilly and Company, a US pharmaceutical company based in Indianapolis, Indiana. Prior to 1980, Eli Lilly exhibited all the classic characteristics of a centralized multinational. Foreign markets, described as "outside the United States" (OUS) were seen as appendages to the domestic market, nice to have but not essential. The company's foreign strategies clearly were seen as a way to leverage domestic products and resources, and national affiliates outside the US were focused mainly on the local implementation of the headquarter strategy and programmes.

Organizationally most value-creating operations were located in the US, with limited resource commitment in foreign markets. Even then, these foreign resources emphasized supporting local product sales, and thus included final manufacturing, clinical support and sales. There were separate domestic and international organizations, and a one-way flow to foreign operations of products, technologies, staff and ideas. Within a centralized decision-making process and usually run by expatriate management, the local companies were judged according to profit contributions. Sales were seen as incremental to those of the home market. While management spoke of the large, global opportunities, the company's consistent success in the US market precluded any strong drive for changing its approach to foreign markets.

Building local resources: expanding local sales

Between 1980 and 1986, Eli Lilly began to emphasize the capacity of national affiliates to expand their local sales. Initially this involved making fundamental changes in where important supporting functions were performed, and how new products were developed and marketed. These changes did not impact all affiliate operation or tasks, but rather initially emphasized expanding the clinical organization at major national affiliates. These operations had responsibility for undertaking all activities necessary to obtain regulatory approval of new products, including building relations with local opinion leaders. The marketing and sales organizations were also strengthened and reorganized to support and expand local sales.

At this initial stage of the globalization process, the focus is on expanding selected local resources. A number of factors complicate this process. Within their home markets, companies are frequently able to attract the "best" available resources. With a much smaller presence and less personal opportunities within national markets, it can be more difficult to attract the same level of resources and expertise within national markets. This complicates the process of not only building up resources, but also transferring home-country expertise to local markets. As a result, the organizational challenges at this stage involve how the headquarters can support the local build-up.

Upgrading local resources: supporting mounting global challenges

By the mid-1980s, Eli Lilly faced mounting competitive pressures on its worldwide operations. These pressures called on the company to begin to utilize its growing resource base now located within national markets to respond to these pressures. While for some operations (sales), national affiliates continued to emphasize their local roles, for others (clinical and manufacturing) the company began to upgrade local resources and align local operations to enable it to draw on national affiliates to support activities outside their local market. For example, it became critical for Eli Lilly to coordinate worldwide clinical trials across major world markets to speed product development and launch. However, before being able to utilize local operations globally, the company had to ensure that the local operations performed tasks at global standards. This upgrading and aligning of worldwide operations in selected tasks required extensive communications and coordination across operations.

For other operations not involved in these activities (sales and marketing), there was also an emphasis on upgrading national resources, and expanding communication and coordination across national affiliates. However, as opposed to helping to respond to mounting global pressures, this upgrading and communication focused on further enhancing local operations. For these operations, the communication emphasized the sharing of experience across markets. These changes were achieved through a reorganization of the worldwide marketing structure, creating four regional organizations of which, significantly, North America was one. To manage worldwide activities, a decision matrix was set up to allocate authority based on the impact of a decision, whether local, regional or global. Regional heads operated within global guidelines, while exchanges across geographic locations were facilitated by means such as common planning systems, product-focused teams for transferring expertise and experience, and frequent meetings among regional and country-based staff at various levels.

Focusing specialized local resources: reallocating resources globally

By the early 1990s, Eli Lilly had redefined its global strategic challenges around "seven essentials for success" (Table 12.3), reflecting the overall pressures and opportunities facing the company. Eli Lilly management spoke less and less of having a separate international strategy, but rather increasingly focused on having a global strategy that reflected the overall pressures and opportunities facing the company. This phase of the globalization process directly built on the strong resource base that had been developed and installed during the 1980s.

Table 12.3: *Eli Lilly's seven essentials for success*

	Essential	Objectives	Global implications
What	Speed to market	Reducing the time to develop and launch new compounds in five of eight major world markets to 2500 days	Common global standards Leveraging regulatory differences Performing trials globally
	Leverage existing products	Identify opportunities to maximize the value of existing products	Identifying opportunities across markets
	Expand global and therapeutic presence	Identify and build a presence across product and geographic markets	Building operations in major world markets
How	Business development	Identify external opportunities to increase sales by leveraging resources and accessing external resources	Increasing partnering with non-US firms across operations
	Customer orientation	Recognize and reflect fundamental changes in industry decision makers	Reflecting the changing buying patterns across markets
	Streamlining business processes	Improve efficiency by re-engineering major activities	Re-engineering processes across previously independent units
	Energizing the climate	Facilitate and encourage contributions of all employees	Expanding role of non-US staff

In terms of roles and responsibilities, the company separated its domestic affiliate operations (actually moving it out of the company's headquarters office) and Lilly's headquarters began to focus on global issues of strategy, technology, resources and products. Increasingly "lead affiliates" began to play an active global role in selected operations as the company moved toward a structure of integrated worldwide operations, with mixed structures across operations.

The overall structure of Lilly's worldwide operations varied significantly by operation. Specifically the structure that emerged was as follows:

- *Discovery*: Dispersed specialized laboratories for product or technology areas to exploit world-class innovation, access scientific talent wherever it was located, and use global specialization of operations to ensure the needed economies of scale in R&D.

- *Clinical*: Dispersed capability to perform trials flexibly across major world markets to speed product approval, and launch and build relations with local opinion leaders.
- *Manufacturing*: A structure built around global bulk facilities, and regional or local formulation and finish facilities, to simultaneously promote cost efficiency in bulk facilities and production, and efficiency and adaptation in formulation and finishing.
- *Marketing/sales*: A strong local sales presence in major world markets, while building more selective positions in other markets to take advantage of selective local opportunities.

At this stage of its globalization process, affiliates expanded resources in selected operations (particularly where there was local expertise or resources that could play a regional or global role), while reducing operations in others (particularly those where the local needs could be provided by other affiliates, leveraging the cross-affiliate linkages previously established). Affiliates assumed regional or global roles in some operations, while maintaining supporting roles in others. Affiliate resources continued to focus on strong downstream activities, but also emphasized specialized resources and roles in other operations.

As these changes occurred, the measurement and control of affiliates became increasingly complex. Affiliate measurement continued to reflect local profitability, but also had to consider formally the measures of their global contributions. Overall, firm control mechanisms expanded to include the development of global processes, standards and procedures, within which there was a growing decentralization of decision authority. Linking the company's global operations was also a strong global culture and mindset.

It is important to remember that Eli Lilly's globalization process did not involve a single move or initiative, but rather a series of changes over time where each change built on prior adjustments within and across the organization (Table 12.4).

Table 12.4: *Eli Lilly globalization process (1980–1995)*

	Early 1980s	Late 1980s	Early 1990s
Global strategy	Expand local sales	Use affiliates to respond to mounting global pressures	Integrated worldwide strategy
Resource configuration changes	Expand selected local resources	Upgrade local resources to world class standards	Specialize local resources Reallocate resources globally
Organizational linkages changes	Support local resource build-up	Transfer expertise and align local resources and activities	Integrate worldwide operations

In terms of building a dispersed global configuration of resources that were effective both locally and globally, initially the focus was on building up resources in local markets, overcoming the challenges of attracting resources to smaller affiliates. Following this initial build-up, the emphasis was on upgrading the resources drawing on expertise and skills located at within the home market or other established operations. As the company built a network of skills resources, the company was able to focus selected operations, and reallocate resources and tasks globally.

Where there are a number of options to speed the entire process, each of the change periods installed critical resources and capabilities that were further developed and exploited in subsequent phases of the globalization process. *The challenge for the management of firms beginning this journey today is not to eliminate phases and jump to an immediate integrated network structure, but rather to understand the overall process and evaluate options for shortening it.*

For example, a company can speed the process of building local resources through acquiring a local company, although this could potentially complicate the subsequent process of developing effective organizational linkages with the operations. Additionally a firm could choose not to own local resources and rather rely on alliances or partners, but this could again complicate the subsequent integration process.

The globalization process challenge for decentralized firms: building and leveraging effective organizational linkages

Previously decentralized firm have different challenges. Such firms usually become international by duplicating resources and operations in every country where they have established a presence. The organization is built around autonomous and powerful fiefdoms. This is the model that has been followed by many European companies. The first step for them is to try and begin to rationalize duplicated resources and eliminate the stifling bureaucracies and inefficiencies. As they do this, they can also begin the process of building cross-border linkages between affiliates. Linkages provide the opportunity to focus operations in a much more streamlined way. Effective linkages enable management to consider how best to allocate resources globally by reallocating roles and responsibilities.

In decentralized firms, important challenges, which again vary over time, include:

* reduce duplication and build cross-border communication;
* build up specialized resources, while formalizing linkages to enable sharing of resources;
* subsequently integrating worldwide resources, reallocating roles and responsibilities, with supporting adjustments in systems and cultures, leading to a fundamental altering of the organization.

Regionalization of Citibank's European Corporate Bank (1979–1994)

Citibank has been a leading worldwide bank for many years. By the 1920s, for example, its international activities already accounted for 20% of its total assets and profits. While from the outset the bank operated through autonomous affiliates, it maintained tight centralized financial and credit controls. The bank's traditional geographic structure lasted until the 1980s, when it began to alter this structure in response to the changing structure of the financial services industry. The following discussion focuses on the changes in Citibank's European corporate banking operation.

In the early 1980s, Citibank's European operations were based on a network of autonomous local banks in separate national markets. Each local bank acted as an independent fiefdom and the linkages between the headquarters and local banks were largely through financial measures. Local banks had within their geography most if not all the resources they needed to operate locally, and these banks were measured based on local profitability.

In the early 1980s as a result of changes in the financial services industry structure, most European national affiliates began to face deteriorating financial performance due to decreasing margins on traditional loan-based products and growing local competition. Initially the bank's reaction to this deteriorating performance was to push each affiliate to increase profitability, leading many to further invest in local infrastructure and expand independently into new products. This initial reaction resulted in a dramatic increase in the cost structure across each affiliate without addressing the underlying causes of the deteriorating performance. By the mid-1980s, senior global and regional management launched a series of initiatives to reverse this trend.

Building informal linkages: the "European Bank" initiative (1985–1987)

By 1985, when diversification had failed to reverse declining returns, a new head of the European operations launched a new set of initiatives to respond to both short- and long-term pressures. Central to this was a focus on immediate cost control, with regional head count being reduced from 7000 to 4500 between 1985 and 1987.

The new European executive also launched a new initiative, referred to as the "European Bank" initiative, that sought to leverage the bank's unique position across the region by targeting large local corporations and selected product markets that could exploit this position. While seeking to lever the bank's unique position across Europe, the traditional organization was not designed to operate regionally. Rather resources were duplicated and locally focused and there were few, if any exchanges or linkages across markets.

Regional management began to address these organizational challenges by creating informal regional units to focus on key products and customer groups. Initially the executives in charge of these units focused on gathering information on market opportunities, as well as the bank's capabilities that were necessary to move toward a regional approach. Without this information and linkages between the previously autonomous units, Citibank would not have been able to pursue effectively this European Bank strategy. However, at the same time, powerful country managers would resist any efforts to alter their traditional power structure and control over local operations. Informal linkages provided a mechanism to collect information while not threatening this power structure.

Formalizing regional linkages: the "Unique European Bank" initiative (1988–1990)

In 1988, Citibank executives expedited the formalization of its regional structure through a series of new initiatives, referred to as the "Unique European Bank" initiative. The goal of this initiative was to create a common vision for all corporate banking activities in Europe, creating a three-dimensional internal partnership among geographies (to prepare country plans, access local customers and provide local administrative support), products (to develop product expertise, prepare product strategies and define product delivery systems) and customer/industry units (to coordinate relations with important customer groups). This initiative drew directly on information and plans on regional product and customer opportunities generated in the earlier European Bank initiative.

To implement this vision, the informal coordinating regional product and customer units were formalized with dual reporting relationships overlaying the geographic affiliates. The new units began to shift actively toward aligning local activities and processes and standardizing operating systems to facilitate further communication and alignment. At the same time, a European Policy Committee was set up with executives from all three streams to review regional strategies and policies, coordinate activities and promote the behavioural changes needed to foster a spirit of teamwork across the region. The formalization of organizational linkages across national markets enabled bank management to focus on regional product and customer opportunities, drawing on resources that remained largely within the national affiliates.

Installing a pan-European strategy and organization (1992–1994)

During the early 1990s Citibank implemented an integrated pan-European strategy and organization based on interdependent specialized and distributed resources and operations. In terms of products, centres of expertise and innovation were established in London and Frankfurt to maximize the position within targeted products. The back office operations were centralized in London to take advantage of scale and efficiency, while being flexible toward local needs. Regional/global industry units were distributed based on local expertise and charged with transferring expertise across markets, while the geographical units became responsible for customer relationship management. In the move toward integrated team-based management, country managers began to assume additional roles based on local expertise.

Overall Citibank's regionalization process is outlined in Table 12.5. As with the globalization process at Eli Lilly, Citibank's regionalization effort was spread over a

Table 12.5: *Citibank regionalization process (1979–1994)*

	Early 1980s	Late 1980s	Early 1990s
Regional strategy	European Bank (regional units support local focused strategy)	Unique European Bank (local units support regional focused strategy)	Pan-European strategy (integrated regional strategy
Resource configuration changes	Duplicated autonomous units within national markets	Introduced specialized regional product and customer units	Reallocate resources and operations across the regions
Organizational linkages changes	Informal regional units overlaying affiliates	Formalized dual reporting, with common operating and control systems	Integrated regional operations

long, 15-year period. The challenges facing managers beginning this process is again to understand the challenges and developments at each stage in the process in order to shorten it as much as possible. In terms of building organizational linkages, Citibank first used informal linkages to gather information on and plan for cross-market opportunities; then it formalized these linkages to re-orient the bank's operations toward these regional opportunities; then it reallocated resources and operations and installed an integrated regional structure. Again each stage of this process created opportunities that were developed and exploited in the subsequent stages of the process.

SUMMARY

This chapter has developed the different roles that national affiliates can play in a company's global strategy. Rather than having either a single role or treating each market differently, it suggests that companies need to segment market strategies based on patterns of similarities in industry and firm-specific factors that influence national market opportunities and profitability. Examples of such systems are Citibank, Coors and Eli Lilly.

The chapter then discussed the evolving strategic roles of individual national affiliates. Typical strategic development patterns involve moving from a global–local role (focused on leveraging global products and know-how within a local market) to a local–local role (focused on leveraging local resources to adapt such products and know-how to local market conditions) to a local–global (using local-based resources to support local and global opportunities) roles. While not all affiliates pass through each stage, with many stopping at intermediate stages, this pattern drives the overall shifting strategic focus of national affiliates.

The chapter then addressed the globalization process within firms, focusing on how companies build and leverage specialized local resources and build and exploit effective organizational linkages. It examined the organizational challenges of globalization by describing the processes of change at Eli Lilly and Citibank. In both instances speeding up the process requires an understanding of each stage.

For management of firms beginning this journey, the question becomes whether and how some of these stages might be circumvented as companies face increased pressure to exploit their scattered international resources in a much more systematic way to create and capture value. An integrated network will not be developed overnight. Experienced managers are critical, particularly those with a plurality of perspectives, general management excellence and who can foster continuity of management teams. There is also a need for special strengths in terms of strategic integration at the top and operational integration at the bottom, since the integrated network approach tends to weaken middle-level management. Roles need to be clearly defined, but without too much clarity or overlap to maintain flexibility, although some overlap is inevitable. In general, informal, *ad hoc* processes work better than rigid, formalized ones.

Crucial decisions will have to be made on what to centralize and what to decentralize, balancing multiple options on how the aspiring global organization can best exploit its strengths. Competencies and connections ought to match where, in the organization, critical success factors and key contingencies are best managed. This calls for a review of both the need for differentiated local responsiveness and the opportunities for international integration or rationalization.

 **LEARNING POINTS**

- Move beyond incrementalism, by building a common understanding of the goal and focusing on the importance of this goal to all operations.
- Communicate constantly, to break down organizational barriers. Use common information and systems to create a common language.
- Do not order changes from the centre. The headquarters needs to support and enable the process. So headquarters' abilities need to be in place first, although affiliates should be involved in the change process early on.
- There needs to be recognition of the dramatic nature of the changes, while it should be kept in mind that many executives might not be able to make the change. Training and support should be an integral part of the process.
- For acquisitions and alliances, focus on integration, not just the deal, since value is created in the stages of integration.
- Managing both the resource and organizational process together will expedite your globalization progress.

Part Six

Putting it Together

13

Accelerating International Growth – And Succeeding

This book has described in depth the five key strategic capabilities essential for globalizing firms: developing strategic capability, managing global partnerships, staffing the global company, fostering global learning and adapting the global organization. But the real challenge, says **Philip Rosenzweig,** is to develop an integrated approach that deploys them simultaneously rather than one at a time.

Overview

We began this book by showing that international growth isn't just a concern for large industrial companies. Companies of all kinds are responding to the combination of wider opportunities and competitive pressures, and expanding abroad. Today, international growth is truly everybody's business. And with more and more companies facing an imperative to reach a strong competitive position quickly and efficiently, they look for accelerated international growth.

We've devoted most of this book to an examination of five key capabilities needed for accelerated international growth. By now they're very familiar: companies must develop global strategic thinking; they must master working in partnerships, both alliances and acquisitions; they need to staff their growing activities, through expatriation and localization; they have to excel at global learning and knowledge management; and they have to adapt their organizations continually.

Over the past twelve chapters, we've described these capabilities in depth. Now, in this final chapter, we look at all five together. We show that successful international growth requires an integrated approach, shifting back and forth among all five capabilities, rather than addressing them one at a time, in a sequential manner. Finally, we turn our attention to international growth in companies that have already achieved a mature multinational position, focusing on improvements in efficiency, and stressing once again that international growth is a continuing process, not a one-time objective.

Five capabilities: not one at a time, but all at once

We've presented the five capabilities in sequence, examining them one at a time. But it doesn't follow that companies can, or should, apply them sequentially. Strategy may indeed be the place to begin – that's where it all starts, after all – but the remaining four capabilities aren't addressed in sequence. It's not as if companies can first address partnerships, then turn their attention to staffing, then learning, and finally to adapting their organizations. Not at all. Successful international growth demands that firms continually identify key priorities, and shift back and forth among them.

INTERNATIONAL GROWTH AS AN INTEGRATED PROCESS

Two leading researchers on multinational management, Yves Doz and C. K. Prahalad, have underscored this point: the hallmark of a multinational company – in fact, its key advantage as it competes against firms that are less extensive in their global position – is the ability to manage growth as an integrated process of organizational learning (Doz and Prahalad, 1991).

International growth takes place along three dimensions – geographic, product lines and functions. But growth along each dimension isn't independent. Successful growth involves sharing expertise among dimensions. Learning about doing business in foreign countries helps further geographic expansion, learning about a given host country enables a sequential line of business addition in that country, and so forth. Of course, experience gained by a line of business in one country not only leads to greater knowledge of that country, it can also lead to greater knowledge of the line of business, which can be leveraged across countries to speed up the entry of that business into other countries. In this way, leveraging knowledge across dimensions results in evolution that is faster and more extensive at any point in time than it would otherwise have been.

The key, as described in Chapters 8 through 10, is to manage learning and knowledge exchange as a global process. By leveraging knowledge throughout the company, multinationals avoid duplication and achieve internal differentiation. The ability to leverage knowledge across and among dimensions is precisely what gives multinationals their greatest competitive advantage. Growing on one dimension - say, entry into new countries - isn't independent of growth along other dimensions - say, adding functions or business lines - but affects and is affected by activities elsewhere.

Sony provides an example. Sony first set up a television assembly plant in the United States in 1972, then entered into additional lines of business over the next few years. In 1974, Sony set up a television assembly plant in Europe, and soon entered into audio equipment. Entry in Europe in audio equipment was facilitated by two kinds of knowledge accumulation: greater expertise about Europe gained through the initial entry to Europe in televisions, and also knowledge about audio products that was transferred from the US operation to the new plant in Europe. By leveraging lines of business knowledge across countries, Sony more efficiently and more successfully added a new line of business in Europe.

Five different capabilities – involving different people

Rather than thinking in terms of a sequence, a better metaphor might be a panel of five controls, with a pilot who pushes on one, then another, eases off on one, pushes on the next, back and forth. Yet even the metaphor of a control panel is misleading, since it conjures up the image of a single person seated in front of the controls. One of the most difficult challenges of coordinating these five capabilities is that they involve different people and different departments – people who must work together effectively if international growth is to succeed.

One of the greatest practical challenges facing organizations is that the capabilities we've described are often thought to be the concern of one or another department. Strategy is often the exclusive province of senior executives, or by extension their planning department. Staffing is sometimes seen as the domain of human resource professionals, who are expected to find solutions to expatriation and localization. Alliance management is sometimes left to those individuals involved directly with a joint venture, but not of much interest to others in key roles. Organizational design is sometimes left to organization development specialists, or may be handled by external strategy consultants – or in many instances is ignored altogether. The result is an awkward mix of action and inaction, of overlaps and gaps.

What's a better approach? Since successful international growth is an integrated process, the managers who guide the process have to share an integrated mindset. Of course any organization has specialists. But coherence requires a general understanding of key issues shared by many, and the active exchange of information among them. Senior executives must not devise global strategies without a clear understanding of organizational consequences. As we showed in Chapter 2, *grasping the globe* involves all stages of the value chain and demands participation of all areas: procurement, finance, logistics, manufacturing, research, human resources and more. For their part, division managers must appreciate the perspectives of their counterparts in different corners of the organization. Human resource professionals have to be clear about the company's strategic imperatives which drive staffing and learning needs. Managers of alliances must not be treated as marginal and peripheral, but brought into the full discussion, recognizing the increasingly central role of partnerships in the success of an international growth strategy. The point is simple: international growth is by nature a complex undertaking and companies must forge a shared understanding of how the various elements fit together.

Examples of successful accelerated growth

In Chapter 1, we presented Lincoln Electric as an example of a highly successful company that stumbled badly when it expanded abroad. Lincoln Electric's story pointed up several distinct failures – of strategy, of partnership management, of staffing, of learning and of organization design. In other words, problems in each of the five key capabilities we've discussed in this book.

Now that we've discussed each capability on its own, let's bring them together through the lens of companies that have grown rapidly and successfully. The story of DHL provides one such example as described in the case study below. In the next section, we'll examine at greater length the international growth of Mobile Telephone Networks (MTN), one of South Africa's leading mobile telecommunications operators. MTN is a very apt example: a small and young organization, growing rapidly in its home market, but at the same time attempting to grow rapidly abroad. Typical of many such companies, MTN is resource constrained – not just for financial resources, but for human resources. Seeing how MTN has successfully managed its international growth is instructive to companies of all kinds.

CASE STUDY: **DHL: RAPID GROWTH IN GLOBAL DELIVERY**

Founded in 1969, DHL created the first door-to-door express service between San Francisco and Honolulu. The company started small and internationalized early. Initially, DHL's international expansion radiated from its San Francisco home. Within two years of its founding, DHL expanded from Hawaii to the Philippines followed by other Asian markets such as Japan, Hong Kong, Singapore and Australia. DHL shifted to a more opportunistic, global expansion strategy as it entered Europe in 1973,

*followed by the Middle East in 1976, Latin America in 1977 and Africa in 1978. In
addition, DHL tried to enter new markets as soon as they opened. For example, the
company was the first air express company in eastern Europe in 1983, the first in China
in 1986 and the first to re-establish service to Kuwait after the Gulf War. By 2000, DHL
was a global company with headquarters in San Francisco and Brussels, operating in
80 000 cities in 228 countries with 63 552 employees around the world.*

*DHL has used a variety of entry modes as it expanded worldwide. While it often
relied on greenfield investments, DHL also used agents and joint ventures in countries
where greenfield investment wasn't possible. For example, the company entered
Czechoslovakia through an agent in 1986, but set up a greenfield subsidiary as soon
as the market opened. Also in 1986, DHL formed a joint venture to enter China. An
agent still operated DHL's office in Korea in 2000. The firm also made use of alliances
to grow abroad. In 1990 Japan Airlines, Lufthansa and Nissho Iwai Trading purchased
equity in DHL, with the strategy to complement the airport-to-airport service of the airlines with DHL's door-to-door service. To illustrate this alliance in action, DHL helps
Russian car producers to document and transport cargo to and from the airport and
Lufthansa carries the cargo on its international routes. In addition, DHL formed an
equity alliance with Deutsche Post in 1998 and a non-equity alliance with the US Postal
Service in 1999 to leverage the international skills of DHL and the local delivery
access of the posts. Versatility in entry mode has been a key reason why DHL has
internationalized so far and so fast.*

*DHL relies on consistent service delivery worldwide, making staffing and training of
the highest importance. Yet given its rapid global growth, sequential assignments of
expatriates aren't possible. When it enters new markets, DHL brings in a few key expatriates to set up the operations, then quickly hires and trains local managers to allow the
expatriates to leave within months. It looks for flexible people with a customer-focused
attitude who thrive in the constantly changing local environments. Then, DHL invests
heavily in training programmes and international job assignments to teach customer
service and business skills to new employees.*

Mobile Telephone Networks (MTN)

Founded in 1993, Mobile Telephone Networks (MTN) is an independently owned and
managed firm with the second largest mobile phone network in its home country. It
has grown rapidly since its founding in 1993, and by 2000 provided a mobile telecommunication service for more than 1.6 million people in its home country. Known for
its high-quality service, MTN was one of only three network operators worldwide to
receive ISO 9001 certification.

The mobile telephone industry experienced explosive growth in the late 1990s,
and companies like MTN were stretched to keep up with domestic demand. But –
typical of many companies in many industries – MTN also felt a keen need to expand
internationally. From its beginning, MTN cast its eyes beyond its home market, and
sought to expand internationally. In part it was a matter of opportunity: mobile

telephony offered huge opportunities for growth in sub-Saharan Africa. In part, too, it was a matter of imperative – if MTN did not capture licences at the time they were offered, it might miss out on entry to key countries. For that reason, MTN had from its earliest days stated a clear strategic vision: "*To be the leading telecommunications operator on the African continent*".

The result was a classic example of accelerating international growth: a company, without abundant resources, and facing high domestic growth, also needed to expand its activities internationally. And just as clearly, the result was a company that exhibited all five key capabilities – global strategic thinking, managing international partnerships, rapid global staffing, global learning and knowledge management, and organizational adaptation – and shifted back and forth among them.

MTN: the early years

MTN began as a joint venture composed of Cable & Wireless, a UK-based firm; M-Net, a South African pay-TV channel; Transnet, the state-owned transport company; and other local investors. It secured the second network operator licence in South Africa in 1993, and began operation in 1994. At the outset, it had a capital investment of 500 million Rand (R), worth about US$150 million at the time. Key technology was provided by Cable & Wireless. The initial staff included some key expatriate managers from Cable & Wireless and a number of local employees.

MTN's first challenge was to build a network of base stations across the country. Within six months it had set up 400 base stations, and offered mobile telephony to the main urban areas of Johannesburg/Pretoria, Capetown, Durban and other major cities. The network "went live" for testing in March 1994 and was launched commercially in June 1994. It met with immediate success. MTN's business plan projected 50 000 subscribers in the first year of operation; in fact, it achieved 95 000 subscribers in its first year. It was profitable after just 22 months.

Over the next years, MTN built a network of 2200 base stations, stretching from Capetown to the border with Zimbabwe, connecting all major cities and towns, and operating along 13 000 kilometres of national highway. It was the largest GSM network in the world, covering an area of 650 000 square kilometres, or 48% of the country – an area 50% greater than all of Germany. In its first year of operation MTN had 200 employees; by 1999 it had more than 2200. Hiring and training the workforce was a constant concern. The workforce was young, with an average age of 29, and most managers were in the most responsible position they had ever held.

MTN's international expansion

Even as it was building a successful domestic position, MTN had its eyes on international growth. Its focus was the African continent. With 700 million inhabitants, Africa was more populous than Europe or North America, yet it had very low teledensity. By one estimate, 70% of all Africans had never used a telephone. The company stated:

> *The incredible potential for cellular telephony within the African market has driven us to explore the opportunities available in each country. In terms of*

securing the future success of our company, expansion in Africa came as a natural decision.

To identify opportunities and prepare bids in foreign markets, MTN recognized the need to dedicate key resources. It therefore adapted its organization, creating a department of International Business Development. Members of the International Business Development department identified opportunities, devised business plans and prepared bids. Bid teams analysed a variety of factors: the host country's geography, its population, degree of urbanization, level economic development, potential for growth and more. They also evaluated possible joint venture partners, since many licences were granted to joint ventures of local companies and foreign network operators.

Building partnerships

MTN entered new markets largely through joint ventures with local telecom companies. It developed a considerable expertise in managing partnerships, working closely with local governmental agencies and telecom companies, as well as other local investors. Although MTN didn't require majority ownership, it insisted on being the lead partner in all its joint ventures. During the planning phase, MTN identified "material decisions" over which it needed to retain decision authority, including capital expenditures and the appointment of top executives. Keeping authority over those key decisions was a necessary condition of any tender offer.

A strategy of growth: bidding for new licences

During 1998, MTN was awarded licences to operate networks in three countries: Rwanda, Uganda and Swaziland. In April 1998, MTN was awarded a licence to operate the first GSM network in Rwanda, a small central African country with a population of 7 million. MTN received a second network operator licence in Uganda, a nation of 19 million inhabitants located on Rwanda's northern border. MTN Uganda began full commercial service on 21 October 1998, six months after the licence had been issued. MTN's third foreign licence in 1998 was in Swaziland, a small country with a population of 900 000 nestled between South Africa and Mozambique.

With the addition of these entities, MTN again shifted its organization structure, creating a subsidiary called MTN (Africa) which held ownership shares in the three African subsidiaries. Yet through 1999, MTN (Africa) was only a holding company, with just one employee, a chief financial officer. All other employees of the MTN Group were either located in MTN (Pty) Ltd, M-Tel (Pty) Ltd or in the three African subsidiaries.

Rapid staffing: expatriation and localization

Once MTN received a licence in a new country, it faced a set of challenges. First, it had to set up a network of wireless transmission base stations quickly and efficiently. It accomplished this task with a dedicated task force that travelled to the new country and quickly rolled out the network – a combination of organizational focus and leveraging knowledge, applying expertise from the home country to the new market. MTN also needed to staff a competent workforce. As a matter of policy, MTN wanted to hire local employees to the greatest extent possible. In each country it entered, word of mouth spread fast, and job seekers sent dozens – often hundreds – of résumés. Many administrative, clerical and sales positions were filled with local hires. Yet many technical and managerial positions could not be filled locally. A company publication described:

> *The technological nature of the telecommunications industry, and specifically mobile telephony, demands specialized skills, especially at the start-up phase. These skills are unfortunately often not readily available in the local market, therefore justifying the need for a largely South African expatriate contingent in initial project implementation teams.*

MTN wished to localize positions as much as possible, replacing a South Africa expatriate with a local hire. But in practice it was difficult to localize many positions so soon. Rather than replace the expatriate with another expatriate, it was often better for a manager who had gained local experience to stay on.

Accordingly, as it began to set up operations in a new market, MTN identified the key positions that would have to be filled by expats. Finding people who were interested in foreign assignments was another matter, made even more difficult by the fact that domestic operations were growing rapidly and couldn't spare lots of talented people. To obviate a drain of talent from South Africa to other African countries, in 1998 MTN created a special pool of managers, hired and trained expressly to take on expatriate assignments. Thirty employees were hired during 1998 and 1999 for this purpose.

Small countries like Rwanda and Swaziland called for about six MTN expatriates each. Uganda, a larger country with a larger staff, had 20 expatriates – the CEO, six direct reports to the CEO and 13 managers at the next level. Finding competent CEOs was another problem. As lead joint venture partner, MTN had the right to appoint the senior executive, but finding people with the right background and experience wasn't easy. MTN recruited its country managers for Rwanda and Uganda from outside the company, selecting managers with extensive telecom experience as well as knowledge about managing in Africa. During 1998 and 1999 MTN sent 48 expatriates to its various African operations, with initial assignments of two years.

Evaluating further international growth

Following MTN's entry into Rwanda, Uganda and Swaziland in 1998, and with its new licence in Nigeria in 1999, some of the firm's managers were more confident than ever about future international growth. Ross Macdonald, head of International Business Development, elaborated:

> *The African market is characterized by massive under-investment in telephony, and this presents us with tremendous opportunity to extend our business outside the South African borders.*

In early 2000, MTN continued to grow rapidly in its domestic market as well as in several African operations. Guiding its expansion in Africa was a vision of three regional hubs: southern Africa, where it was already established in South Africa and

Swaziland; east Africa, where it operated in Uganda and Rwanda; and west Africa, where it was in a strong position to secure a licence in Nigeria.

MTN viewed its activities throughout Africa not only as places to apply knowledge from South Africa, but also as learning opportunities. In Uganda, for example, employees developed a portable telephone cabin, powered by solar panels, that could be transported to distant villages, and run by a local franchisee. The concept worked so well that soon similar cabins were rolled out in South Africa – an example of using international activities as a larger classroom, with applications in the home market.

In February 2000, MTN acquired the newly privatized government GSM and fixed line business in Cameroon. MTN had failed to secure a new licence in Cameroon two years earlier, but the firm had remained interested and was ready when the government privatized and sought a buyer. MTN had acquired 100% of the entity, and was looking for a local partner to take on 30% ownership. Although the operation was small, with just 6000 subscribers, it offered a promising platform for growth. Beyond Nigeria and Cameroon, MTN was looking seriously at acquiring privatized networks in hub countries including Kenya and Tanzania.

Organizational issues

With the growing activities in Rwanda, Uganda, Swaziland, and now Cameroon, MTN felt the need to shift its organization once again. MTN (Africa) had been created as a legal entity, but as an operational entity it lacked the dedicated resources to focus attention and managerial oversight on the growing Africa activities. Without a separate management structure, MTN's African operations naturally looked to the larger and more sophisticated South African operation for guidance. Thus, marketing managers in Uganda, Rwanda and Swaziland had an informal reporting relationship to MTN's key managers in South Africa. Local finance managers looked for guidance to MTN's chief finance officer in Johannesburg; local human resource managers looked to MTN's head of human resources; and the same held true for MTN's other functions, information technology and networks. Yet these managers were busy with the demands of a rapidly growing domestic business. The need to staff African operations, as well as support them, placed a strain on MTN's South African activities. Quite naturally, problems in small, faraway countries were not a top priority for managers in South Africa. One manager described the attitude as: "We can't help you now, we've got a crisis [in South Africa] and the domestic business is far more important."

As a shift in organization design, the Africa Management Committee was created in 1999. Composed of the heads of key functions, ranging from finance to human resources to networks, the "ManCom" met frequently to confer on African managerial issues and coordinate their actions. Yet it was mainly a transitional mechanism as MTN bolstered the dedicated resources of its African division. With the recent addition of Cameroon, and the likely addition of Nigeria, more attention was being paid to the right organizational structure.

Lessons from MTN

We offer the story of MTN in this final chapter, not because it has been perfect – it hasn't been – but because it illustrates a young company with international ambitions. Rather than wait until it had reached saturation in its home market, MTN decided it needed to grow simultaneously at home and abroad. As we see, it had a clear strategy, it learned how to work well with local partners, it found ways to staff rapidly through expatriation and also to localize as far as possible. MTN also paid explicit attention to learning, both in applying expertise from South Africa to new markets, but also in being open to learning from those markets for leveraging throughout its positions. And finally, MTN offers an example of constant adaptation of the organization, first creating a new department to take charge of international expansion, then creating a umbrella organization for new entities, and finally staffing that organization to provide full and dedicated oversight. MTN is, of course, still early in the journey of international growth, but its record so far provides reason for confidence as it continues to grow.

CASE STUDY: IDENTIFYING PRIORITIES: VODAFONE IN 2001

The world's leading wireless telecommunications company, Vodafone, more than quadrupled in size between 1999 and 2001 thanks to the acquisitions of the US firm, AirTouch, and the German carrier, Mannesmann. No company in its industry has pursued such a clear vision of international growth. What must Vodafone emphasize as it pursues its global strategy? A quick comparison against the five capabilities offers some ideas.

Vodafone's strategic vision is unsurpassed in the industry. It has literally grasped the globe. It has assembled an outstanding basis for future growth by taking positions in key markets on almost all continents. But much work remains. Vodafone has shown versatility in its entry modes, setting up greenfield activities, taking partial ownership in many countries and making bold acquisitions, yet its ability to manage minority ownership ventures and to integrate acquisitions is still uncertain. In staffing and worldwide learning, Vodafone is in the early days of forging a coherent global company out of its many disparate units. It has taken clear steps toward organizational integration, a promising sign.

Given the talent of its management, and its leading position in the industry, prospects for Vodafone are bright – but remembering that success isn't just a matter of strategic moves, but an integrated approach involving knowledge management, organizational adaptation and staffing is a sobering reminder of all the work that remains. Focusing on these issues offers a useful road map for Vodafone to realize its promise as an outstanding global firm.

The next frontiers of international growth

So far, our focus has been on the early phases of international growth, as companies expand from an initial position to achieve a mature multinational position. We've described three dimensions of growth: a geographic dimension, meaning entry into new countries; a product line dimension, meaning adding new products in those countries; and a functional dimension, meaning the performance of value-added activities in those countries.

Once a company has achieved a broad global position, it may have fewer new markets to enter, and may also have full positions in each market where it competes. Should we consider its international growth to be over? Of course not. Rather, companies enter a new phase of growth, focusing on improvements in efficiency and profit rather than simply scale and size.

Global integration and local responsiveness

Key in this transformation is the need to achieve global integration and local responsiveness (Prahalad and Doz, 1987; Bartlett and Ghoshal, 1989). Global integration describes the benefits of managing as an integrated whole, rather than as the sum of many parts. Some of these benefits are realized through coordinated sourcing and purchasing, rationalization of production across nations and regions, scale economies in central research, and global branding. Others come from the sharing of best practices and adoption of common systems. Capturing the benefits of global integration is not easy. Most multinationals fail to identify and take advantage of these potential benefits. Outstanding global firms systematically identify and capture these benefits.

At the same time, the best global firms respond to each locality where they operate. They tailor their product formulations, adapt their marketing approaches, vary their labour policies, and find different ways to compete with local rivals. They gain the respect of local communities, and adhere to the norms and expectations of local populations. They attract the best local talent, and provide excellent career opportunities to people of all countries.

Take McDonald's. It succeeds in part on a standard global formula. Its basic business model, its techniques of cooking and customer service, are standardized. Hamburger University – the first campus in Illinois, although there are now many more on several continents – helps bring about global consistency. But in less obvious ways, McDonald's localizes its activities very effectively. It tailors product offerings to local tastes – beer and wine served in some countries, the vegetarian Maharaja Mac in India – and builds advertising campaigns around local themes. As James Cantalupo, head of McDonald's International, explained, "You don't have 2000 stores in Japan by being seen as an American company" (Friedman, 1996). Furthermore, it excels at attracting and hiring talented managers everywhere. Recently it was named, along with French firms, by *L'Expansion* as one of the most attractive companies for local employees.

Dynamic operating flexibility

Achieving global integration and local responsiveness at a single point in time isn't enough. Conditions are constantly shifting – new competitors, new product and process technologies, breakthroughs in logistics, shifting currency values and much more. The best global companies strive for dynamic operating flexibility – that is, the ability to shift sourcing, production capacities, inventories, staffing and other critical dimensions among locations around the world.

Again McDonald's offers an example. For years, its restaurants in Singapore imported chicken from the US. But when Thailand's currency devalued sharply in 1997, McDonald's in Singapore quickly began to buy chicken from Thailand. Similarly, when the Indonesian currency fell in 1998, McDonald's quickly paid off its local debt by drawing on assets elsewhere in the world. This kind of rapid response typifies dynamic operational flexibility.

Global service firms often shift human resources to respond to specific needs. ABB, the global engineering and power generation firm, undertakes large-scale industrial projects in all parts of the world, and assembles project teams using engineers and managers from many subsidiaries. Teams come together, work on projects, and are dispersed to work on others. Professional service firms like McKinsey also combine and recombine teams of experts. These and other outstanding global firms are examples of dynamic flexibility, with constant adjustment and readjustment to shifting forces.

Global rationalization

In recent years, as global competition has intensified due to a convergence of consumer demand, increasing opportunities for economies of scale and scope, and rising levels of industrialization around the world, many multinational companies have begun to restructure their worldwide operations. In some instances they have consolidated existing functions and lines of business, and in other instances have shut down entire subsidiaries. Paradoxically, we find that growth in efficiency and profitability is achieved by consolidating and rationalizing activities. Surely this is not the same kind of growth we have discussed in most of this book, as it no longer denotes expansion of operations into new markets and businesses; but in an age of intensive competition, it is growth of a different nature but no less valuable.

When might global rationalization be most common? Firm factors and industry factors are both likely to be important. Regarding firm factors, the potential for efficiencies through global restructuring might be most common in multinational companies that expanded many years ago. Because close coordination of foreign subsidiaries was relatively difficult, older companies were frequently organized on a country-by-country basis and pursued a multidomestic strategy. These multinational companies often performed *all* functions in each line of business, resulting in a high level of duplication among countries. Recently, because of enhanced global communications and transportation, opportunities have arisen to capture greater scale and scope economies, leading to a consolidation of functions among lines of business, as well as a consolidation of lines of business among country subsidiaries.

A prime example of this consolidation is the example of Matsushita in Europe. Matsushita had evolved in Europe on a country-by-country basis, yet by the mid-1990s it found its organization to be inefficient, and needed to adopt a pan-regional approach. The pressure for restructuring is also likely to be greater in global industries, where competition on a global scale imposes an imperative for worldwide efficiency. As firms in an industry begin to manage their activities on a worldwide basis, other firms will face an imperative to do likewise.

Companies most likely to restructure their activities are those that expanded abroad long ago and now find themselves in highly global industries. Take IBM. When it set up foreign subsidiaries in many South American countries, these subsidiaries performed a full set of functions. Recently, in response to intense pressures to improve efficiency and cut costs, IBM consolidated its South American activities into three regions – Brazil; the Andean region (Venezuela, Colombia, Ecuador, Peru and Bolivia); and the southern cone (Argentina, Paraguay, Uruguay and Chile). In the latter two regions, where several country subsidiaries were consolidated into a single entity and managed jointly, a number of functions were located in a single country and discontinued in the others. In the Andean region, for instance, human resource management was centralized in Peru; the human resource function in other Andean countries was reduced. The subsidiaries in the other Andean nations, which had performed all functions, now experienced the elimination of several functions.

Seeking global integration and local responsiveness, both at a point in time and through dynamic optimization, and rationalizing activities for global efficiency, may seem far removed from the themes of international growth that have been the focus of these pages. And yet, these later stages of growth – intensive rather than extensive, concerned with efficiency and profit rather than size and scale – call on several of the same capabilities we've discussed in earlier chapters.

Clearly strategic capabilities are as critical as ever. The only difference is that in these later stages, "Where in the world?" might not lead to new markets and new activities as much as to a concentration in some places and discontinuation in others. Yet the logic is the same – scanning broadly, searching for the best opportunities worldwide, and grasping the globe. Global knowledge management remains just as vital, perhaps even more so since consolidation and rationalization calls for more intense coordination across boundaries than before. Companies that identify potential economies of scale and scope, and that can restructure their activities swiftly and efficiently, will be in a better position to compete on a global basis than those that evolved in a graduated fashion but now fail to undertake such restructuring.

 **LEARNING POINTS**

- Successful international growth not only calls for the five capabilities of developing strategic capability, managing global partnerships, staffing the global company, fostering global learning and adapting the global organization; it requires companies to shift back and forth among them simultaneously not sequentially.
- Organizational specialization is often an enemy of efficient growth – managers must not focus on one capability to the exclusion of others, but

share a vision of how the various capabilities combine to produce successful international growth.

- Mature multinationals, with broad global positions, may not seek new markets to enter, but enter a new phase of international growth focusing on improvements in efficiency and profit.
- International growth is a continuous and never-ending process – complex, challenging, but essential for almost all companies today.

References

Bartlett, C.A. and Ghoshal, S. (1989) *Managing Across Borders: The Transnational Solution*, Harvard Business School Press, Boston.

Doz, Y.L. and Prahalad, C.K. (1991) Managing DMNCs: A Search for a New Paradigm, *Strategic Management Journal*, **12**, 145–164.

Friedman, T.L. (1996) From America, a Case Study in Successful Globalization, *International Herald Tribune*, 12 December.

Prahalad, C.K. and Doz, Y. (1987) *The Multinational Mission*, The Free Press, New York.

Contributors

PHILIP ROSENZWEIG
Professor of Strategy and
International Management
E-mail: Rosenzweig@imd.ch

Philip Rosenzweig is Professor of Strategy and International Management at IMD and is the programme manager of *Accelerating International Growth*, IMD's one-week course focusing on the challenges of global management.

His research and teaching centre on the challenges of managing multinational firms. Fields of interest include global strategy, foreign investment, multinational organization design; international staffing and career management; cross-cultural management and leadership; and diversity in the global workforce.

Drawing on 20 years of business and academic experience, Professor Rosenzweig has been a consultant to numerous firms in Europe and North America, and has taught executive courses in North America, South America, Europe, Japan, Singapore and the Middle East. Prior to joining IMD, he was Assistant Professor at Harvard Business School. He has written extensively on the management of multinational firms, with articles published in leading journals such as the *Strategic Management Journal*, the *Journal of International Business Studies* and the *Academy of Management Review*. He is co-author, with Paul Beamish and Allen Morrison, of *International Management, Text and Cases*, published in 1999 by Irwin.

He received his PhD from the Wharton School, University of Pennsylvania in 1990; MBA from the University of California, Los Angeles, in 1980; and BA in Economics from the University of California, Santa Barbara, in 1976. Professor Rosenzweig has received several academic honours, including the UNISYS Fellowship, the Dean's Fellowship from the University of Pennsylvania and the Watts Memorial Fellowship.

XAVIER GILBERT
Professor of Industry Analysis and
Strategy
E-mail: Gilbert@imd.ch

Xavier Gilbert is Professor of Industry Analysis and Strategy and holds the LEGO Chair in International Business Dynamics. He was Acting Director General of IMD from early 1992 until June 1993. His areas of special interest are competitive analysis and strategy implementation with specific attention to management development implications.

He has considerable experience in executive education having been Professor of Business Administration at IMEDE – one of the two founding Institutes of IMD – from 1971. During that time he directed several programmes including the Programme for Executive Development and the one-year MBA programme.

Professor Gilbert is a consultant, chiefly on strategy formulation and implementation, to several leading companies in the fields of consumer and industrial manufacturing and retailing.

He is a graduate of ESSEC (Ecole Supérieure des Sciences Economiques et Commerciales) Paris, and has a Doctorate in Business Administration (DBA) from Harvard University.

THOMAS MALNIGHT
Professor of Strategy and International Management
E-mail: Malnight@imd.ch

Thomas W. Malnight is Professor of Strategy and International Management at IMD. Prior to joining IMD, Professor Malnight spent eight years on the faculty of the Wharton School, University of Pennsylvania.

His fields of interest are international strategy and management, global strategy implementation, evolutionary organizational change in multinational corporations, and emerging models of multinational corporations.

Professor Malnight has written for the *Strategic Management Journal*, the *Journal of International Business Studies* and the *Academy of Management Journal*. He has also authored more than 30 case studies on various aspects of global strategy and organization.

Professor Malnight holds a Doctorate of Business Administration from the Harvard Business School, an MBA from the Wharton School of the University of Pennsylvania and a Bachelor's degree from Northwestern University. Prior to his doctoral studies, he worked for 10 years at Mitsubishi international Corporation, including spending two years working in Japan.

VLADIMIR PUCIK
Professor of International Human Resources
E-mail: Vladimir.Pucik@imd.ch

Vladimir Pucik is Professor of International Human Resources at IMD.

Before joining IMD, Dr Pucik was Associate Professor and Academic Director of International Programs, at The Center for Advanced Human Resource Studies at the ILR School, Cornell University, and a faculty member at the School of Business, University of Michigan. He also spent three years as a visiting scholar at Keio and Hitotsubashi University in Tokyo.

Vladimir Pucik has been a consultant and conducted workshops for major corporations worldwide, including British Airways, Citibank, Daimler-Chrysler, General Electric, Nokia, Shell and Sony. He teaches regularly in a number of executive development programmes in the US, Europe and Asia.

His research interests include international dimensions of human resource management, globalization processes, mergers and acquisitions and strategic alliances, and comparative management with a particular emphasis on the Far East and Eastern Europe. He has published extensively in academic and professional journals, such as the *Academy of Management Review* and *Human Resource Management*. Dr Pucik is co-author of a forthcoming book *The Globalization Challenge: Frameworks for International Human Resource Management* and co-editor of *Globalizing Management: Creating and Leading the Competitive Organization*.

Born in Prague, Czechoslovakia, Dr Pucik has a Master's degree in international affairs – specializing in East Asia, and a PhD in business administration from Columbia University.

Index

Printed and bound by CPI Group (UK) Ltd, Croydon, CR0 4YY

16/04/2025

14658501-0005